Peter Hamilton Myers

Thrilling Adventures of the Prisoner of the Border

Peter Hamilton Myers

Thrilling Adventures of the Prisoner of the Border

ISBN/EAN: 9783744753692

Printed in Europe, USA, Canada, Australia, Japan

Cover: Foto ©ninafisch / pixelio.de

More available books at **www.hansebooks.com**

HARRY AND GETTY.—Page 18.

THRILLING ADVENTURES

OF THE

PRISONER OF THE BORDER.

BY
P. HAMILTON MYERS,
AUTHOR OF "KING OF THE HURONS," ETC.

WITH ILLUSTRATIONS.

NEW YORK:
DERBY & JACKSON, 119 NASSAU STREET.
1860.

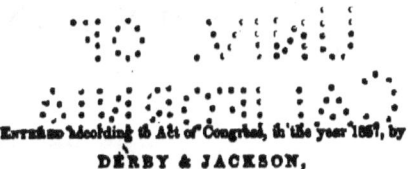

Entered according to Act of Congress, in the year 1857, by
DERBY & JACKSON,
In the Clerk's Office of the District Court of the United States, for the Southern District of New York.

W. H. Tinson, Stereotyper.   Geo. Russell, & Co., Printers.

CONTENTS

CHAPTER I.
Guert Rosevelt and his Grandsons,

CHAPTER II.
A Dutch Belle,

CHAPTER III.
Aunt Becky and the Heiress,

CHAPTER IV.
Abrupt Proposals,

CHAPTER V.
The Eloquent Emissary,

CHAPTER VI.
A Dark Compact,

CHAPTER VII.
Harry and Gertrude,

CHAPTER VIII.
Barak, the Agitator,

CONTENTS.

CHAPTER IX.
The Midnight Army,

CHAPTER X.
The Invasion,

CHAPTER XI.
The Battle of Windmill Point,

CHAPTER XII.
A Recreant Brother,

CHAPTER XIII.
The Magic Rifle,

CHAPTER XIV.
A Tyrant and a Slave,

CHAPTER XV.
Ruth's Story,

CHAPTER XVI.
A Good Samaritan,

CHAPTER XVII.
A Guinea Negro,

CHAPTER XVIII.
A Dutchman's Courtship, and its Consequences,

CHAPTER XIX.
Tidings from the War,

CHAPTER XX.
Gertrude and her Friends,

CHAPTER XXI.
Captain Tom's Fortunes,

CONTENTS.

CHAPTER XXII.
The Hero of the Thousand Isles,

CHAPTER XXIII.
Rainbow Island,

CHAPTER XXIV.
A Thousand Pounds for his Head,

CHAPTER XXV.
Subterranean Councils,

CHAPTER XXVI.
Samson Unbound,

CHAPTER XXVII.
The Express Travellers—An Unexpected Meeting,

CHAPTER XXVIII.
The Prisoner of Prescott,

CHAPTER XXIX.
Light in a Dungeon,

CHAPTER XXX.
A Mysterious Client,

CHAPTER XXXI.
An Unlucky Walk,

CHAPTER XXXII.
Jack Shay and his Gang,

CHAPTER XXXIII.
A Trial—An Unexpected Witness,

CHAPTER XXXIV.
Heroism,

CONTENTS.

CHAPTER XXXV.
Black Brom and the Attorney-General,

CHAPTER XXXVI.
The "Queen's Evidence,"

CHAPTER XXXVII.
Sir George Arthur,

CHAPTER XXXVIII.
A New Advocate,

CHAPTER XXXIX.
A Physician Disappointed,

CHAPTER XL.
A Sad Interview,

CHAPTER XLI.
An Inquisitive Man,

CHAPTER XLII.
A Visit to a Desperate Brigand,

CHAPTER XLIII.
The Outlaw and his Followers,

CHAPTER XLIV.
Nobility in Disguise,

CHAPTER XLV.
A Lawyer with a Small Library,

CHAPTER XLVI.
The Will,

CHAPTER XLVII.
Rough Visitors,

CHAPTER XLVIII.
Conclusion,

THE

PRISONER OF THE BORDER.

CHAPTER I.

GUERT ROSEVELT AND HIS GRANDSONS.

WITHIN view of those mystic mountains, which were long since rendered classic soil by the pen of Irving, and on the banks of that beautiful Hudson, whose charms defy even the power of genius to depict, was the quiet home of Walter Vrail. Not in the days when the ghostly Hendrick and his phantom followers made the rocky halls of the Catskills reverberate with their rumbling balls, and with the clatter of their falling nine-pins, and when their spectral flagon-bearer could be dimly seen at twilight, toiling up the misty ascent to join the shadow revellers, but in these later days, when the quaint old bowlers in doublet and jerkin, have retired deep within the bowels of the mountain, to pursue their endless game undisturbed by the plash of the swift steamboat, or the roar of the linked cars, plunging through dark passes, trembling along narrow ledges, and sending up their shrill scream through all the far recesses of a once holy solitude.

Ah, how much has modern utilitarianism to answer for at the tribunal of Poetry. How many a fairy dream has it dispelled; how many a cherished illusion has it dissipated! How has it measured out with square and compass all the sacred precincts of Romance, and run its surveyors' chains along the moonlit haunts of the Naiad and the Hamadryad! There are no haunted wells, no spell-bound treasures now. No restless spirits tramp along our darkened halls at night, and lead the way, all voiceless, to their hidden gold. No headless horseman scours the plain, frightening belated travellers, and vanishing at churchyard gate. No solemn conclave of grey-bearded men and ancient dames, around the ample hearth, discuss the last new apparition with uplifted hands, and look askance at darkling corners of the room, while the wild tale is told.

Progress has changed all this. Our old men talk of stocks instead of ghosts; our children, fancy dwarfed, prefer philosophy to fairy tales, and laugh at good old Santa Claus, for whom the pendent stockings gaped by a thousand chimneys in the days of yore. We search no more for Kidd's deep coffers, or if we do, a spook-defying joint-stock company, with shares commanding premium on 'change, attempts the work, disdaining other incantation than the power of steam.

Progress has wrought these changes. Progress has opened to us a land of gold, outvieing a thousand fold, the fabled stores of brigand wealth. Progress has—

"Done nothing for your story yet, Mr. Romancer," we hear some querulous reader object, and accepting the rebuke, we bid adieu to goblins, and "chimeras dire."

We said that Walter Vrail lived; yet, almost in the same paragraph, are we to record that he ceased to live. Called, in his meridian years, to relinquish life, he left besides it, two much loved sons, the education and welfare of whom had long been the object of his earnest solicitude. Both had passed out of the age of boyhood, Harry, the elder, having attained to his twenty-third year, and Thomas just verging upon legal manhood; but, although brothers, there was a diversity in their character and appearance which would have prevented a stranger from suspecting them of even a remoter affinity.

Both were handsome in face and in figure, yet Harry alone possessed that indefinable beauty of expression and manner, which we so often see without the power to analyze, and which won many fair hearts whose peace he never dreamed of disturbing, and some far above his aspirations. Aspirations, indeed, he could scarcely be said to have. Never, perhaps, was mortal more devoid of self-esteem, his deficiency in which quality might have been considered almost reprehensible, had it not been a natural hiatus in his character which no education could supply.

Elegant, well-educated, witty and graceful, he really believed himself to be a very ordinary mortal, who owed all his consideration to the extreme good-nature of his acquaintances, and to the great merits of his younger brother. His friends were all quite or nearly faultless in his estimation, but Tom was a perfect paragon of excellence. So talented, so learned, so very, very *deep*, so ambitious, too, that he was sure to become a very great man ere long, and to shed a rich lustre upon the family name. Ah! how he regretted that his parents, whose pet Tom had ever been, could not have been permitted to live to see that coming day which was to realize their predictions and his own expectations.

It was true, he thought, his brother had some failings of character, though perhaps he ought rather to call them eccentricities. Genius is always eccentric, and cannot be expected to be governed by the same laws which bind ordinary mortals. He had thought that Tom lacked in—what should he call it?—thoughtfulness, consideration for others—not for *him*, indeed; there was no need of thinking about *him*—but for his now solitary old grandfather, and sometimes for other friends. Then, Tom was a little irritable—that was the genius, of course, but it was a pity; and sometimes he was a little, a very little vain—yet how could the poor fellow help it, thought Harry, with so much to be vain of?

Mr. Vrail had been wealthy, but in his mistaken anxiety to increase his property for his children's sake, it had been reduced, within the last year of his life, by a failing speculation, to less than a competence. His small farm and homestead, situated in a village on the bank of the Hudson, formed the whole of his possessions, and to this estate the brothers were equal heirs.

Brought up in the expectation of so great wealth, it seemed indeed but a pittance to them, and they became speedily aware of the necessity of making some exertion for their support.

Harry, unfortunately, had learned no business. When his collegiate course had terminated, he had been advised, but not urged, by his indulgent parents, to select a profession and pursue it, and he had often nearly resolved to do so. But what was Harry fit for, in his own estimation ? He thought, at times, of the law ; but what was the use of studying law, when young Tom could outspeak him already in the debating society, and could make more noise in five minutes than he would dare to make in the whole evening. To be sure, Tom was not very perspicuous in his arguments, and often forgot and misstated historical facts, but then he did everything with an *air*, and made the weakest point of his case seem strong by the force and fire of his declamation.

The practice of medicine had also been recommended to Harry as a genteel and easy business, but the idea of ever having a human life dependent on his poor judgment made him tremble ; and as for the pulpit, he thought that a man, like himself, who was good for nothing else, certainly had no right to think of that. So Harry had wasted year after year in a sort of elegant leisure, reading, indeed, a great deal of history, biography and classic lore, and constantly finding among his departed heroes prototypes of what Tom was going to become one of these days.

When Mr. Vrail's losses occurred, his sons were far from knowing the extent of them, for the kind father, still hopeful of retrieving his fortunes, would not look poverty in the face, nor teach his children to contemplate what seemed to him so hideous a spectre. It was not, therefore, until his sudden death that they became aware of their comparative penury, and of the necessity of turning to some account the excellent education which he had bestowed upon them. The younger son had, indeed, for several years been nominally a student in the office of a village attorney, more with a view to the acquirement of that renown which he was sure must follow his first forensic efforts, than with any expectation of making his business a source of profit. But now, when poverty had come so suddenly upon him, he felt entirely impatient of the slow process of regaining his lost wealth which his profession offered, and he longed to discover some " open sesame " to the magic portals of Mammon.

It is difficult to convince a man who has once been affluent that there is not some short and certain road which will lead him back to the golden highway from which he has strayed, and Tom was particularly sanguine on this point.

"We must sell the homestead to begin with," he said to Harry, when, a few months after his father's decease, the brothers had their first business consultation; "we must turn everything into money"——

"Grandfather included, I suppose," said Harry, smiling; "for your plan would leave him no home."

"Oh, I did not *think* of grandfather," replied Tom; and then added, after a pause, "How very old he is—isn't he?"

"Why, bless you Tom, no! He isn't seventy-five yet, and he is as hale and hearty as ever—he is good for a dozen years, at least, yet, I hope."

"And nothing to live on. Well, we must manage some way in relation to *him*, and then we must sell out everything. There are many fields open for speculation when once one has a little money on hand. But nothing can be done without that. At present we can scarcely buy a barrel of flour."

"Tom talks like a book," thought Harry; "but what *does* he mean to do with grandfather?"

Their conversation was interrupted by the entrance of the venerable subject of their remarks, a hale, hearty old man, bent, indeed with years, and slightly crippled with rheumatism, yet with a face red, and fresh, and unwrinkled, shining out of its setting of snowy hair, like the sun breaking through a white fog.

Guert Rosevelt was a Dutchman at all points, and his consent had with difficulty been obtained, twenty-five years before, to the marriage of his loved Katrina with an American who could boast no Flemish blood or affinities—but these scruples had long been forgotten, and he now cherished the memory of his son-in-law with an affection scarcely inferior to that with which he mourned his departed daughter. His grandsons were all that he had left on earth to love, and his old heart clung to them as the oak, riven, but not uprooted, clings to its native soil. Yet it was not with an equal affection that he regarded the orphaned youths, for Harry had been his pet in childhood, and, though unacknowledged as such, was greatly his favorite still.

"I am glad you have come, grandpa," exclaimed the elder brother, impulsively; "we were just speaking of"——

"Of business," said Tom, interrupting his brother, and slightly coloring as he spoke; "and we shall, perhaps, want your advice."

"Vell, den, boys, what is it, now?" said the old man, complacently, seating himself between the youths.

"Why, you see," answered the younger brother, "it is time for us to be seeking our fortunes, Harry and I—we are poor enough now, you know, and we ought to be up and doing. But what we are to do, is the question."

"Yes—yes," said the grandfather, quickly, nodding his head energetically, "I hef been thinking of it too. This reeting of books and blowing on the flute will never make a poor man rich."

"That's *you*, Harry," said Tom, chuckling.

"Neither will this shmoking cigars in a lawyer's shop, and talking politics," continued the mentor, shaking his white locks still more earnestly.

"That's *you*, Tom," said Harry.

"Yes—yes—it is both of you. If Tommy means to be a lawyer, well and goot. 'Tish a trade I don't much like—but he is a shmart lad, and may get to be a Justice of the Peace or Supervisor one of these days."

"Justice of the Peace or Supervisor!" echoed Tom, contemptuously.

"Hush!" whispered his brother.

"Yes—yes," continued the old man, "that you may, ef you are shmart—you will be, a Squire, perhaps a Judge some day, Tommy."

"Like Judge Boory, I suppose, to wake up and say, 'I concur,' when the first judge gives an opinion, and then go to sleep again."

"Yes, like Judge Boory," added Guert, who had not understood the latter part of the young man's reply; "yes, you will do very well, if you try—but as to Harry, here"—

"Oh, I shall rise to be first flageolet to some travelling Punch and Judy, grandfather," said Harry, laughing, and taking down his flute; "you will see if I don't. Just listen to this new air from the Beggar's Opera, which I have been learning."

"'Tish the right thing for you to learn, poy," replied the old man, smiling, and laying his hand affectionately upon the head of his grandson. "The Beggar's Opera—yesh—yesh!" and the old gentleman's head gave a great many little nods, the playful smile still lingering upon his lips.

Harry took advantage of the pause in conversation to play the air half through, and he would have played it over a dozen times before his grandfather would have interrupted him in anything which gave him so much pleasure; but Tom frowned, and Harry stopped.

"We have no time for music now," said the younger brother, "if you call *that* music—but I think I have heard cornstalk flutes give clearer notes than that cracked and patched tube of yours."

"It was *father's* flute," replied Harry, in a low voice, which certainly was most musical, if the instrument was not.

"As to the law," said Tom, recurring to business, and, of course, to his own prospects, "I don't half like it; and, besides, it is too slow a path for me without some auxiliary. I must try something else. I want to get rich first, and then I will practise law afterwards for the honor and *éclat* of it. But the money—the money is what I want now, grandfather, and what Harry wants too, I suppose."

"Why don't one of you go and marry little Getty Van Kleeck?" asked Guert, addressing them both, but looking at his favorite. "She is almost as rich as the Patroon, and a pretty little chub she is too."

Harry rose, and turned aside to lay his flute on the shelf, and Tom replied,

"By George! I never thought of that. It wouldn't be a bad idea—though, to be sure, she isn't exactly the kind of wife a man would like to introduce to—to distinguished circles."

"To distinguished *what?*" said the old man, sharply.

"Why to distinguished people, grandfather—fashionable acquaintances, you know."

"She is a goot girl," said the old man, earnestly; "as clean as a pink and as fresh as a rose."

"She is short and fat," answered Tom; "but she must be very rich, of course. A queer old codger her father was, and he died of a surfeit of sour crout."

"He was a goot man," said Guert.

"And died like a great one," added Harry, smiling. "Frederick the Great killed himself by over eating, and there are plenty of royal precedents for gluttony."

"He was a goot man!" reiterated Guert, sharply.

"I don't know," muttered Tom, musingly, "I don't know but I will take Getty. She is squabby, certainly; but—a—what do you think, Harry? You are much better acquainted with her than I am."

There was the slightest perceptible increase of color on Harry's cheek as he was thus applied to, but he answered without hesitation.

"I think you could get her, Tom."

"*Get her!* You think I could *get her!* Well, I did not want your opinion on that point—but the question is, whether it would be quite the thing?"

"I think Gertrude a very amiable and sensible young lady," replied Harry.

"Well, I guess that is the first time the little dumpling was ever called a young lady, and I don't think she would recognize herself by the title. However, she might be transformed into a young lady—stranger metamorphoses have taken place. I will certainly think about it. Will you go over there with me some evening? I am almost a stranger to her."

"Yes," said Harry, unhesitatingly.

CHAPTER II.

A DUTCH BELLE.

Harry and Getty were very well acquainted with each other. Their homes were indeed a considerable distance apart, Miss Van Kleeck living in a large old farm-house quite without the precincts of the village, and nearly a mile from the residence of the Vrails. Almost alone did she live, too, for her mother had been several years deceased, and since the death of her father, which had occurred only a few months prior to the time now spoken of, she had continued to reside in the family mansion, with an old aunt, who had been one of the household-longer than even Getty herself. The remainder of the family consisted of a hired laborer and two domestic servants, all of whom had occupied their present position so very many years without change, that each seemed to challenge a life interest in the old homestead, and Getty had not the heart to break up the establishment since the removal of its venerable head, nor could she be said scarcely to entertain the least desire to do so. For what idea had Getty of home, elsewhere than in the old brown house, with its antique chimneys, and its long Dutch stoop, whence for so many summer evenings, far back as memory could reach, the smoke of the paternal pipe had ascended.

Getty did not wish to change her abode, nor did she scarcely realize her right to do so. She knew, indeed, that she was the sole inheritor of her father's large property, but she very faintly comprehended its value, or the importance which it gave her in the eyes of others, and she had so long been accustomed to deference to her aunt, that it was with difficulty and by slow degrees alone that she could appreciate her position as mistress of the household.

How or when Harry's acquaintance with Gertrude began it would be difficult to say, but for several preceding years his hunting excursions had extended more often through old Van Kleeck's woods than in any other quarter, and the silvery stream which tinkled across the meadow of Mynheer afforded the finest flavored trout, in Harry's opinion, of the whole country around. It was natural enough, on these expeditions, to stop and chat occasionally with old Baltus, on his stoop, and sometimes to leave a tribute of his game with the proprietor of the domain on which it was bagged. If a string of finer trout than usual rewarded his afternoon's labors, the larger half was sure to be left at Baltus' door, despite of all resistance; and then the servant was to be instructed in the art of dressing, and Getty in the mystery of cooking them in the way which should best preserve their flavor. Sometimes, too, the fatigued youth could be induced at the close of the day, to remain and see if his culinary instructions were properly followed, and at the bountiful board of the Dutchman his seat chanced ever to be beside that of Getty, who saw that he received of the choicest portions of his own gifts. How she loaded his plate, too, with dainties drawn from dark closets, the key of which was seldom turned, save on such occasions as this; how the thickest cream filled the old-fashioned silver creampot to the brim, and was half emptied over Harry's strawberries, or on Harry's currants, while with her own white hand she pitched the large wheaten slices, quoit-like, around his plate, enjoining upon him, in the most approved fashion of Dutch hospitality, to *eat*.

Nor did Harry always find himself sufficiently refreshed to start for home as soon as the evening meal was finished. From the table to the long covered stoop was a natural and easy transition; for there the air was fresh and cool, and while Baltus planted himself, puffing, in his favorite corner, and his silent vrow sat knitting and musing at his side, and pussy, unreproved, now dandled the good dame's ball of yarn in her paws, and now tapping it fiercely, pursued it rolling far across the floor; while the swallows darted daringly inside the pillars, and skimming close to the ceiling, flew chirping out at the farthest opening, Harry and Getty chatted and laughed together—talking only on common themes it is true, yet at times in tones which might have been mistaken by one who had not caught the words, for tones of love. And there *was* a time when yet Harry's father was alive, and was a man of wealth, that the young man had dreamed of love. It was presumptuous in him, he knew, even then, to look up to one so fair and pure as sweet Gertrude seemed to him, and one for whom so many worthier than himself would be certain to aspire.

Yet he could not refrain from hoping, though with so faint a heart that he never found encouragement to declare, or even most remotely to hint at the love which consumed him. But if, while he was the prospective heir of great wealth, he felt thus unworthy of the object of his admiration, widely, hopelessly yawned between them the gulf of separation when positive poverty became his lot.

With a pang of unspeakable intensity he dismissed the bright visions which had gilded his heart, and sought no more to recall so painful and illusive a dream.

Yet, strangely enough, while he held himself thus unworthy of Gertrude, and considered that his changed position precluded him from the right to offer her his hand, he saw no such barrier in the way of his brother. Tom, he thought, was so clever and so handsome, his merits were so many and his fortunes so sure, that he might almost be entitled to wed a princess, and although he was half incensed, he was not surprised at the very confident tone in which the young lawyer had spoken of winning the beautiful

Gertrude, if he chose. Harry thought so himself—he had often thought of it before, and had wondered why his brother had never seemed to notice this sparkling jewel in his path any more than if it were but common crystal.

But true love, even when hopeless, instinctively revolts at the idea of seeing the beloved object in the possession of another, however worthy, and Harry, although not without some upbraiding of conscience, had carefully abstained from saying anything which should set the current of his brother's thoughts in the direction of the great prize he had discovered. Very great, therefore, was his alarm when his good grandsire made his abrupt suggestion, and when Tom so coarsely and ungraciously seemed to approve it. Yet he suppressed his great grief, and replied truthfully to his brother's inquiry, for he not only believed that the latter could obtain the beautiful heiress (indeed, he looked upon them from that moment as wedded), but he failed to see the utter selfishness which had so entirely overlooked himself or any predilections which he might entertain.

So Harry accompanied his brother on his first visit to Getty, not because any formal introduction was needed, for there had been a slight acquaintance existing between all the parties from childhood, but because Tom thought it would serve to put him at once on better and more familiar terms with the lady. And so it did. Getty was delighted to see them, for she appreciated the kindness which remembered her bereavement and her isolation. So very amiable and cheerful did she appear—so naturally graceful and winning, especially when conversing with Harry, with whom she was best acquainted, that Tom was positively delighted with her, and on his return homeward, he announced his fixed determination to offer himself within a week.

"Won't she be astonished?" he said.

"It will be rather abrupt," replied Harry; "she will hardly expect it so soon."

"Very probable; but when a thing is to be done, the sooner it is accomplished the better. Besides, it wouldn't be fair to keep her in suspense."

"Perhaps you are right."

"I shan't hurry her to fix the day, you know, but I abhor long courtships, and these things can as well be settled in a week as in a year."

"Perhaps you would have done well to save time by proposing for her to-night," said Harry, compelling a laugh.

"No, that would not have looked well. Besides, it is proper she should have time to make my acquaintance."

"And you surely do not think a week sufficient for the purpose of forming a mutual acquaintance, and for acquiring that attachment for each other which ought to precede a matrimonial engagement?"

"I surely do. Have we not been neighbors from childhood and does she not know me well enough by reputation? Do not fear, Harry; I will manage it."

"But if"——

"No, no—a 'but' and an 'if' are quite too much in one sentence. I tell you I have no fears. She may possibly be engaged to some boor of a fellow, but even-then, Harry, I think it could be managed. Don't you?"

"I do not think she is engaged—certainly not to any one unworthy of her."

"Then we are on safe ground," said Tom, with hilarity, for he seemed to think his brother equally interested with himself in the success of his plans. "She seems a nice girl, and I have no doubt we shall get on capitally together. She shall soon lead a different sort of life from her present one, cooped up in an old brown farm-house, with a dragon to guard her. Won't she open her eyes when we go to the city, and she gets into New York society?"

Harry began to open *his* eyes a little to his brother's character, but the force of education was strong, and he had been taught to believe Tom almost perfect, and his invincible good nature was busy in meliorating the harsh views which he was at first disposed to take of his conduct, and in inventing excuses for him. Besides, he had a strong affection for Tom, which he believed to be fully reciprocated, and he did not doubt that Getty would inspire him with the same fervent love which his own heart had once felt, and even now with difficulty suppressed. He did not pursue the subject, nor return to it again, excepting when compelled to do so by the other, whose exuberant spirits ran wild in contemplation of the fortunate change which he was about to make in his affairs, and who could not cease to wonder that he had never before discovered such an obvious opportunity for his personal advancement.

The more he thought of his project the more deeply his heart was set upon it, and so bountifully was he supplied with that quality of mind which Harry most lacked, self-esteem, that he had no misgivings as to success.

CHAPTER III.

AUNT BECKY AND THE HEIRESS.

BALTUS VAN KLEECK had left the world somewhat suddenly, and without making any provision for the disposal of that part of it which he claimed to own; and when his pretty daughter Getty became, by operation of law, sole proprietress of several square miles of the terrestrial globe, without any guardian or man of business to guide or instruct her in its management, her position was one of no little embarrassment.

Not that she would have so considered it had she been left to herself in exercising her sovereignty—for Getty was an easy, good-natured soul, who said "yes" to everybody's advice, and to all applications for favors. Not a tenant but would have had his rent lowered, or his house repaired, or some privilege granted or restriction removed, had it not been for the perpetual interference of aunt Becky, a shrivelled, nervous old lady, who was kept in a continual state of excitement by the fear that her niece would be imposed upon.

"Don't you do it, Getty," were the words with which she usually burst in upon these conferences, spectacles on nose, without waiting to hear the specific subject of negotiation.

"I'll tell you what, aunt," said the heiress, one day after one of these interviews, from which the applicant had retired discomfitted by the very first gleam of Madame Becky's glasses. "I must have an agent to manage these matters, for they are quite beyond my comprehension. What with farms to hire, and farms to sell, stock to dispose of, and rents to be collected, I shall go crazy. I know I shall. I must have an agent."

"What for, then, would you have an agent?" said the dame, in a loud key, scowling meanwhile over the black rims of her spectacles; "to cheat you out of everything, and to grow rich on your money? Hey?"

"No, aunt; some good, reliable man"——

"Good, reliable fiddlestick, Getty."

"I say no, aunt."

"I say yes, child. He'll charge you half for taking care of your property, and run away with the rest. Don't talk to me about agents."

Getty had never divested herself of the dread with which from childhood she had regarded her scolding aunt, and so, without fully resolving either to carry or yield the point, she sought to escape from the altercation for the present by not pressing it.

"But these repairs, aunt," she said, "which are so much needed for these poor men?"

"It is no such thing; there are no repairs needed. Why, one would think the houses and fences had all tumbled down the moment poor Baltus was gone. It is no such thing, I say—they are well enough. I have been in every house on the estate within a fortnight, and they are well enough."

"But Mr. Jones, who has eight children, can't make his rent out of the farm."

"Let him give it up, then, to some one who can. What *business* has he with so many children?"

"And Mr. Smith has lost one of his best oxen."

"He must take better care of his oxen, then. He need not expect *us* to pay him for it, I can tell him that."

"But I gave him ten dollars, at all events," replied Getty desperately, and not without alarm.

"Ten dollars, child! Well, now, did anybody ever hear the like of that? Ten dollars to that idle, whining fellow! Why, Getty, you will be in the poor house in a year, if that is the way you are going on—that you will. Ten dollars!"

Becky could hardly throw accent enough upon these two words to express her appreciation of the magnitude of the waste.

"I dare say it was too much," said Getty, "but he told a very pitiful story."

"Yes, yes, they'll all tell pitiful stories enough, if they can only find any one silly enough to believe them. But I'll see to it that there is no more such throwing away of Baltus' money. Give me the key."

Getty submissively took from a side pocket a small bunch of keys, and slipping the smallest off the steel ring which held them together, she handed it to her aunt. No sooner, however, had she done so, than the absurdity of the command and the compliance became apparent to her, and with rising wrath, she was about to recall her act, when her eyes met the dark scowl of the old lady, and yielding to the force of habit, she remained quiet.

Now, Becky's conduct, harsh as it seemed, was altogether caused by excessive anxiety for her niece's interest, and she was to the full extent as honest as she was crabbed. She felt her responsibility as the only surviving adult relative of her brother, and as a sort of natural guardian of both the heiress and her estate, a position which she was by no means desirous of retaining any longer than the welfare of Gertrude required it. Her only hope of relief from her self-imposed duties, was in getting Gertrude married to some "stiddy, sober man." But on this point she had a morbid anxiety even greater than that which related to the property, for she was in constant trepidation lest the heiress should fall a victim to some needy fortune-hunter, in which class she ranked all suitors who did not follow the plough, and wear homespun. She even went so far as to question more than one presuming beau as to his intentions, and one timid young man, who had been a whole month accumulating courage enough to make a first call upon Gertrude, was so frightened by the fierce manner in which aunt Becky asked him what he wanted, that he only stammered out something about having got into the wrong house, and retreated without once seeing the object of his hopes. Strangely enough, too, although Getty knew her aunt's conduct in this instance, and her general asperity towards gentleman visitors, she did not seem to resent it, or to be rendered at all uuhappy by it—nay she was even suspected of rejoicing at so easy a mode of escaping the persecution of lovers. She was unwilling, however, that the imputation of inhospitality or impoliteness should rest upon her family, and on this point she remonstrated with the duenna.

"Let the mollyhacks stay at home, then," said Becky; "what business have they to come here sparking? Let them stay at home then, and when we want them we will send for them."

The visit of the Vrails caused her some annoyance, for she knew that their father had died nearly insolvent, and they were what she called "broad-cloth beaux." But neither of them could yet be regarded as a suitor, and the old dame kept quiet in regard to them as long as there was no repetition of their offence.

CHAPTER IV.

ABRUPT PROPOSALS.

"What has come over you Getty, that you have been singing all the time for these two days, up-stairs and down—hey?" said Becky to her niece, in the afternoon of the second day after the visit which has been spoken of.

"O, nothing, aunt Becky," replied Gertrude, hesitatingly; "I often sing like that, do not I?"

"Not often, I hope. I have counted these stitches over these three times, and every time your ring-tee-iddity has made me forget how many there are."

The dame's tone was severe, and as Getty spied the old scowl taking shape on her forehead, she retreated to her own room to sing away the remainder of the evening by herself. On the morrow, also, her heart seemed equally light, and snatches of old songs were escaping all day from her lips, making every room and closet vocal as she flitted through them on various household duties. Now and then a growl responded to some of these chirpings, silencing them for a while, only to break forth in some other quarter of the house more merrily than ever. As evening drew nigh; her merriment gradually subsided, and she withdrew to her own apartment in a more thoughtful and pensive mood—not long, however, to remain unsought.

Her heart beat quickly when, listening, she heard the voice of a visitor below, and far quicker when a servant girl came up and informed her that Mr. Vrail was in the parlor, and wished to see her. Startled, but not surprised, with a fluttering heart and flushed face, she flew to the glass to add the last touch to the simple adornments of her person, and although far from being vain, she could not forbear contemplating for a moment with complacency the sweet picture reflected by the faithful mirror.

She waited a little while for her agitation to subside: for with that rapid breath and heightened color, and something very like a tear glistening in her eye, she was unwilling to meet her visitor; but, while she waited, she received another and more urgent summons.

"You had better come down, Miss Gertrude," said the girl, who seemed to guess that her young mistress was expecting a not unwelcome visitor; "you had better come down, for your aunt Becky is getting ready to go in and see the gentleman."

This announcement did not have a tendency to allay Miss Van Kleeck's excitement, but it hastened her movements, and in a few moments she was at the parlor door, which she entered tremblingly, and not the less beautiful for her fright. Her step had been agile, but she stopped as if spell-bound just within the doorway, seemingly unable to comprehend or reply to the very civil "Good evening," with which she was addressed by Mr. Thomas Vrail.

The changed expression of her countenance, so radiant on entering, so amazed and saddened now, did not fail to attract the notice of that young gentleman, who, sagely attributing it to the awe inspired by his presence, at once condescendingly resolved to reassure the heart of his charmer by his suavity. But, although Getty recovered herself so far as to say "Good evening," and, after another considerable pause, to ask her visitor to sit down, and then to sit down herself on the farthest edge of the chair most remote from her companion, she did not seem easily reassured.

Tom said it was a pleasant evening, and Getty said "Yes," very very faintly.

Then Tom said it was a beautiful walk from his house to Miss Van Kleeck's, and Getty again answered with a monosyllable, but this time a little more distinctly.

"A very delightful walk," reiterated the suitor; "and one which I hope I shall have the pleasure of taking frequently."

Miss Van Kleeck, thinking it necessary to say something in reply, and entirely failing to comprehend the drift of the remark, "hoped so too."

Tom now felt himself to be getting along fast—nay, with very railroad speed, so he ventured to draw his seat a little nearer to Getty, to her manifest trepidation, for her eyes turned quickly toward the door, and she seemed to be contemplating flight.

But it was one of Tom's maxims to strike while the iron is hot, and if he had been so well convinced of having made a favorable impression on the evening of his first visit, he felt doubly sure now, after the new encouragement he had received.

"I may be a little hasty, Miss Van Kleeck," he said, again slightly lessening his distance from her, "but I have had the presumption to imagine that I—that you—that I"——

"Please not to come any nearer," said Getty, hastily, as her suitor's chair exhibited still farther sings of locomotion.

"Ah! certainly not, if you wish it," replied the lover, very blandly; "I mean, not *at present;* but allow me to hope that the time will come, when you—when I—that is to say when both of us"——

Tom stopped, for Gertrude had risen and taken a step toward the door, with much appearance of agitation.

"I fear you do not understand me," he said.

"I fear I do," she replied quickly and sensibly; "although it is rather your manner than your words which express your meaning."

"Stay, then, and be assured that I am quite in earnest."

"I do not question your sincerity, Mr. Vrail"——

"That I have come to offer you this hand," he continued, extending a very clean one, which bore evident marks of recent scrubbing for its present service, but which the heiress exhibited no haste to accept.

She had attained sufficient proximity to the door to feel certain that her retreat could not be cut off, and her self-possession having in some degree returned, she listened respectfully and replied politely, although with a tone of sadness.

"I will spare you any further avowal of your feelings, Mr. Vrail," she began.

"Do not think of such a thing, dear Gertrude," he replied, still unawakened from his hallucination. "I am proud to make profession of my love for you."

"Will you listen to me a moment before I go?"

"An hour! a week! nay, forever!"

"I shall not detain you a minute."

"I assure you I am in no hurry."

"*I am*. You are laboring under a mistake. We are nearly strangers to each other, and you have scarcely the right to address me in the way you have done; but if it were otherwise, I have only to answer by declining your offer," she said, glancing at the hand and arm which had remained projecting like a pump-handle all this while, with the evident expectation on the part of Thomas, whose whole attitude was quite theatrical, that it was speedily to be seized and clung to.

He now began to look astonished and alarmed, but he immediately rallied.

"Oh, I see how it is," he said; "I have been rather abrupt, I dare say; but we will become better acquainted. I will call often to see you, and then—why, Miss Van Kleeck—*don't go!*"

Getty had now become angry; she left the room and her astonished lover, but paused a moment outside the door, and said, with a very pretty flush on her cheek, and a very bright sparkling in her eye—

"Call as often as you choose, Mr. Vrail, but I shall never see you. You do not seem to understand the plainest words, but I assure you we shall never be better acquainted with each other than we are now. Good evening."

So saying, Getty almost ran out of the outer room, shutting the door after her with a haste that gave it quite the character of a slam, and hurried up to her own apartment.

Tom's panoply of conceit, which was almost invulnerable, and which had withstood so much, only now gave way.

"I really believe she means to refuse me," said he, soliloquizing; "it is very ridiculous—but perhaps she may come back. I will wait a little."

He did wait some minutes, listening earnestly, and was at length gratified by the sound of approaching steps, which he advanced to meet with great alacrity. But what was his consternation on encountering at the door the wrinkled and vinegary countenance of Dame Becky, whose huge spectacles, as she stood confronting him a moment in silence, glowered upon him like the eyes of the great horned owl.

The lover retreated a step before this apparition.

"*Do you want Getty?*" she said, at length, in a voice amazingly shrill and sharp.

"I—yes, I should be happy to see her for a few moments, if—if you please."

"But do you want her—do you want to *marry her?*" she asked, in still more of a scolding tone.

"Oh—ah—yes, madam," said Tom, attempting to win the old woman by a fine speech; "I am exceedingly proud to call myself an admirer of your beautiful niece, and I have indulged the hope that we might find our tastes congenial, and our hearts sympathetic. May I count, my dear madam, on your influence with Miss Gertrude?"

"No, you *can't,* and more than that, you can't have her. So no more of that. You are the *third* this week."

"Good gracious! the third *what*, ma'am?"

"No matter what. You can't have her—you understand—don't you?"

"Y—yes," said Tom, "I suppose I do."

"Very well, then—no offence meant," said aunt Becky, now trying to modify what might seem harsh in her language by a stroke of politeness, but still speaking in the same high key; "won't you sit down?"

"No I thank you," muttered Tom, now decidedly crestfallen; "I rather think it is time for me to go."

"Good night, then," said Becky, following him to the door as close as if he had been a burglar. "*Take care of the dog!*"

"The deuce!" said Tom to himself, clutching his cane, as he walked off the stoop; "is there a dog to be shunned too? I shouldn't wonder if they should set him on me!" and he quickened his step down the lane that led to the highway, and was soon out of sight of the old farm-house, without even turning to take a last look at the solitary light which gleamed like a beacon from Getty's room—alas! no beacon of hope for him.

CHAPTER V.

THE ELOQUENT EMISSARY.

Tom had kept his own counsel, and although his greatly changed demeanor, and the fact that there was no repetition of his visit to Miss Van Kleeck, excited Harry's suspicions, he could not fully believe either that his brother had been rejected, or that he had abandoned his matrimonial views. But much as he had tried to wish for the suitor's success, he had been unable really to do so, and when the latter, fearful of the imputation which his silence would fasten upon him, condescended to define his position, it was greatly to Harry's relief, although not much to his enlightenment.

"I'll tell you what," said Tom, "I didn't like Getty as well the second time I saw her; I hardly think she'll do for me. Then that old dragon that guards her is a horrid old creature. I rather think I won't be hasty about it. At all events, I will wait awhile."

Harry thought all this true, for he could not suspect his brother of falsehood, and he imputed his mistaken opinion of Gertrude entirely to a want of sufficient acquaintance with her. How truly he knew her to be worthy of the most exalted love! But he made little reply, and the subject was soon willingly dropped by both parties.

Their business affairs, in the meantime, did not mend. The younger brother soon grew as chimerical and visionary as ever in searching for short roads to fortune, but without the least idea of seeking her where she frequents most, in the beaten highway of patient and plodding toil. It was about this time that Tom returned home one day from his office, where his occupation was anything but study, and sought out his brother with an appearance of much excitement.

"Now, Harry," said he, "the time has really come for decision and action—such an opportunity as offers but once in a man's lifetime. My most sanguine hopes bid fair to be realized."

"Why, what is it now, Tom?"

"A great chance! While we are dreaming away our time here, others are up and doing in one of the greatest enterprises of the age. I have had a long interview, this afternoon, with a Col. Allen, of Canada, who is to stop here two days, to form a 'Hunter's Lodge,' and I am going to become a member. He says as I am the first volunteer, and am a man of—of note, as he was pleased to say, I shall be in a condition for immediate advancement and a commission."

"Why, what in the name of the seven wonders are you talking about?" asked Harry, laying down his flute, and gazing earnestly at his brother. "Who is Col. Allen, and what is a hunter's lodge?"

"Surely you cannot be so ignorant as not to know about the hunters, Harry? You must have read about them in the papers."

"Oh—ah!—those meddlesome fellows that are trying to get up a revolution in Canada. I remember now, they call themselves hunters."

"Trying to get up a revolution! No, sir; the revolution is already begun, and is rapidly progressing, and in every town on the northern frontier, secret clubs are forming of those who wish to aid, either by personal service or by money, in the cause of freedom. Col. Allen says that the youth and chivalry of the whole nation are ready to rise, and win for themselves just such honors in Canada as Lafayette, and Kosciusko, and other great men, achieved in our Revolution."

"Besides lots of prize-money, I suppose," said Harry, laughing quietly.

"Yes; General Mackenzie, who is at the head of the provisional government, has issued a proclamation, offering three hundred acres of land, and a hundred dollars in specie, to every private; and as to commissioned officers "——

"General Mackenzie at the head of the provisional government! Why, Tom, Mackenzie is in Michigan, a refugee and an outlaw, with a price on his head, and all his own property confiscated."

"No matter for that! There was a price on Washington's head, too, wasn't there? What hurt did it do? Mackenzie is to be the Washington of Canada, its deliverer and its future President."

"But I thought this agitation was subsiding, since the insurgents at home, or the patriots, as you call them, and their sympathizers here, had met with so many and such constant reverses. Surely, blood enough has been spilt in such a hopeless cause."

"Subsiding! Col. Allen says it is but just begun; he says that the burning of the 'Caroline' has lit up a flame in every quarter of the land—that meetings are being everywhere held, and that millions of money are already subscribed for the cause. Did not you read of the great meeting in New York last week?"

"Yes, I believe I saw something about it—but I did not pay much attention to it. It is, at all events, certain that our government has heretofore, and will continue to use all means to enforce neutrality, and to prevent American citizens from invading a country with which we are at peace."

"Very true. But government can't prevent sympathy, and private assistance with money, such as we gave to Greece and Poland—nor can it prevent our citizens from quietly leaving the country, and when they are out of it, joining any standard they choose. That's what the colonel says, and every lawyer knows it's true."

"It may be true," said Harry, taking down his flute; "but I should require more evidence than I have ever seen, either that the Canadian people are greatly oppressed, or that they desire a revolution, or that they will turn out to help those who go over to help them, before I should be sympathizer or subscriber—much less a hunter, as you call it. It may suit the purpose of a few agitators, both there and here, to get up a rebellion in the name of a suffering people, who are very quietly minding their own business at home, and have no remote intention of committing high treason."

"But if the people are trampled down, and blinded by their tyrannical rulers"——

"Let them remain so, until they have spirit enough and sense enough to rise, as our ancestors did in '75, and then, if they can show the world even half as just a cause as we did, they will not lack help. The youth and chivalry of the whole nation would rise in such a cause uninvoked, excepting by the clash of arms in the cause of freedom; armies would start up at a hundred points along our frontiers, like the Highland legion at the whistle of Roderick Dhu; they would pour into the arena impetuous as the mountain torrents, and as resistless as the tornado which strews forests in its path."

"Why, Harry," said Tom, who had listened with gradually distending eyes, "you grow eloquent. You must come with me tonight and join the club—you must, indeed. Col. Allen will convince you that the very time you describe is at hand. You ought to hear him talk on this subject, for I have not told you half of what he said."

"You must excuse me—I have not the least curiosity on the subject."

"I cannot excuse you—I shall certainly take you along."

Tom understood the passive and yielding nature of his companion too well to doubt his ability to carry the point with him, nor was he disappointed. The brothers went to the meeting, and not a few of the young men of the village were influenced by their example to do the same, while many already favorably predisposed to the cause, responded to the call without solicitation, and awaited eagerly an opportunity of expressing their sympathy for the Canadians. Few, indeed, of the large number in attendance entertained the remotest idea of engaging personally in the anticipated war, yet there were some, like the younger Vrail, of military tastes, who hoped to find it an easy avenue to fame and fortune.

No secrecy was observed in this primary meeting, at which its originator did not intend to say or do anything which could infringe the neutrality laws—but out of the elements present, it was his design to form a lodge or secret club, to whom the most daring projects of the agitators could be proposed, and from whom could be expected a quota of men for actual service in the field.

The emissary who had convened this assemblage was a man fully competent to play his part in the important drama in which he was engaged. He was a dark-complexioned man, apparently of about fifty years, with a countenance indicative of great intelligence and sagacity, and it was with an air so serious, a voice so musical, and words so apt and fitting that he began his address, that he could not fail to enlist the earnest attention of all, and at once to inspire them with an interest in his subject. He spoke briefly of the history of the Canadas, of the long standing grievances of the people of the lower province, and of the more recent, but not less severe oppression of their more western brethren. He recited the most glowing parts of that celebrated appeal issued by the leading reformers of Upper Canada, which bears throughout such a striking resemblance to our own Declaration of Independence, and which in frequent instances adopts its exact language to complain of the same wrongs.

He spoke of the premature outbreak which ensued shortly after the publication of this document, and which, but for some erroneous counsels which thwarted the plans of the valiant Mackenzie, must have led to an immediate and successful issue.

How the revolutionary spirit, ripe in both provinces, had been kindled into a hundred distinct, but unfortunately never united flames—how a dozen successive insurrections had been successively defeated by government—and how hundreds of brave men had been dragged to prison and to the gallows, while a still larger number had sought refuge in this Asylum of Freedom—he described in language bold, graphic and startling. He next painted the efforts which were making by these refugees in this country, to enlist the friends of Freedom in their cause, while the throbbing heart of the whole Canadian nation, he said, was anxiously and ardently awaiting the advent of their deliverers.

"Let but an American army cross the frontiers," he said, "and their first bugle blast will be to the disheartened millions of the North, what the voice of the prophet was to the dry bones in the valley of vision—they will rise and stand upon their feet, an exceeding great army. They will rush to your standard from a thousand points. There will be but one blow to strike, and the chains will drop from the manacled form of Liberty, never again to be replaced. Who would not share in this glorious enterprise of liberating an oppressed and generous people from the shackles of tyranny; of creating another independent Republic to rank as a power among the nations of the earth? Strong as is your government, Americans! deeply as it is rooted in the affections of twenty millions of brave people, it is not beyond receiving an accession of strength from the influence and co-operation of a sister Republic springing up at its side. Canada is destined to be free. The event is a fixed and certain one in the womb of the future, and the only question that remains is one of time. Shall it be *now?* Now, when oppression has filled to the brim her cup of bitterness—*now*, when tens of thousands, both here and there, are already armed in her cause—*now*, when all America is sympathizing with her sufferings, and encouraging her struggles? Or shall this golden opportunity, so filled with all the elements of success, be lost, and another cycle of darkness be reserved for my beloved country?"

The great earnestness of the orator, and his impassioned style of speaking, as he proceeded at considerable length to enforce his appeals, were not without a marked effect upon his audience. He was frequently interrupted by applause, and sometimes by loud and long-continued cheers, and at the close of his remarks he was surrounded by a crowd of young men, who remained, in compliance with his intimation that he intended to organize a secret society, or lodge, composed of all who were willing in any way to aid in the cause.

The younger Vrail, of course, was of this number, and he made a strong effort, seconded by the Canadian, to induce his brother to follow his example—for Harry, although not convinced, had been moved by the stranger's eloquence.

"You do not commit yourself in anything excepting sympathy and secrecy," said the orator, "by becoming a member of the lodge. You will still be as free to decline assisting the cause as you now are—but those who join and give the required pledge of secresy will learn much more of the cause and its prospects than I am at liberty to communicate publicly."

Harry's yielding nature gave way as usual to the importunity of his brother, and the young men, together with many of their associates, soon found themselves transformed into "Hunters," fully supplied with all the secret signs and passwords with which to recognize all others of the fraternity, in whatever quarter of the two countries they might chance to meet.

CHAPTER VI.

A DARK COMPACT.

Enthusiastic, ambitious and vain, Thomas Vrail was fully resolved from the outset to accept the tempting offer of a commission in the patriot army, which the emissary was empowered to offer him, many nominations of the kind having been placed at his disposal by those who had assumed command of the provisional government of the provinces.

He exhibited the fullest credentials from his superiors, who evidently placed great confidence in his tact and discretion, and who were as liberal in the bestowal of their chimerical honors, as in the distribution of the yet unconquered soil which they were about to invade. He was, of course, instructed to offer these higher prizes only to the educated and influential classes, to whom the private's pay and bounty could not be expected to prove a sufficient inducement to enlist.

Of course, the majority of these appointments, although conferring rank from their date, were entirely prospective, as far as related to the command bestowed upon the various officers. Colonels of regiments yet unraised, and captains of companies still unformed, awaited with ardor the hour when, stepping upon Canadian soil, they should behold the eager hosts which they were to lead to battle and to victory, and they were content, meanwhile, to perform the duty of privates in the first movements of the invasion.

Col. Allen, after much secret instruction to his new allies, left them on the ensuing day, to pursue his mission in other quarters, promising to visit them again within a fortnight, and to give due notice of the time and place of rendezvous to such of them as should determine to engage personally in the cause.

The intervening period was devoted by the younger Vrail to the most incessant efforts to induce Harry to accompany him to the field. The infection and sympathy was spreading more and more rapidly throughout the country, and Tom brought daily to his brother reports of fresh accessions to the ranks, and new accounts both of the sufferings of the Canadian people, and of the extent and progress of the insurrection.

"Beacons," he said, "are placed on a hundred hills, ready to be fired the moment that the invading army lands, and these are to be the signals for a simultaneous rising throughout the country."

Harry did not lack courage, and his heart was full of generous eelings for the oppressed, but his scruples were not entirely overcome.

But he knew that Tom could not be dissuaded from his own purpose, and his extreme solicitude for his safety in so perilous an enterprise went further towards deciding his movements than all other influences combined. He resolved to go for Tom's sake —that he might watch over his welfare, and keep him from unnecessary dangers. It would be so very dreadful, he thought, if anything should happen to Tom, while his own fate seemed of comparatively trifling moment. Such was Harry's nature, and such is the nature of many whom the world decry as wanting in energy and force of character.

When Allen returned, a lieutenant's commission was easily obtained for the new recruit, although, if he had chosen to make terms, he might easily have procured a higher rank, but he took, of course, what his brother chose to ask, and Allen to bestow. It was true Tom was a captain, but what was that to Harry but a source of pleasure? He did not doubt that the latter would become a major-general if the patriots succeeded.

The returned emissary assembled his lodge, and informed them with much excitement, and with many injunctions of secrecy and caution, that the time and place of attack were fully decided upon. The frontier village of Oswego, he said, was the place of rendezvous for a large part of the recruits, where they were to repair quietly and without arms, which would be provided in due time. They were not to go in numbers of more than three or four together, nor were they publicly to discuss the object of their expedition, lest they might subject themselves to arrest and detention by their own government, which, he said, was taking sides with tyranny against the rights of man. Having imparted these instructions to the neophytes, together with such other information as was necessary for their guidance, he departed northward, to visit other clubs, and give them like notice of the time of the intended invasion.

Secret as had been the proceedings of the lodge, its existence and object, and even the names of the volunteers for service in the field, were generally known throughout the village. True, they were rather whispered than openly proclaimed, and it was said, not that such and such an one had enlisted for the war, but that he had become a hunter. This plan was universal and was everywhere understood. Officers of the United States government were not obliged to understand it unless they chose to do so, and Mr. Deputy Marshal Stone never dreamed of knowing what it meant, when used among his own neighbors and acquaintances. If people chose to go north in search of game, which had become very scarce at home, it was no business of his. But he caused it to be understood that they must not go to the chase with military accoutrements, or with the accompaniments of drum and fife, or he should be obliged to suspect them of other designs. In short, there was a very good understanding between the deputy and his fellow-citizens, upon whose favor he counted for assistance in obtaining a renewal of his term of office.

Old Guert Rosevelt made no serious opposition to the designs of his grandsons, which he very imperfectly understood, but he had great confidence in the good sense of the elder, and he was so impatient of the long idleness of both, that he was glad of any change which gave them occupation and even a remote prospect of success.

But there was another quarter in which the tidings of Harry Vrail's changing fortunes were received with more interest, and were contemplated with more anxiety. Although Gertrude Van Kleeck had long tried to convince herself that she cared little or nothing for her old associate and visitor, she could not repress the fears which continually arose in her mind for his safety, now that he was about to engage in a war of which the theatre was distant and the issue very uncertain. True, he was only a friend, and would never be anything more to her, but she felt that it would be very dreadful if anything serious should happen to him. Yet not for the world would she have him or any one else know that she felt this solicitude in his behalf, and the necessity of so closely locking her emotions within her own breast rendered them doubly oppressive. Again and again she reverted to the subject, only to feel her utter impotency to plan or do anything which should counteract Harry's anticipated movement. She reflected upon the great wealth of which she was the mistress, and thought how freely she would be willing to dispense of it, if there was any way by which she could avert from her friend what seemed to her so very pressing and imminent a danger.

She continued to receive tidings from day to day, through various members of her household, in relation to a subject which, of course, formed a large part of the current gossip of the neighborhood, but her principal reliance for information was upon a negro servant, named Abram, but more usually called Brom, who was almost daily sent to the village on domestic errands. At times, indeed, Gertrude invented little wants, which aunt Becky thought superfluous and extravagant, for the purpose of dispatching Brom to the village store, to bring back his accustomed budget of intelligence. She seldom, indeed, questioned him herself in relation to the news, but she usually contrived to be busy in the kitchen on his return, and thus to hear what he was quite sure to relate to his fellow-servants in regard to the exciting topic of the day.

Now, Brom had become not a little attached to Harry Vrail in former days, having often obtained permission to accompany him in his fishing and hunting expeditions, and he frequently expressed his regret that Master Harry had ceased for the past year to pay his accustomed visits to the Van Kleeck woods and streams.

Of this sable individual a few words of description may not be amiss. He was a man about thirty years of age, who had lived from infancy in the family of Gertrude's father, having been a slave until the general emancipation of 1826. Since that time he had received wages as a hired servant, or rather he had them placed to his account, for Brom never "took up" anything more than was required for his yearly suit of linsey-woolsey, the remainder of his stipend remaining in his employer's hands.

Notwithstanding his freedom, he was in spirit as much a slave as ever, and he possessed that strong attachment for his master's family which characterizes his race, and which is, alas, so often sadly requited.

But Brom was a light-hearted, merry fellow, whose humble condition seemed fully compensated for by a perpetual freedom from cares and anxieties. Everything was food for Brom's mirth, and almost everything was food for his mouth. His appetite and his spirits were equally unflagging.

It was while listening to one of the negro's daily reports in relation to the village recruits, in which he always spoke particularly of "Massa Harry," that the idea occurred to the anxious Gertrude of furnishing her friend with a body-guard in the person of this very African, who manifested so much interest in his welfare. Startled and relieved by the thought, she hastily retired to her room to reflect on the means of carrying it into execution; but this was a task not easily performed with that entire secrecy which was essential to her design. She sent at once for the negro, and after questioning him a little more in relation to the tidings which he had brought, she said to him:

"Brom, you have always been a good servant, and my father ever placed great confidence in you. I think I can do the same."

Brom grinned widely as he replied—

"Yes, Miss Getty, you can trust Brom sartin."

"But can I trust you in a very important matter, far more important than any which you were ever engaged in, and one which requires both courage and secrecy?"

The negro remained silent for a moment and seemed greatly surprised, but at the next instant his large eyes flashed with the earnest spirit of his reply.

"Yes, Miss Getty, you can trust Brom in *anything*."

"Are you willing to go to the war with Mr. Vrail as his servant?"

"With Massa Harry! To the war with Massa Harry! Yes, I is willing, Missis Getty! Dat I is—if you and Missis Becky will let me go."

"You are a free man, Brom, and can do what you choose."

"I will never go without your consent. Besides, I want to come *home* when the war is over, and Missis Becky wouldn't let me do that if I should run away."

"But *I* am mistress now," replied Gertrude, with a very pretty air of command, which she had never before been able to assume, but which the exigency of her position rendered necessary. "Aunt Becky has nothing to say about it."

"Aunt Becky nothing to *say*, hey? Don't you believe it! She has a mighty great deal to say about everything," replied the negro hastily.

"Well, well," answered Gertrude, laughing, "she must be allowed to talk, but you understand that I am the mistress in this house and on this farm—that it is all mine. Don't you understand that, Brom?"

"Y-e-s," said Brom, hesitatingly—" but Missis Becky "——

"Never mind Missis Becky."

Brom looked hastily over his shoulder to make sure that the object of his dread was not within hearing of this treasonous speech.

"And if you choose to go away, you shall be allowed to come back here whenever you wish on exactly the same footing as before, and I will furnish you with plenty of money for the journey; but you will have to enlist as a soldier. What do you say?" Are you afraid?" she continued, as the negro seemed to hesitate in replying.

"Golly, *no!* I isn't afraid of the *war*—but—Missis—Becky"—

The young lady impatiently interrupted him, and, by dint of much argument, succeeded in allaying his deeply implanted fears in relation to the one sole-object of his terror, and when this disenthrallment was completed, there was no limit to the exuberance of the negro's joy at the prospect before him.

"As I said, you will have to enlist as a soldier."

"List? Oh yes, I'll do that, sartin; and then I'll get three hundred acres of land after we've drove the Canaders all out."

"You must not think of that. You may get it or not, and it will probably be worth very little if you do. But remember that you go as Master Harry's *servant*, and that I will pay you liberally for all your time and danger. You will be a soldier it is true, and must do your duty as such; but remember, that you are a volunteer, and that you must enlist on the express condition that you are always to fight at Master Harry's side, and that you are always to be quartered near him, and where you can wait upon him. You are to be within his call at all times of night and day. You are to watch over him in battle, and be always ready to help him when he needs help. If he is wounded (here Gertrude's voice trembled) you are to carry him off the field; and if he is taken prisoner, you are to go with him. Will you do all this?"

"Yes, Missis, I sartingly, will."

"Will you swear to do it?"

"Yes, on all the Bibles in the house."

"But there is yet another thing. Neither he nor any one else must ever know anything of this arrangement between you and me. You are a free man, you wish to enlist as a soldier, but you wish to go with your old friend, Master Harry. All this is true, is it not?"

"All berry true."

"As to the rest, you must not say a word to anybody. You must not even tell Mr. Vrail that you are to be his servant, nor must you ask any wages of him; but you are to do everything for him you possibly can."

Brom was sagacious and discreet. He was easily made to comprehend everything in relation to his young mistress' views except two things. He did not comprehend her reason for secrecy, nor how he was to avoid the wrath of his ancient enemy, Mistress Becky. But he faithfully promised compliance with all the instructions of Gertrude, which she repeated many times over to him, and impressed on his mind with indelible distinctness. Before he left the room he knew his whole *rôle* by heart, and he proceeded at once to business, making his boldest strike first, and the one which he dreaded far more than all the rest. Before the day was over, he gave Miss Becky notice that he was about to quit the service of the family, and was going to the war, and then he stood patiently for half an hour, and bore the expected torrent of invective which his announcement elicited, merely repeating at its close his first remark.

"You shall do no such thing, you black Mollyhack, you. *You sha'n't go!* So just go about your work, and let me hear no more about this nonsense. You sha'n't stir á step, I say. Now, then."

"I *must go*, Missis Becky."

"What for must you, then? I should like to know that, now—hey!" she said, in the very *altissimo* of scolding keys.

"I *must go*."

"You shall not! You sha'n't have a cent of money; and if you do go you shall never come back. You know very well that Baltus would never have let you go on such a wild goose chase as this, and neither will I."

"I am a free man, Missis Becky," said Brom, trembling from head to foot with the violence of the effort to make so bold an assertion, "and I sartingly shall go."

So saying, Brom turned away and walked off to the barn, followed by a rattling volley of words, which came less and less distinctly to his ear until the interposing door of his place of refuge shut out the fearful sounds.

Dame Becky, after scolding for some time at the empty air, went grumbling into the house, and sought out her niece, whom she informed of the servant's audacious design,. which intelligence Getty, to her great surprise, received with much coolness, assuring her that she already knew Brom's wishes on this point, and had consented to his going.

There was something in the air of the young lady as she made this remark which impressed the aunt with a sense of her niece's authority, and it was with some abatement of tone that she remonstrated against the project. Getty heard her through and replied with composure—

"As I said before, aunt, my mind is made up to let Brom go,

3

and I desire that he may be allowed to go in peace, and without further reproof."

"Hoity, toity!" exclaimed the old woman in a subdued tone, turning away from her niece; "these are new airs! Well, let him go then to the old scratch, as he most assuredly will; but he shall never darken these doors again."

"He has my permission to return here whenever he chooses."

"Oh, has he indeed? Pretty management this is! Perhaps you do not know that all Brom's wages for the last ten years are unpaid, and that he holds your father's note for a great part of it, with interest, and that if he goes away it has all got to be *paid*."

The last word was shot out from between the dame's thin lips with much force, and with an air of no little spitefulness.

"I know all about it," replied the niece. "I do not think it is Brom's intention to take up any part of his money yet; but if it is, I am able to pay him without difficulty."

The aunt, after a little subdued grumbling, left the room, and retired to her own department in no amiable mood, and greatly wondering at the change which had suddenly taken place in her niece.

CHAPTER VII.

HARRY AND GERTRUDE.

Harry Vrail was not a little astonished when, on the third day prior to his departure for the seat of war, his old acquaintance Brom called upon him in a state of great excitement, and requested to be allowed to enlist as a soldier and accompany him to the field. To the young man's inquiries the negro replied that he was going to quit his old home, and that he was free to go where he chose, and he chose to go with Massa Harry to Canada.

Harry was delighted with this unexpected proof of attachment in his old companion, and also with the prospect of having always so powerful a friend and auxiliary at his side, and after ascertaining that the negro's mind was fully decided upon going, he assured him that he would arrange everything pertaining to his enlistment, and said he had no doubt that he could so manage matters that their positions should at all times be near each other.

Brom could not restrain his ecstasy at the success of his suit.

"I'll take care of your *hoss*, Massa Harry," he said, "and brush your clothes, and—and"——

"Thank you, Brom. I am not certain that I shall have a horse to take care of, and I fear I shall have but little money to pay for services of any kind."

"Never mind the money, Massa Harry. I don't want any money. Missis Becky has got eight hundred dollars of Brom's now laid up for when I get to be an old man."

The negro could not long divest himself of the idea that Dame Becky was the chief representative of his old master.

"Has she indeed? You are a very fortunate fellow then and I think you had much better stay at home. You can buy yourself a small farm with that sum, and run no risk of getting shot."

The negro was impatient at this advice, and would not listen to it a moment.

"Very well then, Brom," said the young man, "you may go if you wish, and I have no doubt you will make a very good soldier."

"May I take care of your horse?" repeated the negro earnestly.

"Most certainly, if I have one, you may take care of him, and if you like you may call yourself my servant when you are off duty, and in that way we can always be near each other, and I will pay you for whatever services I require of you."

"Never mind the pay;" reiterated Brom, "we'll see about that when you get to be a gineral or govner of Canada; but mind and tell Colonel Allen that I is your servant."

The negro next inquired, pursuant to Miss Van Kleeck's instruction, how much money he would need for his equipment and travelling expenses, and then hastened home to inform the delighted Gertrude of the result of his mission.

The young lady now found it necessary to take another step in the road to domestic authority, by resuming the custody of that part of her property which remained in her father's "strong box" at home, where a considerable sum in gold and silver was stored away, with the family plate. It required some courage to renew the contest for supremacy with her aunt, but animated by the importance of the cause in which she was engaged, she struck for freedom, and after a long and hotly contested battle of words, the old dame flung down the keys in a rage, and retreated to the kitchen, growling deeply in Low Dutch, a language to which she always resorted when much excited.

Getty flew to the box, which had so long been interdicted to her, and took from it the sum which Mr. Vrail had named as necessary for the negro's expenses, and in addition thereto a considerable sum in the smallest kind of gold pieces. This last amount, she told Brom, he must take with him to use in any emergency, either of his own or of his master, and that he must conceal it in some way securely in his clothes, and let no one know that he possessed it.

Brom chuckled greatly, and promised implicit obedience.

"How much will that leave me, Missis Getty, in there?" he said, nodding towards the box, which he supposed to contain an immense treasure, including his own dues.

"It will leave you all that you had before, Brom. This does not come out of your money by any means."

"Golly! Missis, are you going to give Brom all that money"——

"And more, if necessary. Only be perfectly faithful and discreet, and remember all that I have so often told you about—about"——

"Taking good care of Massa Harry?" asked the negro, grinning.

"Yes," said Getty, slightly coloring.

"I will sartingly remember."

"And be sure never to say or hint anything to him about my sending you to the war, or furnishing you with money, or anything of that kind."

"I will be sartin, sure."

Gertrude thought with some trepidation, that Harry might possibly call to bid farewell to her aunt and herself before quitting the country, and such, indeed had been his design for some days past, during which he had frequently requested his brother to accompany him there. But Tom objected.

"It would be quite a waste of civility," he said, "upon old Miss

Van Kleeck, who would as likely as not send for a United States officer to arrest us; and as to Getty, I have really quite relinquished my designs upon her."

Harry hesitated awhile, but at length he resolved to go alone. Common politeness required it from one who had so long been an acquaintance of the family, and he was besides anxious to make sure that he was not contravening the wishes of Miss Van Kleeck by encouraging Brom's military aspirations.

It was on a cool evening, early in November, that Mr. Vrail found himself seated in the pleasant parlor of the Van Kleeck mansion, awaiting the entrance of Gertrude. A glowing fire of wood blazed and crackled upon the hearth, and without the aid of the two candles, which burned almost unobserved in tall silver candlesticks upon the mantel, fully lighted the large room, and was reflected back from every side by the highly polished surfaces of the old-fashioned solid mahogany furniture. Everything was scrupulously clean. The ceiling was dazzlingly white, the carpet seemed guiltless of dust and lint, and the sofa, drawn out corner-wise to the fire, had a most tempting air of comfort and repose, while the tall brass andirons and fender shone as only Dutch servants can induce brass to shine. The hearth, indeed, and its accessories, were the crowning specimens of Flemish neatness. The very ashes seemed to have been taught the duty of falling within certain prescribed limits, while a very clean brush hung in the chimney corner ready for quick service in driving back any intrusive flakes.

When Getty entered the room, it was with an air of much embarrassment, and even alarm, and although she shook hands with Harry, and replied to his questions after her health, her agitation gave the appearance of anything but cordiality to the reception.

But Harry did not expect much of a welcome, and he was not disappointed at this. If it had been Tom, he thought, and he had chosen to make himself agreeable, how differently Getty would have acted, and he could not help thinking, as his eyes were riveted upon the really beautiful face which was before him, yet partly averted from him, how very strange it was that Tom should think of going to the war.

Gertrude had seated herself upon the sofa, and her visitor sat down in a chair at some distance from her; and after he had inquired about her health, and the health of aunt Becky, there was an awkward silence, which it seemed impossible for either party to break.

Harry spoke, at length.

"I am about leaving home for an absence of uncertain duration," he said, "and I have called to say good-bye to yourself and your aunt."

Getty immediately rose and pulled the bell-cord which dangled over the mantel, and then reseating herself, replied that she had heard of Mr. Vrail's intended absence. When she had directed a servant girl, who answered her summons, to request her aunt's presence in the parlor, she felt reassured by the expected arrival, and found courage to say something more.

"Rumor says that you are going far, and on a dangerous errand. I suppose I must not inquire whether this is true?"

"It is true," replied Harry, smiling, "although I do not say so publicly; but the cause in which I am about to engage, is one which, after much reflection, I have been convinced is a just one, and fully worthy of the sympathies and assistance of Americans. I may be mistaken, but if at any time I should see cause to change my views, before it is too late to retract, I shall undoubtedly do so."

"I know very little of the cause," replied Gertrude, "but I fear —I would say, I suppose—there must be more than the usual perils of war attending it."

"It may be so; I have not counted the danger closely, for although I lay claim to no unusual courage, my life has heretofore been one of such dull inaction, that even danger is not with out its charms for me. I confess I do not think, with Thomas and Col. Allen, that our entrance into, and progress through Canada, is to be merely a triumphal march."

"If that expectation is generally encouraged, it may lead many to join the ranks of the patriots who would prove but feeble assistants in the hour of battle."

"Very true."

"May I ask if there are many going from this neighborhood?"

"Only six besides my brother and myself, and one of these, you may be surprised to learn, is your former servant, Brom. Part of my errand here to-night is to inquire if you approve of his going—or, rather, to learn if you had any objections to it."

Getty rose, and adjusted some ornaments on the mantel-piece, and while doing so, if Harry had thought to steal a side glance at her face, he would have seen that it was deeply suffused with blushes as she replied,

"Brom has the entire right to control his own movements, and I have not the least objection to his going."

"He is a powerful fellow, and knows no fear, and will undoubtedly make a very good soldier."

"Will he be in your company?"

"If I should have a company, he undoubtedly will. He has already elected me his captain, and I have promised him that he shall, at all events, be near me. If there is"——

"Excuse me for interrupting you—but I hear aunt Rebecca, and it may be better not to speak on the subject before her. You know she is peculiar in her views."

Harry had only time to thank his fair companion for her caution, when the door opened, and Dame Becky entered, and advanced in a hurried way to the middle of the room, where she stopped.

"I could not come before, Getty, and I can't stay now," she said "the apples are not half pared or strung yet. How do you do, Mr. Vrail? Do you want anything in particular of me?" And the dame lowered her head, and looked sharply at him over the black rim of her spectacles.

"I have only called to say good-bye to yourself and your niece, Miss Van Kleeck," replied Harry, who had risen on her entrance and remained standing; "I am about leaving home."

"Oh, yes! I have heard that you were going away—a pretty sort of wild goose chase it is, too, that you are going on. There's Brom, too—*he* must go. I hope it is not you that has been and 'ticed him into it."

"Aunt Becky! for shame!" exclaimed Gertrude, coloring scarlet.

"When I seek to make proselytes for the cause," replied Harry smiling good-naturedly, "it will probably not be among his class."

"Well, no offence. I am sorry that you are sich a"——

"Aunt Becky!"

"Well, no matter—good-bye—I must go back to my apples. Getty, see to the fire, and—and the front door, and you had better come and help us as soon as you can"—and the old woman departed as unceremoniously as she had entered.

Mortified beyond expression at her aunt's rudeness, Getty knew not what to say; but Harry did not seem to notice it, nor did he offer to resume his seat.

"My aunt is very,—inconsiderate," said Miss Van Kleeck, hesitatingly. "Do not allow her remarks to hurry your departure."

"Certainly not. I ought not easily to take offence in a house where I have received so many hospitalities," replied the visitor, in a voice rendered mournful by the retrospect of departed joys.

Getty's eye glanced at the portrait of her father hanging against the wall, and she would not reject a compliment which belonged rather to her deceased parent than herself.

"I believe my father always thought your visits a great favor," she said.

"He was quite an original thinker, then," replied the young man, with a quiet smile. "I know but very few of that way of thinking."

Getty now looked mournful in turn, and Harry immediately thought what a monster he was to speak so frivolously when her father was the subject of conversation. He added, quickly,

"He was a most kind-hearted and amiable man, and I have every reason to cherish his memory with regard. But I am detaining you from your aunt—good-bye."

Getty gave her hand, but it was utterly impossible for her to speak—her eyes were full of tears, which Harry, blind to the last, believed to be caused solely by the renewal of her filial grief. And so they parted.

CHAPTER VIII.

BARAK, THE AGITATOR.

Of Captain and Lieutenant Vrail's journey to the North, it is not necessary particularly to speak. The few recruits from H—— did not all leave town together, nor of course, with any degree of parade, which could distinguish them as men bound on a military expedition. The brothers were accompanied by Brom, who was allowed an outside seat upon the stage-coach, in company with the driver, with whom, in his frequent stoppings at the village, the negro had long before become acquainted.

He knew well, too, every member of the strong, and glossy team which pranced and curveted beneath the lash of his companion, having often assisted in giving them water in front of the village inn, at a time when he little dreamed of ever arriving at so distinguished an honor as riding behind them on a journey to Albany.

A happy man was Brom, and so exuberant were his spirits that he had frequently to repeat to himself a caution which Harry had impressed upon his mind, to say nothing on the subject of his journey, although, if he had been disposed to be communicative, he could have told the coachman very little which he did not already know, either about his new passengers, or the errand upon which they were bound. He sounded the negro at times, indeed, for his own amusement, when the latter would look very grave, and shake his head, and say that he was travelling for his health.

"The truth is," said Brom, with a merry twinkle of his eyes, "I have been very much confined for the last thirty years" (he had never been ten miles from the place of his birth), "and I don't think it agrees with me, so I'm going to try travelling."

"You are not very pale, Brom."

"Yhah! yhah! yhah! no, I'se got some color left—yhah! yhah!"

"But ain't you really afraid, now," asked the other, sinking his voice into a confidential whisper; "ain't you afraid of going to Canada to fight the red-coats?"

"You jes mind your own business, and give that off leader there another clip—see how he lags. Ef you don't look sharp, I'll go and ride inside with the rest of the gemmen."

One of the places of rendezvous for the attack now in contemplation, by those in command, was Oswego and its vicinity and the point of intended entrance into Canada was near the village of Prescott, on the St. Lawrence river, where Fort Wellington, well garrisoned by the British, was to be the first object of assault. Our travellers were supplied, as has been said, with all the requisite signs and passwords with which to recognize their fellow "hunters," wherever they might meet them; but these signals became scarcely necessary as they drew near the place of embarkation, so general and so wide-spread among all classes was the sentiment in favor of the pending movement. Still, in all the large towns through which the various recruits passed, it was necessary to avoid any open avowal of their destination, if they would have the connivance of the officers of the Federal government, many of whom were willing to wink at the offenders, as far as their own official safety would possibly permit.

Numerous secret agents were on duty at Syracuse, and other prominent points on the Western Railroad vigilantly watching all the arrivals at the public houses, and secretly applying a test question to all whose destination was northward, which, if comprehended, at once placed them on a footing that admitted of giving information in regard to the best mode of advancing to Oswego. Several canal boats had been chartered, and were lying in the basin at the first named village, ready to start for the lake-port, which is only thirty miles distant. They were of the class of freight vessels usually called "line-boats," and were capable of carrying several hundred persons each, in a manner little calculated to attract attention in the emigrating season, when almost every westward bound craft was thronged with human beings. Indeed in so cool a month as November, the voyagers could remain entirely concealed, if they chose, beneath the high decks which extended almost the whole length of the boat. This mode of travel was compulsory upon none, and was designed chiefly for the humbler class of recruits, who were glad to avail themselves of the cheapest mode of progress.

The Vrails, after consulting with several emissaries of the cause at Syracuse, resolved to proceed by stage-coach to Oswego, and they received minute instructions as to the hotel at which they should stop, where they would be certain to find themselves at once in communication with the leaders of the expedition. Harry concluded to retain Brom in his company, a step which Thomas the more readily acceded to, as it gave the brothers the appearance of travelling with a servant, a degree of state to which the young captain was far from feeling indifferent.

At the moment of starting they were joined by a man of very Yankee-like aspect, whose appearance was indicative of much shrewdness, and who was introduced to them as a reliable and influential member of the war party. Mr. Barak Jones, indeed, according to his own account, as narrated to his fellow passengers before he had been ten minutes in their company, was a very mighty hunter, indeed, and one who had already rendered most important aid to the patriot cause.

"May I ask what rank you hold in the service?" inquired Harry, after listening for a long time to the vaunts of his new companion.

"Well, I am not exactly *in* the army," replied Jones, "though I shall probably accept a commission soon. You see I am an agitator. I have been travelling through the country forming clubs, and making speeches, and inducing people to enlist. There are more'n forty of my men now at Syracuse, waitin' for the boats."

"Ah!" replied Harry, "you must have had some influence."

"Yes, sir, although I say it myself, I don't think there's a man that has done more, onless praps it's Col. Allen, who bein' a colonel on the start, natrally had more influence."

"Do you know this Col. Allen?"

"Like a book, sir; a brave man he is, too, and no more afraid of the Britishers than of so many mosquitoes; a right down brave man is Col. Allen, sir. *He* is going over."

"*Over!*" exclaimed Harry, who thought the word sounded like desertion. "What do you mean?"

"Why, over the lines, sir. He's going to *fight*. I presume he is at Oswego now?"

"Well, are not *you* going over?"

"Why, I don't know that I shall *just yet*," said the other, hesitatingly, "as my services may be more valuable on this side. I rather think they want me to keep agitatin'."

"But it will certainly have a better effect upon these men whom you have induced to enlist, if they see you with them in the field."

"Y-e-e-s, praps it would, but *they* think I am going; and, as I said before, I *intend* to go one of these days, you know. Bless you, sir, there's no fear but what there will be enough. The whole country is rising, sir, and all Canada is ready to rise and shake off its shackles the very moment that our flag floats from the battlements of Fort Wellington. Yes, sir, let us but strike one bold blow, and "——

Harry saw that his companion had now evidently fallen into

one of his set speeches, and, not caring to hear it through, he interrupted him by asking what colors it was proposed to plant on Fort Wellington.

"The tri-color, sir. That is the flag under which the patriots fight, who, you see, are chiefly of French descent. By-and-by we shall probably join the stars and stripes with it."

"Where is Mackenzie now?"

"The *great* Mackenzie!" echoed Jones, enthusiastically. "Well, sir, I must confess I don't exactly know. He may be at Oswego, possibly at Ogdensburg, but wherever he is, you may be certain he is not idle. He is moving the machinery, sir; he is moving the machinery."

"Undoubtedly, but I am sorry he is not to command this expedition in person."

"No, sir. Generals B—— and E——, as you, of course, are aware, are to be your leaders, assisted by Colonel Van Shoultz."

"Who is this Col. Van Schoultz, of whom so much has been said?"

This question was answered by another passenger, a middle-aged, gentlemanly man, who had remained silent until now, and of whom Harry knew nothing, excepting that, like all present, he belonged to the secret fraternity.

"He will be to us, we hope, what Kosciusko was to our forefathers in the days of the revolution. Like him, Van Shoultz is a Polander, who has fought for his own country until she has ceased to exist as a nation, and has since sought a refuge and home in America. He is a man of talent and education, and promptly volunteered his services in a cause so similar to that of his own suffering land."

"I have not been able to learn what command the famous Bill Johnson is to have in this affair. It seems to me, that man is more to be relied on than any of these untried officers."

"The commodore will be on hand with some of his immediate

followers; but I believe he is not ambitious of any rank. His great desire is to see the blow effectually struck, and he is willing that the honors should be divided in advance among those to whom they will be an inducement to action. He will be sure to win his laurels in the field."

"He is a remarkable man, and should have some command, which would make his influence and example greater upon the soldiers. There is not a more popular man engaged in the cause than this Hero of the Thousand Isles, as he is called."

"He is a most brave, determined, resolute fellow; there is no doubt of that. A man for whose capture two great nations are offering large rewards must be of some consequence."

"Yes, I am sorry that our Government should seek his arrest; though I suppose he would have little cause to dread such an event after all, any further than as an interruption to his designs."

"Bless you, no sir," replied Barak, "that proclamation is only for show, and to keep 'em quiet over in England. Government don't want him caught by any means, although they would of course have to pay a reward for him, and shut him up a while for infringing the neutrality laws."

"Nothing is more certain than that they would not deliver him up to the British."

"*You may well say that!*" exclaimed Jones, with flashing eyes. "The Government that undertook such a thing wouldn't *be* a government three days. The thing could not possibly *be done*. I should jest like to see the United-States Marshal backed, if you please, by a regiment of soldiers, undertaking to carry Bill Johnson to Canada to give him up to the British. Why, sir, the whole country would rise to rescue him."

"I do not doubt it, nor is there any danger of such an attempt: but if the Commodore should be captured on the other side, his fate is, of course, sealed."

"Yes, sir, he'd swing, beyond a peradventure."

It was on the afternoon of the 4th of November that the travellers arrived at Oswego, where, under the pilotage of Mr. Jones, they readily found the hotel to which they had been directed, and which was situated somewhat remote from the central part of the village. The house, however, was thronged with guests, the most of whom were quiet, sedate-looking people, and not a few were evidently gentlemen. Many little coteries of three or four individuals were assembled in various parts of the piazza and of the adjacent grounds, engaged in animated, but by no means boisterous conversation. Of these a considerable number gathered around the stage coach as it drew up to the inn, and watched the alighting of the passengers with much appearance of interest. Jones was instantly recognized and hailed by several, to whom, much to the surprise of the brothers, he instantly and openly introduced them as Captain and Lieutenant Vrail.

"There's no need of any secrecy *here*," he added, in explanation to them—"these are all picked men, one may say."

"And marked men too," said the landlord, a fat, bustling and very jovial man, who superintended the unloading of the baggage of his new guests. "We are marked men, all on us, ha! ha!"

The young men found themselves treated with much consideration, and were promised that, in the evening, they would have an opportunity of an introduction to the commander of the expedition, and several other of the leaders, including Colonel Van Shoultz. They did not fail to observe that a large number of the individuals present were addressed by titles indicative of the rank of commissioned officers; but Captain Vrail was disposed to regard this as an evidence of the magnitude of the movement, and he did not doubt that there would still be a deficiency rather than surplus of officers, when once they had made a successful stand on Canadian soil.

In the evening the Vrails, together with several other gentlemen who had arrived during the day, were introduced to the commander, General B——, to Colonel E——, the second in command, and to Colonel Van Shoultz. The former was a man of somewhat pompous manners; but, apparently brave, and very confident of success in the great undertaking which he had in hand. He received the new comers with great cordiality, and addressed them briefly on the subject of the enterprise, which he said was destined to prove the most important political movement the world had seen in the present century, and which could not fail to cover its actors with glory.

Col. E——. also was a man whose appearance gave promise of acting a brilliant part in the coming struggle: but neither of the principal officers impressed Harry so favorably as the young Polander, Colonel Van Shoultz, whose grave and manly air, and firm, resolute expression, contrasted favorably, at such a moment, with the more flippant deportment of his superiors.

He was about thirty years of age, and both spoke and understood the English language with tolerable accuracy, and although apparently reserved in his general intercourse with those about him, he seemed disposed to attach himself to Harry almost from the first moment of their introduction. This feeling was fully reciprocated on the part of Lieutenant Vrail, and the young men passed much of their time in each other's company during their stay at Oswego.

CHAPTER IX.

THE MIDNIGHT ARMY.

On the eighth of November, all things being in readiness, it was resolved, at a council of the leaders of the expedition, to dispatch an express to Syracuse, with orders for the immediate embarkation of the recruits, who were in waiting at that rendezvous. Two schooners, chartered by the invaders, were lying at anchor in the Oswego harbor, awaiting orders; and when the canal boats, two days later, arrived by way of the Oswego canal, it was an easy matter, under cover of the night, to transfer their living freight to the larger vessels, which immediately moved out of the harbor, and made sail in a northerly direction, filled with armed men. With the exception of a small number of officers, however, who were placed on board the schooners, the party at Oswego did not embark in these vessels, but remained until the afternoon of the next day in that village, and then when the steamboat United States was ready to sail on a regular trip for Ogdensburg, they took passage in her as ordinary travellers.

The sudden appearance of so many men almost at the moment of the starting of the steamboat, excited no little surprise; but coming from different quarters of the town, being unarmed and deporting themselves with strict propriety, and in no respect like an organized company, there was no excuse for denying them the ordinary right of travellers, whatever suspicion may have been excited in regard to them.

"They look at me very close," said Colonel Van Shoultz whose foreign and military air excited much attention. "I thought that large gentleman, whom you call United States—what?"

"Marshal," said Harry.

"Marshal—I thought he was going to invite me to go on shore with him. Ah! I should not like that," added the Polander, breathing freer at the thoughts of his narrow escape and of the endangered loss of his military glory.

They were safe out of the harbor when this conversation took place, and the young men continued at intervals to discuss the prospects of the opening campaign, as, seated upon the deck they glided down the lake, and watched the various objects of interest which presented themselves to view.

"Do you know the number of our present force?" asked Vrail.

"Not precisely. We count our men by hundreds as yet I believe; but it is said that we are to receive large accessions at Sackett's Harbor and Ogdensburgh. If we should not, however, I doubt not our present force is sufficient for the slightly garrisoned fort we are to attack. Our true strength lies in the disaffection of the Canadian people towards their government, and in the great popularity of our cause in your States. One success you perceive, must bring many thousands to our standard from both sides of the frontiers."

"Of course—and success at an early period becomes consequently of most vital importance to the cause. Doubtless our leaders will neglect no precautions to render the contemplated blow effectual."

"Our arms and military stores are ample, our officers and men are brave and enthusiastic—I see no obstacles. I have known a European State revolutionized by a fewer men and less brave than those engaged in this enterprise."

"I was slow to be convinced," said Harry, "that the quarrel between the Canadian people and their government was such as to justify the interference of our citizens, but I believe that when tyranny and oppression become manifest and manifold, its victims are legitimate objects of interest and aid for the whole human family. Such seems to me the present case, and, unless we are strangely deceived, the voice of the mass of our northern brethren is calling upon us for the assistance which we are about to offer them. It becomes, then, a sort of holy crusade, in which the patriot and the philanthropist may engage with ardor, satisfied that whatever may be his individual fate, the wise and good will everywhere approve his conduct."

This conversation was carried on under some restraint, for the colloquists well knew that they were objects of suspicion to the commander of the boat, who was greatly alarmed lest his involuntary agency in transporting patriot troops should render his vessel liable to seizure.

"Tell you what, gentlemen," he said to Vrail and Van Shoultz, stepping in front of them, in the midst of the dialogue, which was conducted in a mysterious half whisper, "I don't want to know anything of your affairs, but if you are 'hunters' please keep as quiet as possible until my boat is clear of you. I've washed my hands of this affair from the beginning, and yet it seem as if I were destined to be mixed in it some way, in spite of all I can do.

Vrail and Van Shoultz politely promised not to say or do anything which could give offence.

Later in the day, the brothers were surprised to discover among the passengers their stage-coach companion, Mr. Barak Jones, who they supposed had remained at Oswego.

"Ah! gentlemen, I'm glad to see you," said Jones, approaching them with an air of boldness and enthusiasm; "the ball is rolling now, isn't it? The blow will soon be struck—the great—the *de*-cisive—the victorious blow."

Impressed by his courageous deportment, for which quality he had not before given him much credit, Harry replied,

"I am happy to see you so sanguine of success Mr. Jones."

"Sanguine! oh, yes, sir—I have no fears of the result, sir—not I. The whole country is rising, sir, and let us but once plant our flag on the battlements of"——

"Yes, but when did you change your mind about accompanying us to the field?"

"Oh, bless you, sir, I'm not going *over*," replied Jones with great coolness; "I am only going to Ogdensburgh, to address a meeting to-morrow."

"Oh—ah—yes, I see."

"You know, the fact is, I can't be spared."

"I suppose not..'

"But do you see those two schooners about half a mile ahead of us? The wind has failed them, and they are dropping slowly down with the current."

"Can they be our vessels?" asked Harry, in a whisper.

"They ain't anything else," replied Jones also in a low voice; "and although you can't see more than two or three people on board either of them, they are chock full of armed men. Col. Smith is in command there, and I reckon I know what he is after now."

"What is that?"

"He means to get towed down by our innocent captain here, who is already scared half out of his wits, lest he should be suspected of aiding the patriots, and thus should have his boat seized."

Mr. Jones' calculations did not prove incorrect. As the United States drew near, and was about to pass the schooners, the usual signal was given from the deck of each vessel, by some one personating the character of master, that they desired to be taken in tow. As this was a part, and a profitable part, of the ordinary business of the steamboat, it was complied with, without other questions than as to the destination and freight of the weather bound vessels.

We are going to Ogdensburgh, and we are both loaded with flour," was the reply.

The steamer passed between them, and one being secured to either side, she continued her course down the lake, with no material diminution of her speed.

Jones and his companions watched their movements with great interest.

"Do you see that little fellow with the boatman's ragged coat on, and with a jammed hat?" said Barak; "he stands just alongside of the helmsman, on that off schooner here?"

"Yes—a Scaramouch of a fellow."

"That's Colonel Smith—a wide-awake fellow, as you'll see to-morrow. He is disguised now, of course."

"He had better stay below—he may be recognized."

"No; he has something to say to us, you may depend. I shouldn't wonder if he should come aboard."

But Col. Smith manifested no such immediate design, but contented himself with walking the deck of his vessel, apparently much engaged in whittling a pine stick, yet losing no opportunities of observation of the steamboat's passengers. No signs, however, were exchanged, and no communication passed during daylight, but as the day drew to a close, the officers came on deck, and sauntered, as if by accident, to that side of the steamboat nearest the disguised colonel, who, soon after dark, joined them without difficulty. The coolness of the evening had driven most of the passengers below, and there was no difficulty in finding a retired spot where their conversation would be private.

Their deliberations resulted in a determination to continue their present course down the lake and its outlet, the St. Lawrence river, until they arrived near Ogdensburg, and then, after transferring to the schooners all that portion of the party who were passengers on the steamboat, to part summarily with that vessel, and pursue quietly the small remainder of their voyage without its aid. This plan was carried into effect. Smith returned to his vessel, and Gen. B—— caused his whispered orders to be circulated among his party, to hold themselves in readiness to go on board the schooners at the shortest notice.

It was not, indeed, expected to carry out this measure without detection by the officers and crew of the United States, but they cared not, when once their object was accomplished, how soon their unwilling allies should discover the nature of the trick which had been played upon them.

"It will serve them right, the shilly-shally fellows, who are afraid to help such a cause as ours," said Jones; "I only hope their boat will be seized in the first port it enters, for bringing us so far on our way."

It was, perhaps, at his instance, that it was resolved, on approaching the place of intended separation, to summon the men with fife and drum, and depart with all the parade and *éclat* which their straitened quarters would admit of.

Great therefore, was the consternation of Captain B., and great the amazement of his unsuspecting passengers, when they were awakened from the sound sleep of a later hour than midnight, by the loud *réveillé* upon deck, and by the hurried tread of those who had awaited the signal in their berths, and who now hastened to obey the summons.

Rushing upon deck, and vainly seeking to gain an explanation of the turmoil which surrounded him, and as vainly exerting his authority to suppress it, the discomfited captain, whose angry shouts were drowned by the music and by the loud tones of military command, resigned himself to his fate, and waited with what patience he could summon, to see the upshot of so strange an affair.

Still unsuspecting the character of the two schooners at his side, he became impressed with the idea that his boat had been seized, and was about to be pressed into the service of the invaders of Canada, (a feat which would have been by no means difficult to perform,) but he was soon relieved from this apprehension, by the sudden departure of the midnight army over the sides of his vessel. Turning his eyes for the first time toward the schooners, he discovered, by the dim starlight, that their decks were crowded with men, who had emerged from the cabins and holds, and whose numbers seemed scarcely to afford room for the additional forces who were joining them.

As soon as the last of Gen. B—— party had left the steamboat, he gave orders to detach the schooners from their fastenings.

Dropping silently down the stream with no propulsion save that of the current, the invading party found themselves at daylight between the villages of Ogdensburgh and Prescott, the former being a republican, and the latter a royal town, situated, *vis-à-vis*, upon opposing shores of the St. Lawrence. Here it was their misfortune to get into shoal water, and one of the vessels became stranded, an event which, for a while, threatened the most disastrous consequences to the expedition.

CHAPTER X.

THE INVASION.

Both towns, of course, became at once the scene of the utmost excitement—for it was evident to all that Fort Wellington was the point of attack, and thousands of people thronged the shores upon either side of the river, anxious to witness so momentous an event and rife with conjectures as to its issue.

On the American side, however, all were not idle spectators. Captain B., of the United States, had taken the first opportunity of washing his hands of guilt, by stopping at Morristown, and giving notice to the authorities of the movement in which he had been made to play so important, yet so unwilling a part, and an express had been dispatched by land to Ogdensburgh, in order that measures might be taken there to intercept the schooners, or at least to prevent their receiving accessions to their numbers.

This precaution had operated very differently from the design of its originators. No sooner had the United States reached her wharf at Ogdensburgh, where she arrived soon after the express, than a multitude of people rushed with loud shouts on board, took forcible possession of her, and started out to the relief of the grounded vessel. This movement was met by a corresponding one from the watchful citizens of Prescott, at whose wharves a steamboat was also lying. The Experiment (such was her name) had either been armed in anticipation of an attack, or was temporarily supplied with a piece of ordnance from the town, with which she greeted the American steamer several times, a compliment which the latter was unfortunately unable to return, nor could she, on account of the shallowness of the water, get near enough to the disabled vessel to render effectual assistance. But she passed down the river about a mile, to Windmill Point, on the Canadian side, where the other schooner had preceded her, which latter vessel, after landing her forces, returned to attempt to take off the men from her grounded consort.

The United States accompanied, and covered the schooner from the fire of the Experiment, which followed both at a prudent distance; but in the meantime, the excited populace on the American side were preparing other help for the invaders. A small steam ferry-boat, which plied between Prescott and Ogdensburgh, well-manned, and provided with small arms, was sent out to the relief of the stationary schooner, which she succeeded in hauling off, under a brisk fire from the Experiment, returning the salute with muskets and rifles, at the expense of seven lives to the enemy.

The United States, meanwhile, returned to Windmill Point, landed between one and two hundred of her men, and, with a small remainder, returned to Ogdensburgh, where she was surrendered to her owners, and, to the signal dismay of her neutral captain, was immediately afterwards seized by the government.

Among those who had been most forward in this initiatory step of the war, whose courage and skill had been most conspicuous, who had seemed everywhere present at once, who had animated and inspired all hearts with his own enthusiasm, was the hero of the thousand isles, William Johnson. He had now returned in the United States, and proceeded to earnestly harangue the populace, urging and beseeching them to go with him, and join the few hundreds who had already effected a landing on the other side. He succeeded in inducing some, at different times in the course of the day, to cross with him in the schooners, but rumors of a most extraordinary defection from the little army, in the persons of their principal leaders, began to prevail, carrying dismay to the hearts of all the active friends of the cause.

B—— and E—— had re-crossed, like the brave Johnson, to Ogdensburgh with the design, or pretence, of urging the large number of patriots assembled there to cross and join their comrades, but the former of these individuals was either taken suddenly ill, or feigned illness, and both proved inaccessible to their friends on reaching the American shore. They either departed, or remained concealed, leaving the brave Van Shoultz alone to conduct their perilous enterprise, with little chance of farther accessions from the American shore, and deprived even of a large portion of the military stores which had been prepared for the expedition.

The little band of invaders, meanwhile, unconscious that they were deserted, and expecting hourly the return of the schooners, with their leaders and their allies, proceeded to strengthen their position at Windmill Point, and to prepare for the coming contest. They took possession of the Windmill, and of several other large stone buildings, and awaited with sanguine expectation, not only the approach of their American friends, but the accession of that coming multitude of Canadian patriots, whom they believed to be hastening to their standard.

When the desertion of two of their leaders, and the loss of a large portion of their stores, became known, they were saddened indeed, but by no means in despair. The greater, they thought, would be the honor of the Spartan few who maintained their proud position, and became the rallying point of a nation's oppressed and uprising masses.

Colonel Van Shoultz proved equal to his responsible position; he had officers and men of indomitable courage around him, and his gallant ally, Johnson, seemed in himself a host, so great was the influence of his name and of his dauntless demeanor.

But it is time to speak more in detail of the immediate subjects of our narrative, whose fortunes were so intimately connected with the events of the war. Harry Vrail's intimacy with Colonel Van Shoultz had resulted in keeping both himself and his brother near that officer while on board the vessel, and with him they had been among the first to set foot on the enemy's shore. When the Polander found himself chief in command, he consulted his young friend frequently in his movements, and he would gladly have elevated him to a position near himself in authority, if he had been able to do so, but he did not feel at liberty to disturb the settled orders of rank in his little band. In the division of forces, the Vrails became attached to a party under the command of Col. Allen, which was stationed in a stone store-house, that, like the Windmill, served to some extent the purpose of a fort, and Brom, to his great delight, found himself in no danger of a separation from his chosen master.

But there was another member of the invading army who found less cause for exultation. Barak Jones had made some mistake in regard to his expected opportunity for leaving the schooner and landing at Ogdensburgh and to his great dismay he found himself on British soil, in company with the men whom his eager persuasions had induced to enlist. He would have returned when B—— and E—— went back, but he had been so terrified while on board the United States, by the pursuit of the Experiment, and by the cannonading from that vessel, that he did not dare to attempt to re-cross while she was lying in the river, waiting to renew the attack.

There were other opportunities for escape on the first day, in the schooner with which Commodore Johnson crossed several times, bringing over recruits, but here the danger was equally great, and was magnified tenfold by his fears. Yet he would have run the risk of returning, in preference to remaining, if he had not been induced to believe, probably by some of his proselytes, who despised his pusillanimity and wished to detain him, that there would be a chance to cross in the schooner at night, when darkness would shield it from any serious attack. That opportunity of course, did not come, and Barak, more dead than alive, remained in the camp, not in any recognized military capacity, nor directly attached to any division of the troops, but selecting his quarters with those whom he thought most safely stationed, and most remote from the danger of a first attack.

Thomas Vrail's ardor for the war had considerably cooled, and he chafed not a little at serving merely as a private, while carrying a captain's commission in his pocket. Yet he continued sanguine of soon seeing himself at the head of a valiant company, and one of the laurelled victors in the great revolution at hand.

Harry, although more skeptical, was not without similar hopes. He knew well that the spirit of rebellion extended far and wide throughout the Canadas, and he could not doubt the information which had come from so many seemingly authentic sources, that the people had already flocked by myriads to the standard of revolt. Rumors of approaching armies began to reach them, almost from the moment they touched Canadian soil, and they were hourly excited and tantalized by these fallacious tidings. In the meantime, the provincial government was not idle. If the friends of the patriots were tardy, their enemies were not. The garrison was increasing at Fort Wellington, troops were pouring into Prescott, and armed vessels made their appearance in the river. Everything, indeed, indicated that the enemy were not going to await an attack from the invaders, but that they were about to take the initiative step in the approaching hostilities.

Harry Vrail's judgment was too clear to overlook the perilous position in which his comrades and himself were placed. He saw how disastrous must be the result, if their landing should prove to be premature, and if they should fail to effect a speedy junction with the insurgent forces of the provinces. Very valorous he knew their little army to be, but he was not visionary enough to expect that, few as they were, and imperfectly provided with miliary stores, they could maintain themselves against the tenfold force which would speedily be brought against them, and which, if insufficient, could easily be increased yet tenfold more.

But Harry did not quail. He had chosen his part, perhaps mistakingly, but he was a *man* in the broadest acceptation of that significant word. He was prepared to do his full duty to the cause which he had espoused, and to endure whatever destiny it might entail upon him. If he saw the danger, he did not proclaim it; his voice and mien was everywhere that of the courageous and ardent soldier, who, if he did not achieve, would at least deserve success. He knew that help might come in time to save them, and he acted like one who believed it would. To Colonel Van Shoultz alone, in their most private consultations, did he disclose his full views, and in the mind of that brave, but discreet man, he found them fully reflected.

CHAPTER XI.

THE BATTLE OF WINDMILL POINT.

THE invaders were not left long in suspense as to the designs of the enemy. Early in the morning after their arrival, a cannonade was opened upon them, which was returned with spirit by their battery upon the shore, and at "about eight o'clock," says an eye-witness, "a line of fire blazed along the summit of the hill in the rear of the windmill, for about eighty or a hundred rods, and the crack of the rifle and the musket made one continuous roar." This, however, was but the prelude to a more serious attack, which was made by a body of five or six hundred regulars and volunteers, when all the courage and mettle of the little band were in requisition to meet the determined assault of the foe.

Well and bravely did they vindicate their claims to courage in a hotly contested battle of about an hour's duration, which resulted in driving back the enemy to their fort with large loss, while only five of their own men were killed, and about thrice that number wounded.

This striking success, of course, produced the most exhilarating effect upon the patriots, who congratulated themselves upon their triumph with ecstasy, and indulged in a proud presentiment of increasing numbers, and a career of victory. The tidings would reach the interior in a few hours, and summon thousands of the doubtful and the undecided to their side. It would reach the States still quicker, flashing hope, like electric light, through all ranks of their timid friends, and bringing multitudes, eager for the fray, to their victorious banners. Such were the bright hopes and anticipations of the invaders on the second evening of their encampment on foreign soil.

Both the Vrails had acquitted themselves creditably in this engagement, but Harry's coolness and activity had won the especial encomiums of his comrades and his commanding officer. His perfect presence of mind, and his dauntless demeanor, had produced a marked effect upon others, especially upon the inferior soldiers, which contributed greatly to the fortunate result of the day, and he became at once exceedingly popular. Brom, also, won his laurels, acting his part not only with perfect intrepidity, but with a glee which, although unsuited to so serious an hour, had its effect in inspiriting others who might have been inclined to fright in this, their first experience of war. He stood at his master's side, loading and firing with great regularity and rapidity, and keeping up an undertone of ludicrous comment, which more than once elicited an audible laugh from his nearest companions. "Now you've got it!" he would say, as he fired off his piece, and watched for a second to try to distinguish its effects upon the opposing ranks; "tink I saw him drop that time!" he muttered, as he proceeded to ram down another cartridge.

"Now for another red-coat! Golly, if it ain't just like shootin' the Christmas turkeys with their red-heads. Jingo!" he shouted, as a ball passed, whistling, close to his head, "but the turkeys are shootin' back!"

The succeeding day was one of inaction. The intimidated enemy did not renew the attack, and the invaders, who might now be called the besieged party, while holding themselves in readiness for a vigorous repulse of any assault, looked all day long, anxiously and earnestly, for their anticipated succors. Every vessel upon the river, however distant, was closely scanned, and many longing eyes were fastened upon the American shores.

which were plainly visible from the camp, with the hope of seeing some signs of their approaching auxiliaries. Others watched the highways which led into the heart of the invaded province, confident of the bannered hosts which were soon to emerge from distant forests, and advance with defiant tread, timed to the martial airs of freedom. Alas! they did not come. The day waned, the sun went down, and all was doubt, uncertainty and irresolution as to the morrow.

"One thing is sure," said Colonel Van Shoultz, to Lieutenant Vrail, on the evening of that day of dread suspense; "although we may not receive reinforcements, the enemy certainly will, and probably by to-morrow, at the farthest."

"Ours may yet come," replied Harry; "indeed, our friends from the other side would be most likely to cross in the night, when they could most safely effect a landing."

"It is possible, but I am learning not to hope too much. After witnessing desertion in the highest quarters, and faint hearts where the loudest boasts of valor have been made, it is natural rather to fear than hope. This night may diminish rather than increase our numbers."

"There is little chance for desertion. The ferry at Prescott is, of course, strictly watched, and we have no small boats, excepting Johnson's, which he has carefully secured. You do not fear that he will fly?"

"He will fly when this fort does," replied Van Shoultz, looking around at the stone walls of the mill. "Ah! if all were such as he, we should have no cause of disquietude to-night."

The Polander's predictions and presentiments proved alike true. The enemy were reinforced on the morrow, and the patriots were left to struggle alone against the hourly increasing numbers of a foe which threatened their utter extermination.

Attacked both by land and water, cannonaded from steamboats and from field batteries, they maintained the unequal struggle, dauntlessly and hopefully, for nearly two days, still looking for the approaching banners, and listening for the charging shouts of their promised allies.

On the afternoon of the second day, a large force of the enemy drew near the forts (if such they might be called), by land, and were met with a hot and galling fire from the several divisions of the patriot army, stationed in the windmill and the other stone buildings which had been fortified. It would have been madness in the bravest to have met them in the open field while such strong defences were in their possession, almost compensating for the great disparity of numbers between the belligerents.

But this advantage was too great to be left long in their possession, if it were possible to dislodge them from their fastnesses, and it soon became evident that the British had determined to attempt to carry the forts by storm.

The building in which Col. Allen's command was stationed was somewhat remote from the windmill, and was attacked, as was each of the camps, by a separate body of the enemy. The attempt to storm it was twice repelled by that valiant officer and his men, who were stationed in a large apartment in the second story, extending the whole depth of the building, and commanding both the lower entrances, which were strongly barricaded; but a new calamity awaited them in the failure of their ammunition. The slackening of their fire became so necessary, and its cause so apparent to the enemy, that the third attempt to enter the building was sure to be successful whenever it should be made.

The game was too evidently lost to admit of a moment's hope on the part of the most sanguine, and nothing remained to be done, excepting to surrender unconditionally, or to throw away their lives in an obstinate, but useless conflict. Allen was doubtless a brave man, and perhaps his own choice would have been to render

"His last faint quittance with his breath,
While the sword glimmered in the grasp of death."

But he doubted his control over his little band, now thoroughly panic-stricken, nor could he make up his mind to devote so many men to immediate and certain destruction.

While he hesitated, the tumult increased below, another volley of bullets poured into the windows, finding a few more victims among those who were unable to avoid a full exposure, and then, with an impetuous rush, the enemy gained the main entrance to the building, bursting down its barricades, and pouring tumultuously into the lower hall. Their steady tramp was next heard by the besieged upon the very stairway of their citadel, and many a face became blanched with fear. In another moment the large door was burst open with great violence, and thirty muskets, levelled for immediate discharge, were protruding into the room, commanding every part of the apartment, while simultaneously with their appearance a demand was made, in a stentorian voice, for surrender.

It was impossible longer to maintain strict discipline, and although the majority of the men preserved a soldier-like composure, and awaited the orders of their leader, there were a few others who had boasted largely of their valor when danger was distant, who now manifested the most abject and craven fear. Shrieks and cries of " Don't fire !" " Yes, we surrender !" were heard from two or three of these, who were seen scrambling to get in the rear, and farthest from the expected volley. One who carried a commission in his pocket, and who having always had his courage at his tongue's end, had probably allowed it to escape, was seen shrinking close to the wall, crouched down behind a fat private, who was too stupid to stir, or to understand that his body was serving the purpose of a shield. From this shelter he called out, in a tremulous voice,

"Shall we be treated as prisoners of war, if we surrender ?"

"You will be treated as you deserve," was the answer, in a

trumpet-like voice; "you must surrender unconditionally—you are entirely in our power."

"Well, here's *my* musket—so don't shoot *me*," he said, pushing past his protector, and stooping as he advanced to avoid danger from the bristling array of guns which confronted him. In another instant he was hauled outside, and was placed under guard. His example was speedily followed by others, and for some minutes the victors were engaged in receiving the arms, and securing the persons of a portion of the patriots, while the majority yet awaited the reluctant orders of their leader to lay down their arms.

At that critical juncture, when the enemy appeared at the door, Harry Vrail missed the faithful Brom from his side; but so great was the confusion, and so general was the rush for self-preservation, that he did not deem his disappearance a matter of surprise. But the negro had by no means deserted him—on the contrary, all his thoughts were given to devising means for his rescue Ever since he had made his solemn engagement to Gertrude to watch over and protect his master, his mind had been devising expedients to deliver him from whatever danger seemed to threaten, and from the hour they had set foot together upon the enemy's soil, he had calculated the possibility of disaster, and had planned impossible modes of relief.

Ever vigilant and watchful, while others were confident and careless, he had overlooked no remote or minute circumstance which an hour of extremity might render serviceable to one whom he loved so well, and whom he had sworn to befriend. His lodgings, for several preceding nights, had been in a dark corner of the large room in which the scenes last described were enacted, where, with several others, he had occupied the interior of a large, open bin, for a sleeping apartment. On crawling out of this strange dormitory the preceding day, he had accidently dropped his knife behind it, and it became necessary, in order to recover his lost property, to move the huge chest farther from the wall against which it stood. It required great effort to do this, even with the aid of a lever, but when, having succeeded in removing it a few inches, he stooped to regain his knife, he caught sight of another metallic object beside it, which on close inspection he found to be a hinge in the floor. Further examination produced its fellow, and being convinced he had found a trap-door leading to a lower apartment, he hastily shoved back the bin, and sat down to reflect on the discovery, and the possibility of its being in some way turned to account. Circumstances, he knew, might arise which would render it in the highest degree useful to his master, but in order to make it more certainly so he believed it important to keep it secret from all others. When a more favorable opportunity occurred for pursuing his investigation, he removed the bin and, raising the door, ascertained that it communicated with a small store-room beneath, from which a back window, seemingly the only one in the apartment, opened upon the river. Hastily making these observations, he replaced the door and the chest, and quietly resumed his duties.

CHAPTER XII.

A RECREANT BROTHER.

When Harry missed the negro from his side in that moment of horror which has been described, the latter flew to the ponderous bin, which, in his excitement, he thrust aside as if it had been a basket, and standing beside it, with his watchful eye upon his master, he waited coolly for the moment when he might raise the door without detection. The confusion was momentarily increasing, and those who were not pressing forward to surrender, were anxiously watching both the threatening guns and the still silent lips of their leader, who hesitated to speak the painful word of submission. Brom saw that the favoring moment had come, and noiselessly raising the trap-door, he hurried back to the side of his master, whom, without addressing, he began gently to drag toward the rear of the room.

"What is it, Brom?" said Harry, in answer to the violent pantomime of the negro. "You need not be afraid to speak in this Babel—nobody will hear you."

"Come wid me, Massa, come wid me," were all the words which the African could be induced to utter.

Vrail suffered himself to be led as far as the open door, which he no sooner saw than he fully comprehended the plan of escape, and his heart leaped with sudden joy at so unexpected a hope of deliverance. But his thoughts instantaneously reverted to Tom.

"Not without Tom," he exclaimed, and darting off from the spot, he dashed off in pursuit of his brother, whom he had seen last at nearly the extreme opposite end of the room, and near to Col Allen. When he reached that spot, however, his brother was no longer there, and at the very moment when he was hastily searching for him among the crowd who were stacking their arms (for the word of submission had at last been spoken), Thomas had glided around to the rear of the mass in search of *him*, with no other design then that of keeping near him in their common calamity. He was met by the negro, who hastily whispered to him the chance of escape, and implored him to assist in finding Harry.

"It is death to go back," exclaimed the terrified and pusillanimous youth; "let us fly; he will be sure to follow us, since he knows the way. Come, be quick."

So saying, he dashed forward to the trap-door, while Brom turned back in eager pursuit of his master. His excited and nearly frenzied condition was unfavorable to the successful result of his search, and threatened momentarily to arrest attention and defeat his efforts, for that portion of the apartment nearest the door was fast filling up with the enemy. But fortunately as yet, there was a general confusion, in which the shouted orders of the leader of the victorious band, the rattling of the grounded muskets, and the groans of the wounded were the principal sounds.

While Brom was thus wildly seeking for his master, the latter was as earnestly pursuing his quest for the recreant Tom, who had selfishly deserted both. Mingling in the crowd of surrendering men, and borne by the mass toward the fatal point where, with them, he must become a guarded prisoner, the gallant youth did not falter in his resolute purpose, nor once think of turning back alone to seek the means of escape. Of course his search was vain, and while closely scanning every face in the throng of which he could catch a view, his attention was arrested by some execrations behind him, bestowed apparently by different parties, upon some one who was pressing eagerly forward towards the front.

"Blast the blackamoor!" said one, who could jest in his calamity; "he steps on a dozen of us at once, with his elephant feet."

"Stand back, Cuffy; don't be in such a hurry; you'll be hung soon enough to suit you," exclaimed another.

"Why don't he go and walk over the Britishers?" said a third, whose toes had felt the heavy heel of the African; "hang me, if I don't believe he would drive them all out in a few minutes."

Harry could not doubt as to who was the subject of these remarks, and in the next moment he caught a view of Brom, who was, however, too far separated from him by the crowd, to admit of any communication passing between them. As soon, however, as he caught the negro's eye, its expression, together with some significant pantomime, convinced him that his brother was found, and he managed by great effort to commence a retrograde motion against the strong tide which had before borne him onward to a point of such dangerous proximity to the foe. Warning the sagacious negro by a sign to go back, they both succeeded in working their way to the rear, which was as yet unguarded.

"Where is he?" whispered Vrail.

"He's gone long ago—Massa Harry—this way—come along now, I say."

Astonished, bewildered, and half incredulous, the young man hesitated to advance.

"It's sartin sure," repeated Brom; "come quick, now, or you'll be too late. See—see—there comes a lot of red coats this way."

"Don't run, Brom," said Vrail, "or we are lost. Go slowly, and we may not be noticed, or it may seem as if we were only going back for something that has been forgotten."

The negro obeyed, and tremblingly they succeeded in reaching the trap-door, apparently without observation.

"Massa must jump so," said Brom, skillfully letting himself down by his hands, and dropping into the lower apartment.

Vrail followed his example, and they stood together on the lower floor.

"He is not here," said Harry, glancing quickly around the room. "Brom, if you have deceived me, I will not stir a step further."

"He is gone, Massa Henry, I swear it. See here," and he pointed to the raised window, through which the fugitive had doubtless passed. Convinced at length, that Tom was really out of the immediate scene of danger, Harry gave his mind wholly to securing the escape of himself and his faithful companion. Hastening to the window, he saw that it opened upon the river, at the distance of only a few rods from its margin, and that the shore, in that immediate vicinity, appeared to be entirely unguarded. The conflict, indeed, was yet waging in some parts of the encampment, as occasional shots and shouts were heard, and the moment certainly seemed a favorable one for successful flight.

If Harry could have joined any portion of the patriots who were yet making a stand against the enemy, he would certainly have done so, but this was clearly impossible. Leaping, therefore, from the window, and calling upon Brom to follow, he hastened to the shore, with the intention of following the course of the river, and keeping close to its edge. In the opposite direction, which led toward Prescott, of course he could not flee with any prospect of escape. But he had no sooner reached the shore, than the fallacy of his hope to elude observation became apparent.

A little way down the river, but at considerable distance from the shore, lay an armed steamboat, which had been engaged in bombarding a portion of the barracks, before the contest had become so close on land as to render its fire dangerous to the attacking party, and which now seemed to be either guarding the coast, or waiting in inaction whatever duty might be assigned it.

However this might be, no sooner had the flying lieutenant and his servant appeared upon the shore, than a shout from the deck of the distant vessel reached their ears, and at the next instant a cannon ball came booming over the water and buried itself in the bushes behind them. A rattling fire of musketry followed, and Harry dropped upon the beach, to the boundless terror of the negro, who rushed quickly up to him.

"Oh, massa—massa—are you really dead ?" exclaimed the poor fellow, frantic with fright.

"Follow me," said Harry, creeping rapidly behind the shrubbery which grew thickly at a little distance from the shore.

"Where did they hit you, Massa Harry ?"

"They did not hit me at all, Brom," replied Harry, coolly; "and I do not mean they shall. I wish I knew where poor Tom is."

"Never mind Captain Tom, Massa Harry—we've got our hands pretty full enough now, I think, to take care of ourselves. Golly, massa, look at that !" he exclaimed, springing suddenly aside, and pointing at the cannon ball they had so narrowly escaped, and which now lay harmless beside them. "Let us get away from here."

"Never fear, Brom. Sit down on it, if you wish to be quite safe. Lightning never strikes twice in the same place, nor cannon balls either, I presume."

Harry spoke lightly, in hopes of allaying the alarm of his companion, but he felt all the peril of his position, and while he talked thus calmly, his mind was rapidly devising means of escape, and calculating the chances of finding his brother.

"We shall have to skulk around here till midnight, I suppose," he continued, "and then either swim across the river, or find some other means of making the passage. How far can you swim, Brom ?"

"Oh, I can swim all night, I spect; I've swum across the Hudson river, many's the time, where it's wider than this here St. Lawrence—though 'tain't so swift, to be sure."

"It's a pretty long stretch," said Harry, after gazing a few moments at the opposite shore, with a longing to place himself beneath the protecting Ægis which seemed to canopy every inch of American soil.

"I wish we was there," replied Brom, following the direction of his master's eye; "we should not have any Britishers bombarding us over there, should we, Massa Harry?"

"I don't think I can swim it."

"I can help you, Massa Harry."

"I don't know about that—I do not see how you can swim for more than one. If you can swim all night, as you say, you might carry me over in pieces."

"I can help you," reiterated the negro, not heeding the jest; "when you are tired, I can hold you, and let you rest."

"And who will hold *you* in the meantime."

"Oh, I'll be walking up stairs," replied the negro, alluding to a feat well known to swimmers, by which they sometimes sustain themselves for a considerable time in the water while giving rest to the arms.

"More likely we should both be going down stairs to Davy Jones' cellar. No, no, it won't do, Brom—at least, not for me," said Vrail, now speaking more seriously; "I must find a boat of some kind, or I must trust to some of the Canadians for assistance. If I were confident you could succeed in crossing, I would insist upon your doing so alone; but it is an unknown stream, and its waters might prove as treacherous as the people upon its shore, who have lured so many of our brave countrymen to destruction. The darkness, too, would quadruple the peril, as you could not see the opposite shore, and if you became bewildered and frightened, you would be sure to be lost."

"You need't preach all that to me, Massa Harry. I shan't go, 'less you do, any way—so that pint is settled."

A second volley from the steamboat, which sent a few scattering balls among the shrubbery around them, reminded them that they were watched, and induced them to change their position.

CHAPTER XIII.

THE MAGIC RIFLE.

Vrail did not dare to emerge from his hiding-place, but he ventured to draw near enough to its outer edge to reconnoitre the formidable enemy who had seemed to think two trembling fugitives upon the beach a proper subject for his prowess. Great was his alarm on discovering a small boat, containing six or seven men, putting off from the steamer and approaching the shore, very evidently for the purpose of effecting their capture. Both himself and the negro were armed, having preserved their guns, while Vrail had also his pistols, and his resolution was instantly and coolly taken.

"This way, Brom," he said, raising his rifle; "they are after us now, half a dozen of them. If they land, there is no help for us. Stand ready now, to load as fast as I fire."

Vrail was a practiced marksman, and he felt so certain of the fatality of his aim that he hesitated a moment with a natural reluctance, but a random volley from his approaching foe, designed to keep them within their cover, determined him, and he pulled the trigger.

An oarsman sprung from his seat, and fell over the edge of the boat which was nearly capsized by the hasty rush of his comrades to his assistance.

"I am sorry for him," said Harry, coolly exchanging guns with Brom, and raising the second weapon to his eye.

"Golly! I ain't," replied the negro, ramming down another cartridge; "hav'n't the cowardly rapscallions been cannonading us?"

Again the hurtling lead went upon its mission, and another man was seen to fall, but the oars were again speedily manned, and the increased speed with which the boat approached the shore showed a courageous design to effect a landing before the weapons could again be loaded and brought to bear.

"Fool!" exclaimed Harry; "I meant to have spared him," bringing the weapon which Brom now handed him to bear upon the leader of the party, who sat in the stern of the skiff, and who at the next instant was added to the list of victims.

"Golly! there goes the cap'n," shouted Brom with great glee. "Now for another!" he continued, handing up the ready gun.

"Wait a little! I rather think they have enough. I believe they are going back."

"Then it's jes the time to pepper 'em, massa; quick, now, give it to them! Golly! didn't they cannonade us?"

Vrail was correct in his conjectures. The progressive motion of the skiff had been stopped, and after a moment's pause, it was turned about and moved rapidly toward the steamboat, to which it was still much nearer than to the shore. Whether this was by order of the wounded officer, or whether he had given his last orders, it was impossible to tell, but nothing was more certain than that the foe were in full flight. Again the African conjured his master to fire upon them, and the speed with which they fled showed that they expected another discharge, but no urging would induce Vrail to take a human life needlessly.

"We have defended ourselves so far," he said, "but it would not benefit us in the least to take another life. I am really very sorry for those poor fellows, Brom."

"Jingo! massa, *I* ain't. Didn't they *cannonade us?*" repeated the negro, who could not forget his fright at being fired upon by a cannon from a vessel of war, and who did not seem disposed to forgive the offence.

That the steamer approached no nearer the shore during this singular contest, was doubtless owing to some very effective shots which she had recently received from one of the patriot forts, a repetition of which might be apprehended, for the result of the several engagements on shore, if, indeed they had yet fully terminated, was unknown to the commandant on the boat. His remaining forces, however, were not idle spectators of this engagement with the " band of marauders on the beach," as in a subsequent dispatch he styled the two fugitives: but they kept up some random firing toward them, especially during the retreat of their comrades in the boat.

Although temporarily elated by his extraordinary victory, the young lieutenant was far from expecting to make good his escape. He might be considered even to have increased the peril of his position, for his capture, which seemed still almost unavoidable, could scarcely result in anything short of his immediate death from his enraged foe. While daylight lasted, there was no possibility of emerging from his narrow shelter without the certainty of detection and successful pursuit, and scarcely three minutes elapsed after the return of the small boat to the steamer, before it was again sent out by a circuitous route, to gain a distant part of the beach, farther up the stream, and beyond the reach of the magical weapon which had proved so disastrous to its recent occupants.

There were but three individuals in it this time, and the design was very evidently to give notice to some party of the enemy on shore of the lurking place of the fugitives, and to draw down upon them an immediate force which no strength of theirs could resist or evade. It was late in the afternoon, but the sun was yet twice the breadth of his disc above the horizon.

Vrail watched anxiously its tardy movements down the declivity of the sky, hoping against hope for the speedy arrival of that darkness which might afford them one more chance of escape. Never, seemingly, had the great luminary been so slow in its descent, and it almost seemed to him that some miraculous interposition had taken place to arrest the orb of day, like that which stayed its progress down the heights of Gibeon at the bidding of the prophet of God. From the sky to the water and to the flying boat, and back again to the sky, his impatient eye wandered, and he calculated closely the time which might elapse before the sound of pursuit would be heard. Fly he must, but darkness alone could give him even a faint chance of escape. The village adjacent was by no means large, but all its inhabitants, as well as the scattered population of the country for many miles around, had been aroused by the exciting events of the day, and on every road which led into the interior, people were passing to and from the seat of war.

The shore of the river alone remained nearly deserted, but this there was, of course, no safety in traversing under the guns of the steamboat, which had already so nearly proved fatal to them.

While Harry watched in momentarily increasing anxiety, the skiff had passed far up the stream, and began rapidly to approach the shore, and yet the sun had not touched the horizon; but the breeze which so often springs up at the day's decline was rising with unusual strength, and soon the summits of some ascending clouds became visible in the west.

They rose too, with such a breath of base, so "volumed and vast," as to promise an effectual extinguishment of the remaining daylight, from the moment they should receive the descending luminary within their capacious folds. Such, too, was their effect. The night drew suddenly on, unpreceded by the usual twilight, and the still rising clouds promised to make it one of unusual darkness. Of course the fugitives lost no time in emerging from their place of concealment, although with no well-defined idea of the route they were to pursue; but Vrail resolved to leave the river shore, which would be sure to be the first place of search by their pursuers. Being nearly exhausted by fatigue, and suffering with cold and hunger, he knew that he might be compelled to trust himself temporarily to the mercy of some Canadian family, yet he was unwilling to wander far from that stream, which afforded the only means of return to his native land.

There was little time, however, to choose roads, for he had scarcely gone forth from the bushes before he heard the clamor of pursuit, and he hurried forward, attended by his sable friend, not knowing whither he went, excepting that he was leaving the lights of the village behind him.

CHAPTER XIV.

A TYRANT AND A SLAVE.

The course of the fugitives was nearly northeasterly, and not diverging far from the river. They followed a road which led at times through dense woods, and at times through an open country, where an occasional farm-house was revealed by its evening light, and by the barking of its watch-dog as they passed. Their progress was necessarily slow, as the darkness was intense, and the way unknown to them, and they had not wandered long or far before Vrail began to contemplate making a trial of the hospitality of some of the inhabitants. His fatigue was very great; he had eaten nothing since early in the morning, and Brom, though far from being exhausted, was, like him, pinched with hunger. Besides, he thought the chances of meeting a friendly reception as good in one locality as in another, and being well armed, it would be an easy matter, if repulsed, or if he had reason to suspect betrayal, again to take to flight.

Thus arguing, he selected for his hazardous experiment a house, the faint light of which seemed not only remote from the road on which he was travelling, but far from any other dwelling. It proved very difficult of access, and as he travelled slowly across the meadows towards it, the flickering rays which guided him danced bewilderingly before his eyes, seeming at times, like the *ignis fatuus*, to recede as he approached it.

At length he drew near the building, but ere he came near to the door, he heard the sound of angry voices within, and he thought for a moment of passing on in search of more peaceful indications in other quarters; but impelled by his desperate and destitute condition, he dismissed his fears and knocked for admittance. The reply was gruff, but it bade him enter, and flinging the door open, he passed in, followed by Brom.

In a small room, beside a rough deal table, an elderly couple sat, with a meal of brown bread and potatoes before them, while a miserably clad, but pretty and gentle-looking girl, of about thirteen years, stood by the fireside, apparently the patient recipient of the joint rebukes of the other two. The man was small, sallow, and dirty, with harsh and homely features, rendered doubly repulsive by the scowl of wrath lingering upon them, and the woman, though possessing the remains of beauty, had a bold and cunning expression, and a general slatternliness of appearance more disagreeable than ordinary ugliness.

Vrail was not skilled in physiognomy; he had seen too little of the world for that; but if he had been so, the woman's countenance changed almost too suddenly after his entrance to admit of his analyzing its first expression, or retaining the effect it produced upon him. Her civil "good evening" was free from all rudeness or appearance of surprise, while her more blunt partner turned hastily to the intruders, and asked who they were and what they wanted.

"We want food, and assistance to cross the river," replied Harry, advancing nearer the table, throwing down some silver, and seizing a piece of bread, which he began eagerly to devour. "I can make it worth your while to assist us," he added; "besides, I think we ought to be friends."

"Oh, yes," replied the other, with a sudden change of manner; "I see what you are now. You belonged to the patriot army, I s'pose, and you want to get back home."

"Exactly so."

"They've been terribly cut up there at the Windmill, poor fellows—they are all killed or taken, excepting a very few who have fled, but even they will be taken, you know."

"Is it really so very bad?" asked Harry, who had not before learned the full extent of the disaster to his companions.

"Yes, shocking," was the reply, with a baleful gleam of the eye; "I've been down to the Point to see about it. There's dozens lying around there dead, and the prisoners are all marched to Prescott for to-night, with their general; and troops of people following and looking on. But come, sit down and eat, both of you, and we'll talk about that afterwards. You are safe enough here for the present; to-morrow it would be quite another thing."

The famished men waited for no second invitation, but sat down side by side, and attacked the homely fare with as much eagerness and relish as if it had been composed of the choicest viands.

"You think we shall be safe here for a short time?" asked Vrail, scarcely gaining the leisure to speak so long a sentence.

"Oh, certainly," replied the host, exchanging a look of intelligence with his wife; "there isn't a doubt of it, is there Hannah?"

"Not the least, I should think," was the reply, in a very bland voice. "Lock the door, Ruth."

The girl obeyed, and at the next instant the Canadian rose, and glancing again significantly at his wife, approached the negro, who, like his master, had retained his gun at his side when he sat down.

"Let me set your guns in the corner, out of your way," he said to Brom, in the mildest of voices; so mild that it would not have been recognized as belonging to the same speaker who had addressed them on entering.

He laid his hand on the weapon as he spoke, and Brom, who had a whole potato in his mouth and another in his hand, seemed like to acquiesce in the movement without any remonstrance: This was far, however, from his design. Clutching at the depart-

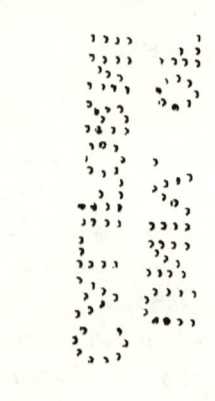

"The negro, clutching at the departing gun with his unoccupied hand, and shaking his head, drew it back to its former position."—Page 101.

ing gun with his unoccupied hand, and shaking his head, he drew it back to its former position.

"No, I tank you," he said, as soon as he could speak.

"Ah, very well, perhaps, it is better to keep them near you, in case of surprise. You would like to cross the river to-night, I suppose?" said the Canadian, addressing Vrail, very quickly.

"Of course," replied Harry, "as soon as possible, and, as I said before, I will pay largely to any one who will take us over."

"Golly! yes—a hundred dollars," added the negro.

Harry looked in surprise at Brom, not understanding the secret of his liberal offer.

"Don't talk about pay," replied the accommodating man; "I am ready to help a friend in need, I hope, without being paid for it. You just sit here and finish your meal, while I go and see if I can get Larry Smith's boat, and him to help me row you across."

"For mercy's sake," said Harry, jumping up, "do not let us lose the time, nor run the risk of trusting our secret to any one else. Let us help ourselves to the boat, and we will give you abundant means of satisfying your neighbor afterwards for it use. As to the rowing, we can do that ourselves."

"But the stream is very rapid, and I could not row the skiff back; besides, he keeps it locked. No, no, you need not be afraid to trust Larry—he is as true as steel—isn't he, Hannah?"

"That he is; every body knows that. The poor man's feelings would be dreadfully hurt, if he thought that anybody distrusted him."

"Very well, if it must be so—but do not be gone long."

"It is about a mile to Larry's, and the night is dark—it will take some time to go and come, but all you have to do is to keep quiet; and as soon as you have done eating, perhaps you had better put out the light, so as not to attract attention if any soldiers should be passing. If they really do come, why you can jump out of the window and make for the woods, and then you will be as well off as you were before."

"It is well thought of, about the light," replied Vrail, at once extinguishing the blaze of the single tallow candle which had very faintly illumined the room; "I think it would now be difficult for any one to find the house in such a pitchy darkness, unless they knew exactly where it stood."

"Of course it would, for you can't begin to see it from the road. But good-bye—keep up good heart till I return, which won't be very long."

He went out, and the woman followed him to the door, enjoining upon him in a loud voice to take care of himself, but saying something in a lower tone, as she drew the door nearly shut after her, standing on the outside.

At this moment the girl, who had stood nearly motionless in the chimney-corner ever since the entrance of the fugitives, advanced quickly a few steps towards Harry, and upon the door re-opening, as hastily retreated to her former position.

The faint light which gleamed from the embers upon the hearth revealed this movement, and the young man supposed that she had meant to take some food secretly from the table, having probably been kept fasting as a punishment for some offence. He began to make some inquiries about her, when the woman, in a whining voice, which was intended to be very gentle, said that she had been a bad girl, but that she might have her supper now, and bade her come to the table.

"I ain't hungry," replied a very faint voice, the articulation of which seemed to indicate a violent trembling of the speaker.

"Then go to bed," was the reply.

The girl remained motionless until the mandate was twice repeated, when she very slowly obeyed, passing near, and pausing a moment close to Vrail, who distinctly *heard* her tremble as she stood beside him

He was about to speak to her, when the voice of the woman again urged her along, and she passed into a corner of the room and ascended a ladder which led to an upper apartment. The hostess, in the meantime, became very voluble, and seemed bent on entertaining her guests until the return of her husband.

Nearly an hour passed away, which, of course, seemed to the young man fully quadrupled in length, and yet there was no sign of the man's return, and still his garrulous partner talked on with unflagging rapidity.

The rebellion was the theme, and as she could relate many an interesting incident connected with it, she found in Harry an eager listener. But he grew impatient, at last, and would hear no more.

"He has been gone long enough to have walked four miles—something must have happened to prevent his return," he said.

"It is very dark—he will certainly be here soon," replied the woman; "I will go and listen if I cannot hear him coming."

She went, as before, outside the door, quite closing it after her, for the night was cool, and at the same time Vrail heard a half whispering voice from the top of the ladder.

"They are cheating you. Larry Smith lives very near us, and he has no boat. Uncle Shay has gone after soldiers to take you."

Harry started up, and was about making his exit through the window, when reflecting that such a course might bring the poor girl under suspicion and procure some terrible punishment for her, he resolved to wait a few moments longer, intending to depart as if not suspecting his host.

"Do you know of any boat?" he asked hastily.

"Yes—about two miles down the river, at Mr. Wells'. But you must hurry. They will go directly there to find you. Do not wait a minute. Oh, I hear voices now."

Vrail sprang to the door and locked it, resolving not to be taken alive, as he knew that his capture would be equivalent to death. He next ordered Brom to jump out of the window, a command which the negro was not slow in obeying, and he stood ready to follow him, yet waiting, in hopes of obtaining further information in regard to his way. The next instant the door was tried, and then the voice of their returned host was heard modulated to a tone of mildness decidedly winning.

"It is I and Larry—I have found him at last. Be quick, and open the door."

"Oh, don't open it," added the voice from the ladder. "There are six or eight men. I have seen them from the window. There is a short way to the place where Wells' boat is kept, if you can find it—but you must hurry."

"I fear I can neither find the short way nor the long one; I do not even know the way to the river, and the night is very dark."

Harry advanced as he spoke with a foreboding heart, and with a conviction that if he failed to make good his escape across the river before daylight his capture would become certain, as the country would be thoroughly aroused by his pursuers, and all the passes would be secured.

The girl's warning and his reply had been quickly spoken, and the reflections we have recorded had been instantaneous; but already another, and an impatient summons was heard from without, accompanied by a violent shaking of the door.

"What is the matter there—can't you find the lock?"

"Wait a minute," replied Harry. "Good-bye, my good girl; you have saved our lives for the present. Take this."

As he spoke he felt a light grasp upon his arm, and heard the whispered words—

"Hurry, hurry, they are coming around the house."

She had glided down the ladder, and now fairly dragged the young man forward to the window, and when he leapt out she followed, seeming almost frantic with the desire to save him.

"I will show you the way to the river, and will go a little way with you," she whispered, again grasping his arm outside the house, and dragging him forward.

They advanced as rapidly as the darkness would permit, followed by the negro, who had been waiting for his master, and stimulated by the momentary expectation of hearing the sounds of pursuit.

CHAPTER XV.

RUTH'S STORY.

As soon as it seemed safe to slacken their pace, Vrail earnestly advised his gentle guide to return to her home, and leave them to their own resources, at the same time offering her some gold.

"No, no," she replied, "I will go on; you never can find the boat without me."

"But your uncle?"

"I do not care. He may kill me if he chooses, I do not care. Come on," she said, almost breathlessly.

"But you will have to return alone, two miles, in the dark—I cannot permit it."

"It is nothing. He often sends me further for rum, on worse nights than this. Nobody will hurt me, for I have nothing for them to steal."

When Harry still counselled her to return, she urged that if she went back now, she could not enter the house unperceived, and if her absence had been detected at all, it would make no difference in the degree of her punishment, whether she went the whole way or part with the fugitives.

The young man reluctantly yielded, and they proceeded on their way with renewed speed; yet he found time to question the poor girl about her history, which was so evidently one of suffering.

Her story was brief, and very pitiful. She was an orphan, and had lived since the age of six years with the man whom she called uncle, but who, it appeared, was not thus related to her. His first wife, long since deceased, had been her aunt, and in her lifetime Ruth had been adopted as their daughter, and had ever since borne the name of Shay, but his present partner was her oppressor, himself her tyrant, and she but the trembling slave of both. A menial child, friendless, overworked, poorly fed, and half clothed, she yet had forgotten her own miseries in her sympathy and alarm for the strangers whom she saw in distress, and whom, after effecting their deliverance, she could never hope to see again.

The contemplation of this picture drew tears from Harry's eyes, and as he listened to the poor child's story, told in the gentlest of voices, he was busy with devices for her relief, and half forgot his own danger.

"Why do you not leave people who treat you so badly," he inquired.

"I have nowhere else to go," she replied.

"But you can earn your own living. I will give you money enough to-night to last you for many weeks, and to buy clothes with."

She did not think she could earn her own living. They had told her she was good for nothing, and could do nothing well. Besides, she did not dare to make the attempt. *He* would be certain to find her out anywhere in that part of the country, and to drag her back.

Such was the substance of her reply.

Vrail began to reflect whether it was not a duty to take this poor child, thus providentially thrown upon his hands, along with him to his own country, if he should succeed in finding the means of escape.

"Would you be willing to go with *me?*" he asked, suddenly.

"When? Where? How?" she inquired with great eagerness.

"This night, if we can find a boat to cross the river—to my own home. I will do the best I can for you, and you will be certain never to see your uncle or aunt again."

"Oh, yes, yes, take me—take me!" she exclaimed; "I do not care where, if they will never get me again. I will do anything for you or anybody. I can work from daylight until dark without rest. I have often and often done it for them, and then been beaten after all. Oh, take me! take me!"

Harry assured her, with tears, that he would take her with him, if it were possible, and that in her new home she would have no such tasks or privations as she had been used to; but while so great uncertainty shrouded his own fate, he hesitated to say more to kindle a hope which might prove so painfully illusive. They continued to hasten forward during this conversation, and after some reflection, Harry took some gold pieces from his pocket, and said :—

"Take these, and conceal them about your person, and if we should become separated, and I should be captured"——

"I do not want them *then*," said the girl, interrupting him shudderingly; "they would be of no use to me."

"Listen to me; they may be of service both to me and to you, if you are prudent and courageous, as I know you are, far beyond your years. In my own country I have friends who will, perhaps, never know my fate, unless you can carry them the tidings. Dare you undertake this?"

"Yes; but can they do anything for you?" she asked, quickly.

"It is possible: but it is scarcely with that hope I send you to them. If I am taken, my doom will probably be a speedy death —perhaps before your eyes. Whatever it is, I wish my friends to know it, and I wish them to take care of you. Will you promise me to go to them?"

"Yes, but if they cannot help you?"

"If they cannot help me, no one else can. I do not mean to be taken; but if I am, I have no hope of escaping death, either immediate, or more remotely on the scaffold."

Harry proceeded to give the attentive girl minute instruction in regard to her journey, and the necessary preparations for it, all of which she seemed readily to comprehend. She was to proceed before daylight to Prescott, there to purchase, at an early hour in the morning, such articles of apparel as she thought essential to her comfort in travelling. Crossing the ferry to Ogdensburg, and availing herself of the ordinary public modes of travel, for which she was amply provided with funds, she was to pursue her way to Albany, and thence to Vrail's native village on the Hudson river. There she was to seek out old Mr. Rosevelt, and communicate to him her tidings, and the various messages which Harry intrusted to her memory.

It was with a sad earnestness that the orphan girl listened to these instructions, as she hastened along beside the stranger, whom she had temporarily saved, and who was in turn trying to confer benefit upon her.

"You have heard and understood all that I have said, and you will remember, and try to perform it well and faithfully, if I am taken or slain, will you, Ruth ?"

"Yes, yes, I will do it," she said; "but you will not be taken, if we hurry and get first to the boat. Let us go faster—we must be almost there."

"I hear the river now, massa Harry," said Brom, "off this away."

"Yes, that is the way, and Mr. Wells' house cannot be far from here."

"How large a boat does he keep?"

"It is only a skiff, but it will hold five or six. It is plenty large enough for us."

"Will it not be locked?"

"Only with a padlock, which can easily be broken."

"Why do you think it is likely that your uncle will lead the soldiers in this direction?"

"He will be sure to do so, if he thinks that I have accompanied or directed you ; for he knows that I know about the boat, and there is no other within several miles, excepting the ferry at Prescott, where, of course, you would not dare to go."

"Does he know of this short way, which you have brought us ?"

"Yes."

"Then we cannot be too quick or too vigilant."

The fugitives now ran as they conversed, and in a few minutes they were at the river side, in the immediate vicinity of the place where the skiff was usually kept. Darting eagerly forward, Ruth uttered a slight scream, as she stopped beside the post to which the little vessel, when not in use, was always chained, and discovered that it was absent.

"*It is gone !*" she exclaimed in a trembling voice.

Harry's heart sank, but the next instant revived with the thought that perhaps Tom had taken it, and had escaped.

"Is the chain or lock broken ?" he asked, coming up to examine the post.

"No, massa Harry, I guess not. There ain't any part of it in the ring, and the ring ain't broke, too."

"Then it has probably been removed by the owner, to prevent its being taken by any of the flying soldiers. This is the way the Canadians *help* us," he added biterly. "Where does this Wells live ?"

"Only a very little way from here. Look, you can see the light from his house through the trees."

"Come on, then Brom—the boat is probably in his door-yard, and we must bring it from there, it is our only chance."

They started, Ruth following, and now, for the first time, unnerved with fright.

"Golly !" exclaimed the negro, "I hope there ain't any dog to set up a barking, and call out all the folks."

"If there is an alarm, we must bring it off by force. See that your gun is in order, Brom, and pay close attention to my directions."

"I will sartin, massa Harry: of Mr. Wells comes out, I pop him right straight over, see ef I don't—and knock the rest of 'em over with the breech."

"You will do nothing of the kind, unless we are attacked with weapons, and nothing, at all events, without my orders. If we find the boat, and if any one appears to dispute our taking possession, we will do nothing more than to compel acquiescence. No life must be endangered, unless in self-defence."

A few moments brought them to the premises of the Canadian, whose house stood on a slight eminence, and fronted the river, about a dozen rods from the shore. It was enclosed by a fence, in which was a small gate directly fronting the main entrance of the house, and a larger one a little further to the left, designed for the passage of vehicles. Setting this gate open, with as little noise as possible and enjoining upon the trembling girl to wait for them beside it, Harry and the negro stealthily entered the grounds. Although acting in accordance with what is usually called the first law of nature, the instinct of self-preservation, Vrail could with difficulty overcome his repugnance to the task he had undertaken. But if he hesitated, a moment's reflection reassured him, and he went forward. It became necessary to pass the building in order to attain the rear yard, where they expected to find the object of their search, and through an uncurtained window they plainly saw several of the occupants of the house, including its master, a large coarse man, who was seated listlessly by the fireside.

Stepping lightly and quickly forward, they gained the yard, and almost at the same instant, to their great joy, they discovered the long-coveted prize. The boat stood upon a sled, which, notwithstanding there was no snow upon the ground, had been used to draw it up from the river, and Vrail at once concluded that the same mode would probably be the easiest for re-transfering it to the water's side. The oars were in the vessel, and as there seemed nothing in the way of at once effectually securing the safety of the whole party excepting the few rods of terra firma which lay between them and the water, hope grew into something like confidence in the breasts of the fugitives, and they began vigorously their task.

Placing their guns within the skiff, and stationing themselves on either side of the tongue of the sled, they started it with difficulty, and, of course very slowly. The necessity for silence also impeded their movements, and it was many minutes before they were able to drag their cumbrous vehicle past the house, whose windows, disclosing so much to them, threatened also to reveal their movements to its inmates. But, shielded by the darkness which enveloped everything without, they succeeded in passing the house and the gateway, from which point their progress was assisted by the declivity, and by all the strength of their feeble, but energetic auxiliary.

Ten minutes had taken them far beyond hearing-distance from the house, and every moment was giving additional assurance of safety; the sound of the river was in their ears—its pebbled margin beneath their feet; in imagination, the prow of their little bark was already ploughing the parting waves, and pointing to the land of Freedom—when Harry felt a vice-like grasp upon his arm, and at the same moment heard a scream from the negro at his side, which told that he also was seized. Before he could relinquish his hold upon the sled, or turn to defend himself, three or four men were upon him, a rope was passed around his arms, and he was secured beyond the possibility of escape.

Brom, despite the most violent struggles, and the most extraordinary vituperations against his assailants, was similarly treated, and the attacking party, which was the detatchment of soldiers guided by Shay, at once set out on their return to the fort, jeering their helpless prisoners, and promising them a speedy treat, either to a breakfast of bullets, or to a morning dance in the air.

CHAPTER XVI.

A GOOD SAMARITAN.

RUTH had fortunately escaped observation. At the moment of the attack she was in the rear of the vehicle, assisting with all her strength in its propulsion, and during the brief struggle which had ensued, she had sunk, stupefied with terror, to the earth, where she remained motionless.

When she found herself alone, she arose, still trembling with alarm, and overwhelmed with grief for the friend who had been so suddenly wrested from her side and hurried away probably to prison and to death.

She had no thought for herself. She knew not that she was suffering from cold and hunger, nor did she reflect on the dangers which surrounded her, but collecting her thoughts, she recalled as minutely as possible all the instructions which she had received from Vrail, and then, without a moment's hesitation, she set out on her adventurous journey.

She took the river for her guide, keeping upon its shore, and travelling in an opposite direction to the course of the stream, for this route she knew must bring her to Prescott, which was not many miles distant, and which even in the darkness she hoped to reach in a few hours. But faint and weary, chilled with the damp breezes from the river, and dejected by the dreadful scene she had witnessed, and which she could not cease to contemplate, she soon faltered, and with difficulty dragged herself forward, even at the slowest pace.

She tried to pray, but her words seemed to fall to the earth. No hope accompanied them. She believed, indeed, that there was a God, who was all goodness, for well she remembered and cherished the instructions which, in infantile days, her beloved mother had inculcated in her mind, but so many and so severe had been her early trials, that she had learned to consider herself in some way an exception to the universality of His providence. With childish simplicity, she believed herself overlooked or forgotten, or in some way too insignificant for Divine protection.

She did not murmur; there was no rebellion against Heaven in her heart; it was only an utter want of belief that she could be remembered or thought of by that great Power which created and guides the world.

Alas! how many far wiser than this neglected girl are equally at fault in discerning the bow of promise which forever spans the clouds of affliction, faintly indeed for the faint-hearted, but bright and gorgeous to those who gaze with the telescopic vision of Faith.

Fearful of falling by the wayside, perhaps to perish, Ruth resolved to seek for a dwelling-house and ask for admission and assistance, notwithstanding her great fear that she might be recognized and detained, or sent home.

A little refreshment and an hour or two of repose she believed would enable her to proceed upon her journey, and she could still reach Prescott long before day, and be able to cross at the ferry in the first morning boat. Thus resolving, she left the river side and wandered across the fields until she discovered a light in the distance, towards which she at once directed her steps. It proved to proceed from the upper window of a farm-house, and, at so late an hour, indicated, as she supposed, sickness in the family. She drew near and knocked at the door tremblingly, but without hesitation.

After considerable delay, an elderly woman came to the door, and, without opening it, inquired who was there, but when she heard a response in a female voice, she quickly drew the bolt and bade the stranger enter.

Ruth heard the permission uttered in kind accents; she tottered across the sill, and, overcome by exhaustion and by her emotions, she sank upon the floor in a state of complete insensibility. A desolate object indeed, and well calculated to move the hardest heart, was the poor child, pale, thin, and miserably clad, and almost without signs of life; but it was not a hard heart whose sympathies were now appealed to. With many expressions of commiseration, the good dame, who was a stout and florid Englishwoman of the lower class, hastened to bring restoratives to the sufferer, assisted her to rise, and conducted her to a vacant bed in an adjoining room.

"Now tell me, child," she said, as she bent over the shivering girl, "what has happened to you, and how is it that you are out alone so late, and on such a night as this?"

"I am going to Prescott," replied Ruth, faintly, "and I got very cold and tired—and—and I saw a light here and stopped in to rest."

"To Prescott—in the night—and all alone, and without any shawl or cloak? Where do you live?"

"Please don't ask me now; I must go on soon. Will you be good enough to give me a piece of bread?"

"Oh! mercy, yes," exclaimed the good woman, at once forgetting her curiosity, and flying to the cupboard.

"Here, eat this," she said, returning with a plate of bread and cold meat, "and I will make you a cup of tea, poor child; I suppose you have had no supper."

"I have eaten nothing since morning," answered Ruth, eagerly devouring the food before her.

"You have run away from somebody, I know; but do not be frightened; I shall not stop you nor ask you any questions, but I hope you know where you are going. You have friends somewhere, I suppose?"

Ruth hesitated and looked puzzled, but finally replied that she supposed she had.

"Can I stay here a couple of hours?" she asked, after a pause.

"You cannot go from here until to-morrow," replied the woman, "and you may stay longer, if you choose."

"I must go to-night; I must be in Prescott early in the morning—I must, indeed."

The woman gazed in astonishment at the child, who spoke with such a surprising energy of manner, as to leave no doubt of the invincibility of her resolution.

"Very well," she said, "but lie still now, and get some rest. Three or four o'clock will be plenty soon enough to start, and perhaps I can send our boy Jem with you, if I can get the lazy fellow up so early; and then I can lend you an old shawl or cloak to wear, and he can bring it back."

"Thank you," said Ruth, gladly, laying her head upon the pillow; "but I must not be late."

"Never fear; I will call you in time. I have to get up every hour, to give medicine to my daughter, who is sick. It will take you but a few hours to walk to Prescott after you are rested."

So saying, the good Samaritan withdrew to her own room, and left the little traveller to her repose—a repose so sound, and rendering her so oblivious of all things, that it seemed to her scarcely ten minutes had elapsed, when she was shaken by the shoulder and called to arise.

"The clock has struck four," said the hostess, "and I have got sleepy Jem up to go with you with a lantern, and here are some cakes to eat on the way, and you must wear this shawl, which is thick and warm, and Jem will bring it back. It is a raw morning."

Ruth look wildly around, and for a while was unable to comprehend her position or the words addressed to her.

"Bless the poor child," exclaimed the woman. "I hope you have friends at Prescott, or somewhere near there. You will perish if you have far to go, with nothing but that thin dress."

"Oh! I have got money to buy clothes," said Ruth, suddenly remembering her treasure, and drawing several gold and silver pieces from a pocket in her dress.

Lazy Jem, who had stood dangling the lantern in his hand and looking sleepy and surly enough before, suddenly brightened up, took a step forward, and became a very interested listener to the conversation.

"I wish you would take some of them," Ruth continued, holding it out to her benefactress, "for you have been very good to me, and you have saved my life."

The woman had seemed greatly astonished when she first saw the gold; a troubled and sorrowful expression next settled upon her face, but at the girl's offer of the money she drew back, and raised her hands as she replied—

"No—no—child, not even if you had come honestly by it, which cannot be. Ah, I see how it is; and you so young and so innocent looking, too!"

"We oughter stop her, mem, and send for a officer," said the boy, putting down the lantern. "I'll go immediately and fetch one, if you please."

Ruth did not at first comprehend the suspicion she had awakened, but as soon as she did so, she protested her innocence with the greatest vehemence, and at the same time with an ingenuousness of manner which carried conviction to the mind of her hostess.

Jem, if not convinced, pretended to be so, and remained silent. He left the room, however, and was absent about ten minutes, after which he returned hastily, and Ruth being now ready, after many kind words of farewell and of admonition from the dame she started upon her journey, accompanied by the boy, who trudged by her side, lantern in hand. She had no fears of a companion provided for her by so kind a friend, and she made several efforts to converse with the lad, who replied but briefly to her remarks, and seemed surly and unsocial. He was a stout boy, of about seventeen years, with dark skin, very black, straight hair, and a shelving forehead, underneath which a pair of glittering black eyes rolled perpetually, even while the head remained motionless.

Ruth noticed, after they had gone a little way, that he had a small bundle in his left hand, which she was certain he did not carry when they left the house, and she wondered much what it could be. She thought that, perhaps, he was angry with his mistress, for the unusual service put upon him, and that he was about to run away. The bundle, she thought, might contain his clothes, which he had carried a little way from the house before they started and might have picked up as they came along, unobserved by her. These suspicions passed throgh her mind, but did not make any permanent impression, for she felt refreshed and comparatively light-hearted, and not disposed to imagine or forbode evil.

Jem walked very fast and seemed impatient to get on, at which Ruth did not much wonder, nor did she complain, although she was forced to almost run at times to keep up with him.

He grew more and more surly as they advanced, and frequently urged her along with harsh language.

"Come on, you lazy baggage," he said, to the frightened girl, "a pretty business it is for me to stop every minute and wait for you to come up. Come along, I say!"

Ruth quickened her steps without reply.

"I tell you what; there's a long piece of woods to be gone through, about a mile ahead, and the sooner we get through with it the better. It ain't allers the safest place in the world."

The girl trembled, and asked whether there were any wild beasts there.

"No; but there are robbers there sometimes. Last winter a man was robbed and murdered in them very woods."

"But nobody would think of *us* having any money—they wouldn't try to rob *us*."

"Don't know—they might. Pr'aps you'd better let me carry them gold pieces of yours, 'cause they couldn't get 'em away from me as easy as they could from you."

Ruth said, perhaps it *would* be best, and she put her hand in her pocket and drew out her money.

They had been walking very rapidly during this conversation, but now the boy stopped so suddenly, and turned to receive the treasure with such an eagerness of manner as to awaken something like suspicion or fear in the mind of his companion, who immediately replaced the coin, and said:

"Perhaps you might lose it, Jem. I will keep it now, and if we see any robbers, then I will give it to you"——

"Then it will be too late, you fool. Give it to me now!"

"No—no—no!" exclaimed the girl, as the lad drew nearer, seemingly bent upon enforcing his command. "Let us hurry on!"

"I will not stir a step further until you give it to me. It isn't safe."

"Then I will go alone!" said Ruth, starting as she spoke; but the boy's hand was at once upon her arm.

"No you won't," he said. "I was sent to take care of you, and I mean to do it; so just give me the money. Be quick!"

"Oh, no, no, no! I durstn't. I—I—am afraid."

"Afraid of what? You don't mean to say you're afraid I'm going to keep it?"

"I—I—don't know."

"If I should it wouldn't be much, for you never came honestly by it. So hand it over now, and be quick about it, too."

The fierce and peremptory manner in which the boy now spoke

fully convinced Ruth of what she had before suspected, that he meant to rob her, and, snatching her arm suddenly from his grasp, she darted forward and ran from him at her utmost speed. It was in vain. Jem followed still faster, overtook her, threw her to the ground, and, holding her down, took forcible possession of the gold, despite her screams and lamentations. No longer making pretence of friendship to her, he extinguished his light, and leaving her still prostrate, ran off across the fields, but not in the direction of his home.

CHAPTER XVII.

A GUINEA NEGRO.

APPALLED by the magnitude of her misfortune, Ruth slowly arose from her recumbent posture, but remained sitting upon the ground almost in a state of stupefaction.

The robber had already disappeared from view, and she knew that it would be vain to hope for his return, or to seek redress. He would be certain not to go back to his late place of service, which he had evidently quitted with this very crime in view, as was apparent to her now, when she remembered the bundle which he had brought clandestinely with him, doubtless containing his own apparel. Ruth's grief, however, was not for herself; she scarcely considered her own destitution; she only thought how fatally her loss might result to her unknown friend, as she had no longer the means to fulfill a behest which he deemed so important, and, on the faithful performance of which she thought his life might depend.

Goaded by this reflection, she suddenly arose and hurried forward on her journey, with a vague hope, that she might still in some way be able to perform the task she had undertaken—a hope so faint, it was well-nigh akin to despair.

The road to Prescott was a direct one, from which she could not stray, and after a long and weary walk, and many alarms, she entered the village soon after the dawn of day.

She resolved to beg a few pennies to pay her ferriage across the river, and when once in the States, she would perform the journey on foot, if she could find no other means of progress, and she would make such great speed as might yet leave a slight chance for the success of her mission.

But the mendicant's art was a new one to the poor girl, and for more than two hours she paced the streets in a spirit of indecision, gazing wistfully into every face she met, but unable to utter a petition for charity. When at length she succeeded in asking, it was only to meet with repeated rebuffs, and occasionally with a silent look of contempt, until worn out with fatigue, she sat down on a door-step to rest, and, in her hopeless manner, again to pray.

She had stopped undesignedly opposite to the jail, and her attention was soon attracted by the assembling of a crowd around its walls in apparent anticipation of some unusual spectacle. From some passers-by, whose conversation she overheard, she soon learned that some of the American prisoners had been confined there through the night, and were soon to be brought out and sent to Kingston under a strong guard. They were some who had fled at the time of the surrender, and had been subsequently taken, but at too late an hour to admit of sending them to Kingston at the same time with the main body of captives, and she at once concluded that the young officer whom she had befriended was among the number. Inspired with the hope of seeing him again, and informing him of her great misfortune, she at once went over and mingled with the crowd; but a little reflection convinced her that there she would not be allowed to speak to her friend, when he was brought out. She pressed desperately forward through the throng; she saw the sentinel pacing his rounds in front of the building, and animated with such courage as carries soldiers to the cannon's mouth, for scarcely less would have nerved the timid child for such an act, she ran up to the fierce-looking man, and asked him if he would allow her to go in and see one of the prisoners, before he was taken away. The sentinel turned quickly, and was about to order her off, when something evidently in her desolate appearance, or in the very piteous accents of her voice, seemed to arrest his attention, and he replied mildly, as he continued his walk, that he had no power to admit her.

"Is there a friend of yours in there?" he asked, as she ran along at his side, looking up anxiously into his face.

"Y-yes, sir," she replied, hesitatingly.

"I am sorry for you, my child. Is it your brother or father?" he asked; and then, without waiting for a reply, he added, hastily, "possibly the jailer might dare let you in; he is a very good-natured man. That is him standing in the door-way, and if you will ask him to step this way, I will speak to him for you. I cannot leave my post."

Emboldened by this encouragement, Ruth ran to the jailer, addressed a few earnest words to him, and soon returned to the sentinel, followed by the wondering man of authority.

"Hale," said the soldier, "this poor girl has a friend among the prisoners, and she has travelled a great way, I believe on foot, to see him before he is sent away. As she will never see him again, don't you think you could manage to let her in?"

The man reflected a moment, and replied, "It could do no harm, I suppose, but I do not like to do it without permission. However, I will tell you what she can do. The poor fellows have not had their breakfast yet, and the girl may go into the kitchen, and when the food is sent in, she may carry something in."

"Oh, yes—yes—thank you!" exclaimed Ruth; "that will do."

"What is your father's name?" asked the jailer.

"It is not my father, sir, that I wish to see," replied Ruth. "He is a young man, and he has a black servant."

"Oh, yes, I know the man. He is supposed to be an officer, by reason of having a servant, but he will not admit it, which would be rather perilous. I know where he is—he and the negro occupy one cell. Come with me."

The girl followed the warder into the interior of the building, where she was given in charge to a servant, who, after some whispered instructions, conducted her to the kitchen, and directed her to lay aside her bonnet and shawl.

She met with ready sympathy among the servants, and was supplied, on request, with the means of making a hasty toilet, which she had scarcely done, before she was summoned to the performance of her solicited task.

A trencher, containing meat, potatoes and brown bread, was placed in her hand and she was directed to follow a large, surly-looking man, whose capacious arms contained the piled dishes for a dozen different cells. Her own load was designed for a single room, and that, of course, the one which contained Lieutenant Vrail and his sable companion. She trembled as she passed the massive doors and heard them close with a jarring sound behind her, and she started at the clangor of the sliding bolts, which, echoing along the dismal corridors, told her that she was locked in among the hapless prisoners whose fate she had bemoaned.

It was with much agitation that she drew near the cell of Vrail, which was pointed out to her by her companion, but fortunately she was not at first recognized, by either of its inmates.

Harry was sitting on a bench, looking pale and dejected, and Brom was standing beside him talking, and apparently attempting to console and cheer him.

"Here comes your breakfast, massa Harry," he said, as the girl appeared; "now you jes eat this, and you feel better right off."

Ruth had no time to waste, and she immediately spoke.

"You do not know me," she said, "I am the little girl"——

"Who tried to save our lives, and would have done so but for my own stupidity," exclaimed Harry, springing up and approaching the door. "How have you come here Ruth, and why? This is a very dangerous experiment, for your uncle is probably among the crowd in the street."

The girl replied by telling him the whole of her sorrowful story as rapidly as she could, not omitting to relate the manner in which she had gained admission to the jail.

"I feared," she concluded, "that I never could get to H—— in time to do you any good, if I went on foot, and I thought I ought to come first and tell you all about it, and do as you say. I hope you will let me go still, for I will walk day and night, if you can only give me a few sixpences to buy bread. I am very, very sorry that I lost the money, but the boy was so much stronger than I that I could not help it."

Vrail turned away to conceal his rising tears. "Here is a child," he thought, "capable of performing the most heroic deeds, and utterly unconscious of her intrepidity and excellence." Then addressing her he said, "I have no longer the means to help you, and I cannot permit you to undergo such perils and hardships for me as you propose. The men who surprised us last night took from me all my money and my watch."

"And my watch too, by jingo!" said the negro, who had carried a silver "bull's eye" for many years, and who had given it up only with the greatest indignation; "I hope it won't *go* for the rapscallions."

"You must consult your own safety now, my poor child," Vrail continued, "for you can no longer do anything for us. Return to your uncle; or the man you call so, and bear your sad lot until some more favorable opportunity offers for improving it. If I should ever regain my liberty, depend upon it, I will not forget you. Good-bye."

"Oh, no, no. I will go for you to H——. I will beg my way, and perhaps I shall be in time for them to come and save you. I will certainly go: but I will return afterwards to uncle Shay's if you think I ought."

"If you go, you must not return; but great as is my anxiety for you to go, both for your sake and my own, I cannot permit you to run so great a risk. You are a mere child, certainly not strong, and the weather is cold, and may be very inclement. No, no, I should not deserve assistance if I could seek it by such means."

Vrail pondered a few moments in great perplexity. He had little reason, at the best, to hope for any effectual interference in his behalf by his friends at home, but that little was much for a man in whose face the gallows might be said to be staring.

If he had dared to make known to his captors his name and his rank in the patriot army, the intelligence of his position would have been conveyed to his friends, through the medium of the public press, more speedily than he could communicate it to them in any other way, and the agency of Ruth would have become unnecessary. But such a step would have been hazardous in the extreme, for on the officers of the expedition, of course, the severest punishment would alight.

He hoped to pass for a private soldier, and in order to increase his chances of doing so he was careful not to divulge his name. Of course he could not dispatch a letter without the certainty of espionage, and the trembling child before him was the only reliance for sending a verbal message a distance of three hundred miles into the interior of a country which she had never seen.

If his friends did not hear from him, nor see his name reported among the prisoners, they would doubtless suppose him killed in battle, and would mourn him as lost, without making an effort in his behalf. Yet if they knew all, what could they do for him, or who was there to whom he could look for aid?

While he pondered thus, and while Ruth waited tearfully for his attention, in order to renew her petition to be permitted to continue her journey with her own resources, Brom had retired to the back part of the cell, from which he now returned laughing.

"How much money did you lose, Missa Roof?" he said.

"I don't know," replied the girl; "there must have been a great deal."

"About twenty dollars," said Vrail.

"Well, how much is *dar*, Massa Harry?" he said, laying down a dozen quarter eagles on the bench.

Harry started in the utmost astonishment as the golden pieces met his gaze; and Ruth, with clasped hands, bent forward towards them, in an ecstasy of delight.

"What does this mean, Brom?" Vrail asked in a whisper, placing himself at the same between the gold and the door of his cell, so that it could not be seen by any one from without. "Whose money is this, and how did you manage to keep it from the soldiers last night?"

"Golly! they never searched *me* for money. I mout have had it in my pocket for all *them*—but I didn't, though."

"But is all this yours, Brom?"

"Nebber mind whose it is—it isn't safe to talk too much in an enemy's country, Massa Harry. Didn't I tell you I had money laid up."

"Yes, but I did not suppose you had brought it with you."

"How much *is* dar, I say?"

"Thirty dollars."

"Give Missa Roof twenty; den she will have as much as she had before, and I'll take the rest, and put it where it was before;" and the negro retreated again to a corner with four of the pieces, which he re-concealed in some part of the lining of his coarse vestments.

Without further waste of time in seeking explanations, Harry gave the remainder of the unexpected treasure at once to Ruth, with the unnecessary warning not to exhibit it before strangers, and having repeated his former messages and instructions, which she had by no means forgotten he bade her farewell, and advised her to depart.

"And Roof," said Brom, pressing his face against the bars of the door, and speaking in a loud whisper, "if you ever should get to H——, which I don't much 'spect, p'raps you will see a colored gal called Sally, that lives in the lane close by old Mass' Rosevelt. Ef you will have the goodness to tell her you saw me, and say that I am comfortable, and 'spect to be back home one of these days; ef you just will do that, I will tank you very much."

"I certainly will, sir," said the girl; "I will go to her and tell her. What is her other name?"

"Her *other* name?" asked Brom.

"Yes, sir—her *surname?*"

"Oh, Jiminy! Missa Roof, I don't know. I don't think she has got any other name 'cept Sally. It isn't the fashion 'mong the first colored people to have two names; but the woman's name that she lives with is Brown."

"Very well, I'll find her—you may depend on that."

"Tank you, Missa Roof—good-bye."

CHAPTER XVIII.

A DUTCHMAN'S COURTSHIP, AND ITS CONSEQUENCES.

From the day that Harry Vrail started on his military expedition, Gertrude Van Kleeck, saddened by his absence and solicitous for his safety, yet unwilling to own even to herself the interest which she felt in his welfare, became an eager listener to all tidings of the Northern war.

No rumor of the successes or of the reverses of the insurgents and their American coadjutors reached the village but found its way to her, and she was kept in a constant state of painful anxiety by the conflicting reports and conjectures which she heard.

Of the merits of the contest she did not suffer herself to judge, but the opinion of Harry, and the prevailing sentiment of the neighbors, she supposed to be correct, and the same authority induced her to expect the triumph of the patriots.

She had no longer Brom for a newsbearer from the village, but there were other sources of daily intelligence of which she could avail herself, besides the weekly installment of news furnished by the village gazette, which was always sure to be startling and exciting, if not authentic. There was one individual too, who, to some extent, supplied the place of Brom in furnishing Gertrude with information, and, like him, without suspecting the nature of the interest which she felt in his tidings.

This personage was a second cousin of Miss Van Kleeck, who, like her, rejoiced in a Dutch lineage, and in the very Dutch name of Garret Van Vrank. He was a young man, scarcely the senior of his fair relative, and although of unusual size, and of great physical strength, possessing a boyish and handsome face, and a childlike simplicity of disposition.

Garret was the owner of a small farm, which had been left him by his father, on which he lived nearly alone, and cultivated quite in the way that his father had done, despite all the improving innovations of the day. His route to the village, which he frequently had occasion to visit, led him directly past the house of Gertrude, and he had a good-natured habit of stopping there on his way, to learn whether he could do any errand in town for the family.

He did not always see Gertrude on these occasions, but on his return call, she usually so managed as to encounter him, when a very little tact served to extract from him all the news he had picked up, without herself manifesting any but the most casual interest in his story.

These frequent calls of Garret induced dame Becky to think he came in the character of a suitor, an idea which had never most remotely occurred to the unpresuming youth; and the prospect of such a match was entirely in accordance with her wishes. Young Garret was a man entirely after her own heart. He followed his own plough; he carried his own grain to market, himself perched upon the topmost bag, in his smock-frock, and with his ox-goad in his hands; and with his smock-frock and his ox-goad did he stand chatting by the half hour to Getty in these, his courting visits, if courting visits they were.

What need she care that he was broad-shouldered, elephant-footed, wide-waisted, and with hands in size and hue like a loaf of brown bread? He was an honest fellow, with a kind heart, a fresh, handsome face, boyish blue eyes, and teeth as white by nature as others were rendered by laborious art.

Becky, indeed, made up her mind that he was the very man for her niece; she encouraged his daily calls, and was as careful to keep out of the way of the supposed lover as she had been before to obtrude herself in the presence of such of Gertrude's visitors as she did not like. But when these interviews had been continued a long while without any approximation to a nearer intimacy, she grew impatient, and resolved to hasten the *dénouement* which she so gladly anticipated. She rallied Getty on the subject, but Getty laughed broadly, and said nothing. She rallied Garret, who did not even comprehend her sallies, broad as they were, and who, being greatly puzzled, made some random replies very wide of the mark.

Becky, however, did not let matters rest thus. The cousins evidently liked each other, and she believed that nothing but a little management was necessary to bring about the result she desired. To effect this she left no means untried. Garry had hints enough wasted upon him to have drawn a dozen lovers to the feet of Gertrude, but they did not draw Garry there.

When he began to comprehend the old dame, he thought she was jesting, or was becoming silly, for the idea of his marrying Gertrude seemed altogether preposterous. He had no such aspirations. He was sensible enough to know that she was in every respect his superior, and that the difference in their fortunes, great as it was, was the least of the differences between them.

Aunt Becky tried an appeal to his cupidity.

"Your little farm," she said to him one day, "joins one of Getty's, don't it, Garry?"

"Yes, it joins on to Squire Jones' farm—that's Getty's; but why do you call my farm *little*, aunt Becky?" he added, with commendable pride; "there's e'enamost a hundred acres, counting the marsh and the pond."

"Yes, yes; but what's that to fifty hundred acres, and more, that you may have one of these days, you know, and have other people to work 'em for you, and you nothing to do but to sit still and take in the rent, unless you choose, like poor Baltus, to keep on working until you are grey, just for the fun of it—much good did it do *him!*"

Van Vrank opened his eyes wider and wider, during the delivery of this speech, as if the distension of those organs would assist him in taking in the meaning of the speaker.

He did take it in at length, but considering it a renewal of the old badinage on that topic, he only shook his head and laughed.

"Why don't you come over, and see us sometimes on Sundays, Garry?" continued Becky, her voice subsiding to a lower and more confidential tone.

"Sundays?"

"Yes, in the afternoon or evening. You have a nice new suit of clothes now, I see."

"Ain't they nice, aunty? The wool came off my own sheep."

"Yes, the cloth looks like store goods, and they fit you as if they had been made by a tailor. Dress yourself up in them next Sunday afternoon, and come round to see us, will you?"

"Yes," replied Garry, looking very much pleased, and quite failing to connect the invitation with the prior subject of their remarks.

"Have you got any pomatum?"

Garry stared at this singular question, but replied that he believed he had.

"Then *use* it!" she said. "Cut your hair first, then comb the tangles out of it, and put on a little pomatum—you don't know how much better you'll look."

The young man promised compliance, and the next Sunday evening saw him, punctual to his appointment, at the door of Gertrude's house.

He did not inquire for her, however, but for aunt Becky, whom he was about to seek in the kitchen, but a servant had been directed to conduct him to the parlour, where, to his great uneasiness, he soon found himself seated alone.

He was apparelled, according to agreement, in his best suit, set off by a very fair show of linen; his hair was trimmed and pomatumed, his thick boots were freshly greased, and altogether he was quite a presentable specimen of a country beau.

Aunt Becky, meanwhile, had kept her own counsel. She allowed no one to know that Van Vrank had called upon her invitation, but she caused Getty to be informed of his presence, and sending her into the parlor, she herself kept out of the way.

Yet, not altogether out of the way was aunt Becky, for she had her hiding places, where, unseen, she could hear all that was said above a whisper in the parlor, and if Garry and Getty came to whispers, she would be satisfied without understanding their words, for then she would know that all was right.

She was not destined, however, to be gratified by any such evidence of confidential intercourse. What Garret had to say, he spoke boldly and in a manly tone, at least after the first embarrassment arising from the unusual position in which he found himself.

In vain aunt Becky listened for something of a wooing character, or for something that might be construed into a hint matrimonial. There was nothing in word or tone which intimated any such sentiment in the visitor's breast.

He talked of the weather, of the farms and the crops, of his horses, his sheep, and even of his new clothes, which he called upon the young lady to admire, but all was in a spirit of frankness and simplicity which rather elevated than lessened him in Gertrude's estimation. In turn, he praised Getty's new pink dress, and the handsome furniture of the parlor, and when conversation flagged, he at length said, jocosely:—

"I suppose you'll be getting married one of these days, cousin Gertrude—there must be lots of fine fellows after you ?"

The dame's hopes revived, and she listened more intently.

Gertrude laughed, and said she did not expect to be married very soon.

"No, I s'pose not—you're young enough yet these half dozen years," replied Garret; "I wouldn't be in a hurry if I were you."

Gertrude replied that she was not.

"It will be somebody quite grand, I suppose, when it does happen," continued Garry; "some of the big bugs."

"I hope not!" said the young lady, laughing.

"Yes, it will, I know—a lawyer or a congressman, or something of that sort. Why, you are good enough for the best, and any on 'em will be glad enough to get you."

Aunt Becky now grew restive under this strange specimen of courting, and she emerged from her hiding-place by a back-way, and came to the parlor door, with resolution stamped upon every feature of her expressive face.

"Getty!" she said, as soon as she had entered the room, "Garry *wants* you! He is afraid to ask, I suppose, but he wants you to marry him."

"Why, aunt—*Becky!*" exclaimed Van Vrank, as soon as he could interpose a word.

"Hold your tongue," said the dame. "If you can't *speak*, let some one speak for you. Garry is a good fellow," she continued, addressing her niece; "and he will make you a good husband, and will take the best care of everything, and, as I said before, he *wants* you!"

"I *don't*, Getty—I never thought of such a thing!" replied Garry, who had risen, and in his haste to vindicate himself from the charge of so great presumption, did not stop to choose words. "I did not come here sparking at all."

"Did ever anybody hear such a—mollyhack?" exclaimed aunt Becky.

"I may be a mollyhack, aunty—but I am not foolish enough to s'pose Getty wants such a hawbuck as I am for a husband. Why

I should never know what to do with such a fine lady for a wife. I tell you she is too good for me—a dozen times too good.

"Ah! that's talking something like! That's the way lovers always talk. Now, Getty, what do *you* say? You will have him, won't you?"

Gertrude was too much amused to be very angry, but she had much kind regard for her coarse, but sincere cousin, and she was embarrassed by the fear of adding to the awkwardness of the position in which her aunt's manœuvring had placed him.

"I cannot accept or decline an offer which has not been made," she said, hesitatingly.

"You don't want me for a husband, Getty, I know—do you now?" asked Van Vrank, who had no sensitiveness on the subject, and was willing to come to a full understanding.

Getty, greatly relieved, now felt at liberty to reply plainly.

"No, cousin Garry," she said, "I do not. I think, like you, that we are not suited to each other, and I know you are too good and too sensible to be offended at my saying so."

"I offended? Never fear that, Getty—you have done nothing to offend me; you have only answered a plain question which I should never have asked, if it had not been for aunt Becky, but she meant well enough."

"I think you are both very foolish, but perhaps you'll grow wiser one of these days," said the aunt, leaving the room in no amiable state of mind.

Van Vrank prolonged his visit a considerable time, giving Gertrude many details of information, which he had picked up on the preceding day in relation to the war, and when he departed there was a mutual friendly understanding between the cousins which admitted of no further misconception.

CHAPTER XIX.

TIDINGS FROM THE WAR.

A DAY or two subsequent to the events just related, the young farmer again sought the village market with a load of produce, having disposed of which, he strolled, while his horses were baiting, to the principal inn, to hear and discuss the current tidings of the day. He met some acquaintances, with whom he conversed for a while, and was about to depart, when a distant horn announced the approach of the mail stage-coach from the North, a daily event of the greatest interest in H——, and one which was sure to assemble all the idlers of the village in front of the hotel.

Great was the admiration of the dashing and rapid style in which the rattling vehicle was always sure to be brought up to the tavern door, no matter how snail-like may have been its progress before; and the reverberation of a tin horn, which was made to resound without cessation, accompanied by the frequent pistol-like reports of a dextrously-wielded whip, cracking around, but never touching the leaders' ears, added not a little to the liveliness of the scene. The motley throng, among which, and surrounded by which, the coach always came to a stand, gave it not a little the appearance of having been stopped by banditti, and it is said that on one occasion a foreigner, waking suddenly from sleep at such a moment, hastily handed out his purse, and begged that the carriage might be allowed to proceed.

The village blacksmith, with sooty visage, and perhaps with his hammer in his hand; the barber, with his apron unremoved; the coatless cobbler, limping from his stall, with most of the loafers and all the negroes of the village, were sure to be there, and interspersed among them not a few of a better class, whose curiosity was equally unrestricted.

A desire to see the passengers, and their apparel and their baggage, to learn who stopped at H——, and what new passengers were taken in, and the hope of hearing some news from some communicative traveller—these were among the motives which drew together a crowd of people, to whom every incident became of value which could detract from the monotony of their lives.

There was but one passenger to stop at H—— on this occasion—a young, slight girl, coarsely, but neatly apparelled, who alighted with trepidation among so many people, and looked timidly around, as if seeking some one she might address.

"Point out your baggage, miss," said a noisy, bustling porter from the inn, addressing the child with the usual officiousness of his class.

"I haven't any baggage, sir," replied a very faint voice. "Will you please to tell me, sir," she said, catching sight of Van Vrank's good-natured face, " whether there is a Mr. Rosyfield lives in this village—an old man?"

"Rosevelt, you mean, don't you—Guert Rosevelt? Yes, come with me, and I'll show you where he lives."

Garry led the way through the crowd of people, who looked wonderingly after the child for a moment, and then gave their attention to other matters.

"Are you sure it is *Guert* Rosevelt you want to see?" asked Garry, as they went along. "There are other people of that name in this neighborhood."

"I don't know, sir. I shall know him when I see him. He is a very old man, with very white hair."

"That is Guert—and a very good man he is, too."

"Yes, sir."

"Is he a relation of yours?"

"No, sir; I have never seen him."

"Never *seen* him! And how can you describe him then so well?"

"Oh, sir, he has a grandson in Canada"——

"Yes"——

"Who was a soldier, and is taken prisoner, and who is going to be hung or shot, if somebody don't save him. Please, sir, let us go faster."

"Come on," shouted Garry, starting off on a run; "but this is dreadful news, and I am afraid to have you tell the old man, who is very feeble now! How did you hear of it, and which of the boys is it, for they both went to the war?"

"His name is Harry, sir, and there was a black man with him."

"Ah! poor Harry—but how did you hear about it, and are you certain it is true?"

"Oh, I am very certain, sir, for I came from there myself. He sent me."

"From Canada! You came all the way from Canada alone?" asked Van Vrank, surveying the pale child with astonishment and half disposed to doubt her story.

"Yes, sir; let us hurry, if you please."

Garry did hurry, and without further questioning his companion until they reached Mr. Rosevelt's house, which he entered with her, hoping to prevent too abrupt a delivery of the worst features of her intelligence, and hoping also to afford some consolation to his afflicted neighbor. His precaution was well-timed.

Old Guert's infirmities had greatly increased within the few preceding days, and he had taken to his bed, and called a physician, who being in attendance when the visitors arrived, positively forbade the communication of their painful intelligence to his patient.

Ruth was in great tribulation at this discovery. She had entertained an indefinite hope that the old gentleman would in some way be able to rescue his grandson from his imminent peril, and she knew not to whom else she could apply for help.

She was requested by the housekeeper to remain a few days, until Mr. Rosevelt's improved health might admit of imparting to him her news, and although with the most harrowing fears that such delay might be fatal to her hopes, she had no alternative but to comply.

Van Vrank himself, painfully impressed with a sense of the imminent danger which threatened Harry Vrail, towards whom, in common with all the neighborhood, he entertained the most friendly feelings, set out on his return home, and being freighted with news of such, unusual interest, he, of course, did not pass the residence of his cousin without stopping. Entirely unsuspecting how agonizing his tidings would prove to Gertrude, he used no reserve in disclosing them.

"Bad news from Canada to day, cousin Getty," he said, as he met Miss Van Kleeck at the front doorway, and without noticing the pallor which overspread her face at so ominous a beginning, he continued:

"The patriots are defeated, and almost all killed or taken prisoners."

"And Harry Vrail—what did you hear of Harry Vrail?" she asked, grasping his arm, and looking eagerly into his face, for that fearful moment was no time for maidenly reserve.

Still obtuse as to the nature of his cousin's emotion, he replied,

"Harry Vrail is a prisoner, and is probably hung by this time, or will be in a few days."

Getty sank to the door-sill, and resting her head upon her hands, remained speechless some moments, violently trembling.

"Why, Getty!" exclaimed the young farmer; "what is the matter, Getty? I did not know you cared so much about Harry.

I am sorry I told you; and perhaps, now, it is not so bad, after all. *Don't* Getty, *don't* now."

"Never mind me, Garry, but tell me, how did you hear all this?"

"That is the strangest matter of all. A little girl, not over twelve or thirteen years old, has come all the way from Canada alone, and she says that Lieutenant Vrail sent her, and gave her money to travel with, and that she saw him in jail at Prescott, only three days ago."

"*Only three days ago!*" exclaimed Gertrude, springing up, her eyes flashing with an unusual light. "Then he is not hung *yet?* They would not do it as soon as *that*. Where is the girl?"

"I left her at Rosevelt's."

"Go bring her to me. Lose not a minute's time. Take a span of my horses and the light wagon. Never mind your team; I will have them taken care of. Quick, Garry! Call Jake, and let him help you harness."

Getty spoke with the air almost of command, and she was not disobeyed.

Greatly wondering, but catching a portion of the young lady's excitement, Van Vrank flew to execute her orders, and while doing so, Miss Van Kleeck waited upon the back piazza, absorbed in thought. Suddenly, seeming to resolve some painful doubt, she came forward to meet her messenger, now prepared to start, and said to him in a low voice,

"Garry, do you know Mr. Gray, who was my father's lawyer in that suit about the south farm?"

"Squire Gray? Yes, I know him very well, and a very good man he is, too."

"Father thought him trustworthy. Can you see him this afternoon?"

"Yes."

"And ask him to come and see me this evening on business?"

"Yes."

"Remember, *this evening*. Do not let him fail."

"I will bring him with me."

"Do so, if you can—and now let us lose no more time. It will be dark before you get back, and you will find supper waiting for you."

CHAPTER XX.

GERTRUDE AND HER FRIENDS.

WITH such post-like haste did the young farmer travel that he falsified Getty's prediction, and returned while the sun yet lingered in the horizon, bringing with him both the Canadian girl and Mr. Attorney Gray—each not a little surprised at the summons they had received.

Leaving the latter to ruminate upon the mystery, Miss Van Kleeck conducted Ruth to her own room, where, by questioning, she drew out her whole story, including what the girl had not before divulged, Harry's betrayal by her uncle, her own heroic attempt to save him, and his subsequent capture.

Gertrude wept at the recital, both of Vrail's misfortunes and of the young child's sufferings in his behalf, but she did not allow her tears to obstruct her questions until the whole truth was elicited in all its harrowing details.

If her resolution had not been already taken, the noble example of Ruth would have inspired her to the task she had set for herself, regardless of those flimsy barriers which the conventionalities of society interpose in the path of affection and duty.

She descended to the parlor with Ruth, and finding the attorney there alone, she immediately addressed him."

"You know something about my father's estate and its value, I believe, Mr. Gray?"

"Yes—considerable."

"You know that I am his only heir—that it is all mine, and that I am of the legal age to dispose of it."

"I know it all."

"How much money can be raised upon it—on an emergency—at once—before to-morrow noon?"

"Do you wish to sell?"

"Not if it can be avoided, but I want a large sum of money—say twenty thousand dollars."

"It is a large sum, but it is only a small part of the value of the estate. There is bank stock to half the amount you require, which, at a little sacrifice, could be made available by the time you name."

"I will make the sacrifice; how shall I get the remainder?"

"I can easily obtain it for you on your mortgage upon two or three of these farms, but I must have a few days' time."

"Not a *day*, Mr. Gray—I must have the money by to-morrow noon. Think again. You shall be paid liberally. I will put the whole estate into your hands for security, if necessary, but the money I must have."

"I will try, Miss Van Kleeck."

"That will not do. If you cannot say that you can do it, I must send to town to-night and employ some one else."

"If the case is so urgent, I think I can promise it, for I can advance five thousand dollars myself, if necessary, and I certainly know where I can get the remainder."

"O, thank you, thank you, Mr. Gray."

"But we shall have to be up half the night drawing writings."

"*All* night, if you choose. What does that matter? Can I help you?"

"No, I believe not, except by bringing me your father's title deeds."

"Yes, you shall have them in a minute," said Getty, darting to the door; "shall I bring them all?"

"No, only those which relate to this farm, and the south farm. That will be abundant security."

"I will bring them all, and you can choose for yourself."

The deeds were brought and Mr. Gray, after selecting those which he had required, concluded to return to the village, and make the necessary writings in his office.

"I will bring them to you early in the morning for your signature," he said to Miss Van Kleeck. "How early shall I be able to see you?"

"At daybreak," replied Getty.

"That will not be necessary; I will call at seven o'clock."

"Very well, but do not be later. I must have the money by noon."

"You shall."

"And with as little publicity as possible, if you please, Mr. Gray."

"I understand."

"You have clerks who *talk* "——

"My clerks all *talk*, Miss Van Kleeck," replied the attorney, with a quiet smile, "but I will attend to this business in person."

"Thank you, again. But there is another thing requisite. I want the money in a shape in which it can be used in Canada. Can this be arranged?"

"Not very easily; but by going to Albany, I can procure you drafts on banks at Kingston or Quebec, which will be as good as gold there, and can be turned into gold at any time."

"Will you do it? Will you go to Albany to-morrow, and procure the papers? Will you be at the ——— Hotel in that city with them to-morrow evening?"

Getty asked these questions in a lower tone, and in a hurried manner.

"I will, if such is your pleasure, Miss Van Kleeck," replied the lawyer, looking much surprised. "I shall not be able to arrive there until after bank hours, but in an urgent case I can obtain the facilities which I shall need for your business. Let me suggest that your agent comes well accredited, or I shall not dare to surrender to him papers of so great value."

"Thank you; I will see to it that you have no cause for doubt."

Mr. Gray declined an invitation to supper, and took his leave, being conveyed back to town as he had been brought, but with the substitution of black Jake for a driver, in the place of Garry, who remained, at Gertrude's request.

Ruth Shay had been present during the whole of the interview between the young lady and the lawyer, and she had listened with astonishment, and with mingled hope and doubt to the strange conversation which had passed. The large sums of money which had been named seemed like something fabulous to the mind of a child, whose experience on this point, during the greater part of her life had been confined to the occasional sight of a few shillings, and to whom the gold intrusted by Vrail had seemed a mine of wealth. Miss Van Kleeck became to her excited imagination a sort of fairy princess, who, with a pen for a wand, was about to conjure up from some unknown source, the vast treasures of which she had spoken, and which Ruth could not doubt would be efficacious for whatever purpose they were designed. But what was their intended use? For whom and in what manner was this great power to be wielded?

She listened earnestly, and as the conversation progressed, she became convinced that it must be intended in some way for the service of Harry Vrail, and that her own painful mission was not to terminate without setting in motion other agencies far more potent and promising.

Yet it seemed strange to her that she had not heard the name of the young lieutenant mentioned, for she did not comprehend the delicacy which had sealed Gertrude's lips on this point, and she had longed for the departure of Mr. Gray, hoping that her painful curiosity might be gratified. Nor was she mistaken. No sooner was she again alone with Gertrude, than the latter, turning suddenly towards her, as if impressed by a new idea, said:

"You have come alone from Canada; will you go back there with me."

"Yes, oh yes! Are you going to save *him?*"

"God only knows what will be the result. I am going to try. Mr. Van Vrank, I hope, will go with us. He at least shall not die without an effort being made in his behalf."

"Is he a relation of yours?" asked Ruth.

"No—a friend of my father's. There is no one else to help him, and we must do what we can."

"I will do anything that I can," replied Ruth, "if anybody will tell me what to do."

"You are a good girl, you have done a great deal already, and now I want you to tell me something more about yourself and about the people with whom you lived when Mr. Vrail came to your house."

Ruth told her simple but melancholy history in a few minutes, and Getty shed not a few sympathetic tears over the narrative.

"You have no wish then," she said, "ever to return to those people who call themselves your uncle and aunt, and who have treated you so unkindly?"

"Oh, no—never, if I can help it."

"Let that be my care," replied Gertrude. "You shall never go there again. You shall return here and live with me."

"Oh, I am so glad that you will take me for your servant."

"Not my servant, but my sister. I need such a friend as you are like to prove; I will provide for your education and for all your wants, and you shall have a comfortable home as long as I have one to share with you."

Ruth fell upon her knees at the feet of Gertrude: she rested her head upon the young lady's lap and tried to speak her thanks, but she gave utterance only to sobs.

"Do not try to thank me. Indeed we are all your debtors yet, and shall ever be. But we have much to do, and we must not waste our time in words. Please to go now, and ask Mr. Van Vrank to come to me, for I cannot rest until I know whether he will go with us or not."

Ruth wiped her eyes and went out, and in a few minutes returned accompanied by the young man, who was in a state of great perplexity and amazement at the strange conduct of his cousin.

She did not leave him long in doubt.

As he entered the room, she advanced to the door, closed it carefully, and said:

"Garry, you will think strange of what I am about to tell you. You were surprised to-day when your news about Harry Vrail's misfortunes affected me so much—but "———

She hesitated, and Van Vrank interposed—

"It is none of my business, Cousin Getty, and I shan't think strange of anything you choose to say or do. You need not be afraid to say anything before me, Getty. It will be all right, I know."

"Thank you, Garry; you relieve me very much, and I can now speak freely. To be brief, then, I am going to Canada."

"To *Canada? You?* What can you do there? How can you help *him?*"

"I do not know. I can only hope, and pray, and try; but I shall certainly go to-morrow."

"Not alone?"

"No. Not alone—for this heroic child will accompany me, if no one else does; but Garry, I am in need of a friend and a protector. You are my relative, almost my only one."

"I will go with you, Getty. Of course I will, if that is what you mean, though I don't believe anything can be done for Harry Vrail; but I will go with you wherever you choose to go, if it is to the North Pole; and I'll protect you, too, against all harm, as far as it is possible for one man to do it," and Van Vrank instinctively closed his huge hand as he spoke, and brought down the embrowned fist with a jarring emphasis upon a table beside him.

Getty seized the threatening member with both her tiny hands, scarcely encircling it at that, and poured forth her thanks as best she could.

She then related to her cousin all that was necessary for him to know of her arrangements for starting, and the appointed hour for departure, and by the time their plans were decided, they received a summons to the supper table, where aunt Becky was presiding, looking not a little glum, and exhibiting upon her forehead that ominous scowl, which was the usual precursor of a social storm.

"These are high times, very high times I think," she began, as they seated themselves around the table, "when people come and go like the wind, and tired horses are sent off in the night to carry lazy lawyers home, who are to come back next morning, and nobody is to know what it is all about. High times these are, I am sure; it wasn't so in Baltus' day."

A great many short jerks of the head accompanied this speech, and the dame's hands passed rapidly to and fro among the cups and saucers before her, making a great rattling, but not any progress in her official duties.

"Why *aunt!*" exclaimed Getty.

"No, no—don't '*aunt*' me, *I* ain't your aunt; I am only a nigger waiter to get the meals, and pour out the tea, and hold my tongue." A scream from the angry woman interrupted her speech, for in her excitement she had caught hold of the metallic spout of the teapot, instead of the non-conducting handle, and in her haste to disengage her fingers from the burning tube, she upset the silver creampot, and dashed several china cups in fragments to the floor.

Her consternation, arising from this disaster, and especially from contemplating the ruin of the china set, fortunately superseded her wrath, and she proceeded in silent dismay to pick up the scattered pieces of the wreck, assisted by Getty, and, between the intervals of his uproarious laughter, by Garry also. When quiet was restored, and all parties were again seated at table, Miss Van Kleeck said.

"I have been too busy and too hurried, aunt Becky, to tell you sooner that I intended to leave home, to-morrow, for an absence, perhaps, of several weeks. You will oblige me if you will not ask me where I am going, or for what purpose, all of which you shall know hereafter, and you will be satisfied that I am safe when I tell you I am to have cousin Garret for a companion."

The severe expression which settled upon the dame's face when Getty spoke of leaving home relaxed as suddenly at the mention of the name of her companion, and she jumped at once to the conclusion that the match she had deemed so desirable was certainly to be effected, although in some secret and unusual way, suited to the notions of a romantic or whimsical girl. She elevated her eyebrows and her spectacles; her lips were wreathed into a grim smile, and she uttered several expressive "ohs" and "ahs," which were intended to indicate that she saw clearly through the whole affair, and that she was very well contented with it.

Much desultory conversation passed, and Becky gave utterance to some sly jokes on the subject of her hallucination, all of which were received by Garry with a loud guffaw, but too deep anxiety rested on Gertrude's heart to admit of any approach to merriment. She had not entertained the least idea of misleading her aunt, and she would even have tried to undeceive her, had she not known how difficult the task would be, without a full explanation of her designs, which she was by no means disposed to make. She did not think it her duty to make a great effort to disenchant a pertinacious mind of an illusion so baseless, and to the creation of which she herself had in no way intentionally contributed.

She contented herself by the simple remark: "You are mistaken, aunt," in reply to one of the sallies of the dame, and her uniform truthfulness entitled her to be believed. Gertrude, indeed, was at all times above deceit; but now, animated by a lofty motive, and about to engage in an enterprise of self-sacrificing magnanimity, she could not stoop to even the semblance of duplicity.

She had overcome, too, in a great degree, the habit of mind which caused her so greatly to dread her scolding relative, having fully learned her right to regulate her own movements in all respects, yet neither her manner, nor her words, nor the remembrance of her direct negative to the forced proposal of Garry in the preceding week, nor Van Vrank's own irrepressible laughter whenever her sagacious hints were thrown out, disturbed the settled conviction in the mind of Becky that the match was *made*, and that the parties were about to proceed on a tour matrimonial. The attendance of the lawyer, who chanced to be also a magistrate, empowered to tie the mystical knot, of course confirmed her views; but whether the ceremony had already taken place, or was to be performed in the morning before starting, or afterwards at some village on their route, aunt Becky neither knew nor cared. It was sufficient for her purpose that she firmly believed Van Vrank was the man of her niece's choice, and that they were to become, if they were not already, man and wife.

The meal being concluded, though with great difficulty on the part of Garry, by reason of the repeated necessity either of violent laughter or a violent suppression of it, he hastened home to make his own arrangements for the journey, while Gertrude, eagerly assisted by her now willing aunt, occupied a considerable part of the night in similar preparations. Ruth was thoroughly rigged by contributions from the wardrobe of the young lady, which, as they were successively bestowed upon her, drew forth continual expressions of childish delight, though accompanied by a manifest reluctance to receive so much.

"I will only take them to travel in, Miss Van Kleeck," she said; "they will be yours again when we come back."

"They are yours, Ruth; say no more about them."

The child laughed as she tried the fine garments, and seemed greatly pleased, but at the next instant a painful emotion was visible in her face.

"If we can only save *him*," she said.

"Ah, if we only can!"

CHAPTER XXI.

CAPTAIN TOM'S FORTUNES.

It will be remembered that Captain Thomas Vrail, forgetful of all fraternal ties, ignominiously sought his personal safety, by availing himself, alone, of the very means of escape which had been provided for Harry, and which the latter had nobly rejected, until assured of his brother's flight. When he had gained the open space in the rear of the building from which he had fled, where the tumult of the assault was yet resounding, he ran to the river, and on reaching its margin he took the only course which gave any promise of safety, and the same that was, a few minutes later, selected by the unfortunate fugitives who followed him. The desultory nature of the battle, or rather of the separate engagements which had taken place, and the uncertainty which yet prevailed in each victorious quarter as to the extent of success in other localities, produced a state of affairs favorable to the escape of the few who had been fortunate enough to take the first steps of flight unobserved.

The vessel which fired upon Harry was lying in the stream when Thomas reached the shore, and caused him no slight alarm, but he was either unobserved, or from some other unexplained cause, he was not assailed from that quarter, and he hastened forward, although in great trepidation.

He had not proceeded far down the stream, before he discovered, about half a mile in advance of him, two other individuals, whose singular and cautious movements indicated that they, like himself, were members of the vanquished army, seeking to make good their escape. The ground over which they were passing, was the pebbled beach of the river, edged, at irregular intervals, with clumps of bushes, which grew at the distance of a few yards from the water, and served as convenient dodging-places for the stealthy travellers. They could not go far, however, in that direction, without approaching the vicinity of numerous dwelling-houses, whence they would be almost certain to be seen, and so imminent seemed the peril of progressing in the route they were pursuing, that Vrail, much as he longed for companionship in his distress, had not the temerity long to follow them.

But if he did not dare to proceed, still less had he courage to return over his dangerous track, or to attempt to seek the open country, which could only be gained by passing through a part of the settlement. Concealing himself, therefore, in one of the clusters of shrubbery which have been named, he watched with painful anxiety the course of his predecessors, until, having stopped briefly in several hiding-places, they finally entered one from which they were not seen to emerge. Not doubting that they had resolved to remain there until the darkness of evening should favor their flight, Tom exulted in the hope of joining them then, and sharing their chance of escape, and with this hope he watched the distant bush, with little intermission, until the declining sun withdrew his beams, and left him no longer power to discern an object of so much interest.

He had heard, meanwhile, the firing a little further up the river, which had so nearly proved fatal to Harry, and the return salutes of his valiant brother, but, of course, without in the least suspecting the extraordinary character of the engagement they betokened. He had seen, too, the second boat which had been sent from the war-vessel, and which, in taking its circuitous route to avoid the magical weapon, had passed in view of both the concealed parties, and had landed at a point considerably above them. Tom also saw, and watched with an interest not inferior to that of his intrepid brother, the clouds which rose to engulf the descending sun, and which enveloped the landscape in a sudden night.

Then, eager with hope, he rushed from his hiding-place, and fast as his cramped limbs would permit, he ran towards the spot which he had so long and vigilantly watched. He knew that his footsteps would be suspected as those of an enemy, and that the fugitives, if they were yet in the bush, or near it, would wait quietly for him to pass. He did not, therefore, attempt to approach them noiselessly, but having gained, as nearly as he could, their immediate vicinity, he suddenly stopped and ejaculated in a quick, sharp tone, one of the mystic words, which served as a counter-sign, and an evidence of membership among the fraternity of patriots.

To his great joy it was instantly answered by another signal, and the two individuals of whom he was in search, without further reserve, approached him. It was too dark to see more than the outline of their figures, of which one was tall and stooping, and the other stoutish and broad-shouldered; but Vrail soon recognized the one who spoke, although he conversed in a half whisper.

"We took you for an enemy," he said, "and we were hesitating whether to cut you down quietly, or let you pass, when fortunately you gave the signal, and now I can't rightly make you out in this light. I guess you warn't in our division."

"No, I believe not—indeed I don't know exactly where you were, Mr. Jones."

It would have been difficult to tell where Barak was during the engagement, and as he did not offer to define his position, Tom continued:

"I am Captain Vrail, that is, if there are any titles left to us now, and I was in "——

"Oh! you are Captain Vrail, are you? How do you dew? and

how did you get off?—and what is become of your brother, the lieutenant—a mighty clever fellow *he* was—I hope he ain't killed or taken?"

Tom replied, hesitatingly, that he believed Harry had escaped, and he was about to add something more, when they were interrupted by the third person, who spoke in a voice of command.

"Silence!" he said; "there will be time enough to talk when we are off British soil. We must go forward now."

"Who is that?" asked Vrail, quietly.

"No matter," was the stranger's reply; "I am your commander for the present, if you remain with us—if not, pass on or return."

"I prefer to remain with you, and willingly place myself under your orders," said Tom, perceiving from the speaker's tone, that he was accustomed to be obeyed, and having a suspicion of his character, which greatly increased his hopes of ultimate escape.

"We are coming at once to the most dangerous part of our way," said the stranger, "as we shall be compelled to pass near many dwellings, and we must proceed with great vigilance."

"Why not wait until a later hour?" interrupted Vrail.

"You can wait if you choose, young man," was the cold reply.

"I forgot—I beg pardon, sir."

"There is reason enough for haste," added the leader, mollified by the apologetic words and tone of Vrail. "At any moment troops may be expected scouring the beach in search of fugitives, and before morning there will be sentinels all along the coast for miles, to see that no boats put off without inspection. This is our only chance, and if we can get three miles further down, without getting caught, I will answer for the rest. We must advance now in single file, and as silent as moccasined Indians. Not a word must be spoken, except to give warning of danger. I will go first, and Mr. Vrail must take the rear."

In this order the three proceeded along their perilous route for the space of nearly an hour, passing frequently within near view of men whose discovery of them would have led to certain capture, and often pausing at the most critical points to wait a favorable opportunity to advance.

The strictest silence was preserved, not a word being spoken; and, indeed, as far as related to Jones, the order for taciturnity was quite superfluous, for his excessive terror had quite deprived him of the power of articulation. Fragments of his own public speeches were floating at times through his mind, and his often-repeated assertion, that the whole country was rising to meet the patriots, seemed to his excited imagination about to be realized, although in a painfully different sense from that in which he had used it.

A happy man was he, and scarcely less so was Vrail, when their mysterious leader, suddenly pausing near a large granite rock, and waiting for them to join him, announced their safety, with an air of confidence which nothing in appearance around them seemed to justify.

"But we ain't off British sile yet, Commodore," said Barak.

"Don't 'Commodore' me here, if you please, and don't talk quite so loud, and if we should be taken yet, which isn't very likely, seeing they won't have more than five minutes to do it in, remember there are no titles to any of our names. Every title will cost its owner a halter. We are but plain Sam, and Tom, and Bill."

"I reckon they'd know *you* though, quick enough."

"Well, possibly they might, but we won't give them a chance to try. Come on," and the speaker advanced rapidly towards the river, which was but a few yards distant.

"Blast the man!" muttered Jones, following; "I believe he means to swim across. I have heard of his doing almost as wonderful things; I say, Commodore, *we* can't do that, you know."

"Hush!" was the only reply of the leader, as he proceeded with rapid and hasty strides until he stood half boot deep in the edge of the stream, when he stopped, and facing shoreward, peered earnestly through the darkness for some seconds, as if trying to recognize some of the neighboring landmarks.

"Mr. Vrail," he said, at length, taking a small box from his pocket, and handing it to the young man, "I must know the exact bearing of the south end of the rock which we have just left, but I can see nothing in this darkness. Go back to the rock, feel your way to the lower part of it, and when you are sure you are at the right spot, light one of these matches, and show it near the ground for a moment—as long as you can count three—I shall see it."

Though greatly mystified by the stranger's conduct, Tom did not for a moment hesitate about compliance with his orders. With some difficulty he found the spot designated, and having made quite sure of the correctness of his position, he exhibited his sulphurous signal the required time, and then returned to the place where he had left his companions, but where he now found Jones quite alone, and in a state of extraordinary excitement.

"I might have known it," he said; "I have often heard he was in league with the Evil one, and now I know it. He's gone, sir!"

"Gone? Where?"

"Right straight across the river, sir—a bee line, sir—by the light of that match. I see him go as far as I *could* see, and after that I heerd him for some time walking through the water, as easily as you would walk on dry land."

"Nonsense, Jones; your head is turned. He can't be far off."

"Far or near, *we* shall never see him again. Listen, you can hear him going now."

Vrail did listen, and very distinctly heard a splashing in the water a few rods down the stream, and not far from shore, as his affrighted companion had supposed, his alarm not admitting of his retaining any correct idea of the course of the river. At the next instant they heard their missing comrade's voice, modulated to a tone which was designed to reach them, and to extend as little further as possible, calling upon them to approach. Barak hesitated and drew back, until Vrail, who had caught a glimmering of the true state of affairs, plunged into the stream and proceeded in the direction of the voice, when the former, afraid to be left behind, followed the path of his companions, groaning bitterly at every step in the cold water. As they approached their mysterious leader, guided by his voice, he said,

"I've got it at last, my boys, come and take hold with me, and help draw it out. Where's Jones?"

"Here," said that worthy, whose chattering teeth rendered his articulation scarcely intelligible. "Here I am up to my knees in water. What on airth are you trying to do and what is that you want me to take hold of?"

"This rope, and pull with a will, and when you see the bow of a boat come to the surface, catch hold with me, and drag it to the shore. Now, then."

"A *boat*, Gineral? You don't mean to say so? Now if that ain't what I call cute! A boat hid away under the water, and that's what you've been fishing for, is it, when I thought you was half way over to the States."

The skiff was sunk in considerably deeper water than that in which the fugitives were standing; a rope of considerable length intervening between them and the prow of the vessel, the end of which cable had been fastened to the bottom of the river, as near the shore as its length would permit. The united efforts of the three men soon raised the boat, and brought it within their reach, after which they found little difficulty in dragging it to and upon the beach, and discharging its cargo of water by turning it upside down.

The promising prospect of immediate safety thus held out to them gave them strength and courage to work with great alacrity, and but a short time elapsed before they were fairly embarked upon the river, for of course the sagacity which had planned such a resort for the hour of danger, had not overlooked the minor means to render it effectual. Two pairs of oars were found fastened to the sides of the skiff, and both being put in action, it was the work of but a few minutes to leave the dreaded and now abhorred shores of Canada far behind them.

It was an easy task, too, to row to an island sufficiently remote from the northern shore to form a safe refuge for the night, and the wearied men were glad to avail themselves of the first resort of the kind which offered. They drew their boat up on shore, and sought the depth of a wood, where a fire was soon kindled, the cheering warmth of which revived their strength and spirits, and round which, on couches of boughs and bushes, they passed the remainder of the night.

They had fasted since morning, but so great was their fatigue that, despite the pangs of hunger, they sunk readily to sleep, to partake of those endless and unsatisfying meals which tantalize the hungry soul in dreams. But soon after daybreak Vrail and Jones were awakened and alarmed by the report of a gun, which proved to be that of their leader, who was already purveying for breakfast. They immediately joined him, and in a short time they had secured sufficient game of the smaller kind to serve for a substantial repast, and around the rekindled fire they cooked and ate it with a relish denied to costlier viands at luxurious boards.

Thus strengthened, they returned to their boat, and under the pilotage of their mysterious leader whose word had become a law to both his companions, they resumed their voyage, leisurely discussing the perilous scenes through which they had passed, and lamenting the fate of their less fortunate associates.

They at length approached a large cluster of islands, forming one of the many divisions of that northern Archipelago, which when summer smiles away its ice, and lulls its Borean blasts, may vie in romantic beauty with the classic shores of the Ægean sea.

Gliding around the coast of one of these isles, and pursuing their way for a considerable distance through narrow channels, which separated different members of the group, the voyagers emerged at length into a sort of watery amphitheatre, lake-like in the lucid beauty of its calm surface, and girded and guarded on on all sides by islands of every size, and of all conceivable shapes. Some of them were separated by a channel scarcely allowing the passage of the tiny boat, which was gliding among them, and some even permitted of an active man's leap from shore to shore —while between others wide spaces intervened, across which a musket ball could be sent with no certain aim.

A marked and peculiar change came over the leader of the little party as they entered within the sheltered precincts just described. His eye dilated, his face brightened, his voice took an exultant tone, and he seemed a monarch returned to his rightful realm.

"We are safe enough here, Mr. Vrail," he said, " and we might be happy enough too in such a place as this, if one could be content to forget wrongs and lose aspirations."

"I am not wrong then in supposing that you are"——

Thomas hesitated and looked around him as if he feared the name he was about to pronounce might conjure up armed foes even in that watery wilderness.

"You need not be afraid to speak here," interrupted the other; "there is none to hear, excepting yonder eagle, who is sailing above us, and he is a fellow monarch of mine, who will betray no secrets."

"You then are 'the hero of the thousand isles,' the brave Johnson, whose name is on every patriot's tongue, whose praise is spoken in every lodge of our order, both in Canada and in the States."

"I am William Johnson," replied the other in a voice of mournful cadence. "A man without titles or possessions, proscribed and hunted by two great nations between which I dwell, daring to go openly in neither."

"And do they not seek you here?"

"Yes, even here the myrmidons of the Canadian government have followed me, but they have grown tired of a sport which always proves fatal to a portion of the pursuers without their even obtaining sight of an enemy. Fired upon from every island which they approach, every island is found tenantless and unoccupied when they reach it, and the discharge of a single gun, waking a hundred echoes, always seems to them like a volley. They have returned to spread stories of my being backed by hundreds of followers, who lurk among the thousand isles, and who could destroy a regiment, if sent against them, without the loss of a single man."

"And you have followers in these wilds?"

Johnson did not reply for some moments, and when he did so, it was in a voice at once musical and melancholy.

"Yes, I have followers. You shall see them."

"Is it far to your *hum?*" asked Jones, who had been a very interested listener to the old man's remarks, "and are we going to it now?"

"All roads lead to the home of the outlaw," replied Johnson. "My abode is like that of the hunted hare, wherever safety requires—but at all times in dens and caves of the earth."

Although Thomas had heard so much of the exploits of his present companion, he had not personally encountered him before their flight, Johnson having joined the invaders on their approach to Prescott, and they having been connected with different divisions of the little army during their encampment at Windmill Point.

Continuing their conversation and their voyage, they at length approached one of the smaller islands of the group, towards which Johnson, who had the helm, guided the vessel, informing his companions they would stop there.

CHAPTER XXII.

THE HERO OF THE THOUSAND ISLES.

Having moored his boat, he proceeded towards the centre of the island, and approached a gnarled and knotted tree, which was partially decayed about the base, and had many holes capable of serving as receptacles of small packages.

"This is my post-office," said Johnson, thrusting his arm deep into one of the openings, and drawing out a small box, "and here I shall find information as to the whereabouts of those I seek. My domains are so extensive, and it so often becomes necessary for my followers, as you call them, to change their residence during my absence, that something of this kind becomes necessary to enable me to find them."

He took from the box a paper, which apparently contained a very brief memorandum, and he immediately exclaimed,

"Is it possible? Why, they are close at hand. I wonder they have not already seen us. They have been in danger too."

Vrail asked him if he were not imprudent in exposing his private resorts to strangers who might betray him, to which he replied:

"No, I do not fear you, or if I should, these things are easily changed; besides, my letters tell no secrets to strangers. See what you can make of this?"

Vrail took it and gazed at it a few moments with a puzzled air, but could make nothing of it. There was not a single line of writing, but simply a few rude hieroglyphics, representing a deer pursued by hunters, and a tree of unusual shape; the first symbol of course denoting the danger which Johnson had understood it to imply, and the last intimating the present place of refuge of his friends.

"We must cross over to Rainbow Island," said the outlaw, pointing to a locality where the forest foliage, presenting even more than the usual diversified hues of autumn, looked as if a rainbow had become tangled in the tree-tops, and had broken up into a million glittering fragments.

The voyagers returned to their boat, and in a very few minutes its prow touched the desired coast, at a point where a profusion of bushes, growing close to the edge of the water, admitted of a perfect place of concealment for the vessel without drawing it upon shore. Leaping ashore the commodore hastily secured his skiff, and rapidly led the way into the interior, followed by his companions.

Rainbow Island was of considerable dimensions, being nearly half a mile in length, and having a width varying from eighty to a hundred rods, and it was more densely studded with woods than any of the surrounding members of the group. This circumstance, together with one which will presently appear, had made it a frequent and favorite resort of the outlaw, to whom it afforded both shelter and the means of subsistence, game being abundant within its borders.

As they advanced, a rugged hill of considerable height rose before them, at the base of which, on their right, gaped a deep ravine, black with the shadows of the interwoven boughs which hung above it, almost impervious to the light of day.

They clambered over this hill, and descending a more gradual slope towards the opposite side of the island, soon found themselves at a distance of about thirty rods from the shore, and in the midst of trees, shrubbery, and underbrush, more dense and tangled, if possible, than those which they had left on the other side of the eminence. From their present position the ravine, which crossed the island and divided the hill into two sections, was more accessible, and seemed a shade less forbidding in its gloominess, and yet it was sufficiently repulsive to cause Vrail and Jones to pause upon its edge, and hesitate about following their leader into its Avernus-like shades.

"Come on!" exclaimed the outlaw. "What do you fear?"

Ashamed of his irresolution, Tom began to descend, followed by Barak, who clung with desperation to the marginal bushes, and made a dismal groaning over his task. To the gratification of his followers, however, Johnson paused upon a ledge about a third of the way down the declivity, and announced the close proximity of one of his homes. A vocal signal, somewhat resembling the call of a squirrel, drew almost instantly forth, seemingly out of the very side of the hill, but in fact from a cavern, the mouth of which was concealed by bushes, an agile boy of about fourteen years, who with every demonstration of delight and surprise, rushed into the arms of the outlaw. Following the lad more timidly, for her eyes had caught sight of the strangers, was a young woman of decidedly handsome and graceful exterior, whose relationship to the hardy warrior a glance was sufficient to determine.

She was dressed with a neatness which seemed incompatible with the place of her abode; but where will not the ingenuity of the gentler sex find means for the gratification of refined tastes? Johnson hastened to meet her, and having kissed her tenderly, he introduced her to his companions as his daughter.

"These are the followers of whom I spoke," he said, smiling. "Do you think Canada has much to fear from them?"

There was a responsive flashing in the eye of the lad, which seemed to intimate that the time might come when his name would not be altogether insignificant in the ranks of England's foes.

The maiden fastened an inquiring look upon her father, anxious to hear some tidings of the war, and uncertain whether to look upon him as a fugitive or as a conqueror—yet afraid to ask in the presence of people of whom she knew nothing.

Equally solicitous in turn to know the particulars of the peril which had threatened his children, and which might, for all he knew, still impend over them and him, Johnson led the way into his cave with a view to a mutual explanation. The bushes which served as a concealment to the entrance were partly of natural growth, and partly transplanted, and were so thickly set as to make the passage difficult to one unaccustomed to the path. The mouth of the cave was small, requiring to be entered in a stooping posture, but its interior was of a size more than sufficient for all the purposes of its occupants.

Expecting to find a squalid den, vying with the lowest cabins of savage life, the visitors were surprised, on entering, to discover something decidedly like a furnished room, wearing a general air of neatness and comfort. Its active and industrious proprietor had supplied himself, from time to time, in the obscure American towns, where he was unknown, with all the necessary articles of furniture for more than one subterranean abode, and such of his chattels as were easily portable, were removed at times from one of his country seats to another, as convenience invited, or danger drove to the exchange.

His grotto, as his daughter fancifully called it, on Rainbow Island, was his favorite resort, and on this he had bestowed the greatest degree of attention and care. Its uneven flooring was covered with a coarse carpet; a table and chairs stood in the centre of the apartment, and near the entrance a fire burned in a small stove, the pipe of which found the outer air through an artificial opening above the doorway. Two bedsteads, apparently well furnished, occupied opposite corners of the cavern, and near the smallest of them a little mirror was fastened against the wall, surrounded with other toilet appendages.

The obscurity of the apartment was relieved only by the light of a single candle, and by the few rays which found entrance at the doorway, yet the eyes of the visitors became sufficiently accustomed, after a while, to this state of semi-darkness, to admit of a partially distinct view of all the objects in the subterranean chamber.

There were, indeed, remote corners which presented no definite outline, and which, fading away in the distance, became painfully suggestive of unexplored recesses, reaching back far into the bowels of the earth, and tenanted, perhaps, by some wild animal, whose glaring eyes might at any moment announce its presence and its approach.

CHAPTER XXIII.

RAINBOW ISLAND.

When the little party had found seats, Johnson hastened to answer the questions which his children anxiously asked in a half whisper about the war and its results. It was a painful task to tell of his new misfortunes, and of the crushing of his high hopes, yet he spoke of the defeat of the patriots only in general terms, and hinted at triumphs yet in reserve for them, which should amply atone for present reverses. The daughter seemed prepared for sad tidings, which she had long been accustomed to hear, but she could not grieve violently over any disaster which left her father unharmed. To his side she clung with an affectionate interest, which lightened the warrior's heart of its load of grief and inspired his failing spirits with new hope and resolution.

"Tell me now," he said, "about yourselves. Your letter hints of danger and of pursuit, but it has been, doubtless, some childish alarm. There can be none of our enemies among the islands now."

"You are mistaken, father."

"That you are," exclaimed the boy. "There's a party of eight or ten men among the upper islands now, all well armed, and led by a Canadian officer. I saw them while I was deer hunting on Fire Island, and they were in two boats, and were not more than half a mile distant from me. I saw them distinctly."

"When was this?"

"The day before yesterday. We came down here the same night; and I advised Ellen to let me take her to old Flynn's, on the American shore, but she said we must wait first a day or two, and see if you returned from the fight, which we knew would be very soon."

"This is certainly serious, if true, but you may have been misled by some hunting party."

"No," replied the boy, "I saw soldiers with guns and bayonets, I cannot be mistaken. Besides, I saw a deer within sixty rods of them, which no one attempted to shoot."

"Then we must be on the alert, and the first thing to be done is for you and Ellen to go to Flynn's to-night, and stay there till you hear from me."

"Not me, papa; I will return, for you know I can help you if they should come. I can at least load the guns, if you don't think I can fire straight enough."

"No, you must stay with Ellen. I could do nothing with either of you here. Besides, I shall have help enough now," and the speaker glanced at the guests, who might be said each to owe him a life.

Jones replied very hastily,

"I think I shall have to be going, Mr. Commodore; 'cause you see, I must be wanted to *hum* about these days. My folks didn't know as I was to be gone so long when I left 'em."

"Where do you think your *hum* would have been now, if it had not been for meeting me at Windmill Point last evening? In a Canadian jail, with a full view of a gallows before you."

"P'raps so—it's orful to think on, and I'm sure I don't want to run no more such risks. I think I'll be going when Miss Johnson and the boy goes. I can help them row the boat, you know."

"You will not go with *me*, sir," replied Ellen, with flushed cheeks and flashing eyes. "I will not trust myself with a man who deserts his friend in the hour of danger."

"Why, bless you, girl, I ain't going to desert nobody. Your father don't need *me* here, and I'm in a hurry to get home. I won't hurt you."

"Why not go yourself to this Flynn's to-night, and remain there till the search is over?" asked Tom.

"Because I am no safer on the American shore than I should be in Canada. Every marshal on the frontier, from Michigan to Maine, has a warrant for my arrest. No, the children must go alone, unless you also wish to accompany them."

"No," said Tom, to whom the poltroonry of Jones had seemed so great that he could not make up his mind to imitate it, notwithstanding his own previous feats in that line. Perhaps his very regret and shame for the desertion of his brother had influenced him to a different line of conduct now, for, whatever were his faults, he did not altogether lack courage. "No, I will remain, and do what I can," he said. "I do not think we have much to fear among these islands against a dozen men."

"And you?" asked Johnson.

"I rayther think I'd like to go, seeing that 'Im "——

"In a hurry," added Johnson. "But there don't seem any way left for you to travel. We have but two boats here—one we must keep, of course, and the other the children must take."

"But, as I said, I will go with them."

"Ellen has made up her mind on that subject. She won't take you. I saw that in her eye before she spoke, and it is useless to try to change her mind. But I tell you what, if the enemy comes, Mr. Jones, I can hide you where you will be as safe as a toad in a rock."

"In this place here?" asked Jones, looking about the cavern.

"No—a safer place than this; for there are some signs and marks hereabouts that a practiced woodsman would soon take notice of. I have a safer place than this, when worst comes to worst."

"Wal, as I said, I'd rayther go," reiterated Jones, "'cause I'm in a hurry, and our folks don't know where I am, but if I hef to stay, p'raps you may as well put me in that place that you speak of; not but what I would stay and help you fight very willingly, if I thought it was lawful to shoot them fellows."

"Lawful?"

"Yes—you see this ain't like killing in war exactly, and these folks ain't arter *me*, and if I should shoot any of 'em, or shoot *at* 'em, and they should capter me, it might be a hanging matter."

"You may make your mind easy on that score, for if they catch you, you'll be hung beyond a doubt, though you never fire a bullet."

"Do you think so?" asked Jones, really turning pale.

"Of course you will—*you*, the great orator and agitator, who went over with the patriot army to Windmill Point."

"But I didn't *mean* to go over, Mr. Johnson, you know."

"No, I know you didn't—I can swear to *that*."

"And I don't think I killed anybody."

"I presume not. By the way, Jones, what division were you in? I never saw anything of you until I saw you running away."

"Well, I was in Colonel Smith's party in one of the storehouses. They fought like bull-dogs there, too; but I wasn't exactly in the lines, not having listed, you know, and not bein' obliged to fight."

"But you gave the affair your countenance?" said Johnson, suppressing a smile.

"Y-e-s," answered Barak hesitatingly, as if reflecting how far the answer might commit him in case of capture.

"But as to running away," he added, for he did not exactly like the phrase; "you know when you overtook me, you were doing the same thing."

"Of course I was. After our commander, Colonel Van Shoultz, surrendered, and there was no more chance to fight, I fled, and took my chance among a dozen bullets which followed me, for I knew there was no hope for me if taken. A dozen men followed me, and probably a hundred more would have joined them, if I had been known."

"How far did they follow ?" asked Jones.

"All but three turned back within five minutes, the rest followed *all their life-time.*"

"All their life-time ?"

"Yes, and they are now lying unburied on the shore, if they have not been found by their comrades."

"Wal, that shows there ain't any harm in running away when the right time comes."

"Certainly not, but judging from the place where I found you, and the time you said you had rested there; you must have taken a pretty early start, probably rather before the surrender."

"Yes, rather, I believe. The fact is, I saw how things were going, and I took a timely start, especially as I didn't know but I might get home in time to send reinforcements."

Johnson burst into a loud laugh at this remark, and although he tried repeatedly to repress it, the ebullitions of his merriment became more and more violent, until all the cavern reverberated with the sound, and the whole party were compelled to join in the contagious mirth. Jones looked a little abashed and was about to add something further, when the conversation was changed by Vrail inquiring of Johnson why, if he had so secure a hiding-place, he did not avail himself of its shelter, and thus avoid all danger.

"Well, sir," replied the outlaw, "a moment's reflection will convince you that that would be very poor policy, even if I could content myself to hide, and inflict no punishment on the men who are seeking my life for the purpose of obtaining a reward of a few hundred pounds. Let it but be understood that I can be hunted in safety, like a deer or a moose, or some tame animal, and in three weeks these islands would swarm with my pursuers. No, no, those who come on such an errand must be taught its peril, in order to proclaim it, if any of them should go back. One man, the last of his party, who was entirely in my power, I spared, for that very reason."

"It's dreadful business though, ain't it commodore?" said Barak.

"Yes, but those who come on such a chase are presumed to know something of its danger. They must take their chances, and I must defend myself."

"Wal, now about this hiding-place?"

"Oh, there's time enough for that when the enemy comes in sight. I must go out now and procure a little game of some kind, for these children have had nothing but dried meat and hard biscuits for a week, and we ourselves have not been overfed."

"But how do you know the enemy is not near?"

"We have a watch among the top boughs of the highest tree that crowns the hill above our heads. Do you not miss my boy from our circle? Never fear being surprised when George plays the sentinel." The lad had slipped out at a signal from his father, and had taken his post of observation, soon after he had first told his story of danger.

"But you certainly will not run the risk of betraying your position by firing guns at game, when your pursuers may be within hearing?" asked Vrail with much earnestness.

"By no means," replied Johnson. "I have more silent weapons, and equally sure at a short distance, both for man and brute."

As he spoke he rose and went to a dark corner of his room, whence he soon returned, bringing a large ashen bow, which might have done honor to the woodcraft of Robin Hood himself, and a bundle of arrows fully fitted for the formidable weapon which accompanied them.

"I bought this bow," he said, "of an Indian chief, who said it had belonged to a famous hunter in his grandfather's time, and had long been preserved in the tribe with a sort of religious veneration, and that for many years, one of the tests of all candidates for the degree of a Brave, was their ability to wield this weapon with effect. The tribe had dwindled nearly away, and of the few who remained none could even spring the bow sufficiently to string it."

"Not the chief ?"

"No, for he was generally too much *sprung* himself for any such feats," said Johnson laughing.

"And did these arrows descend from his great grandfather too ?" asked Barak, who had been handling a bunch of them, and examining their black, hardened points.

"No, but the chief taught me how to make them, and the secret is really very valuable. George prepared these, and they are every one as good as a bullet. Come with me, and I will show you how they work, and you may as well bring the guns in case of surprise."

There was one case of surprise already, for Barak's eyes opened very wide at this invitation, and his head presently began shaking like a mandarin's.

"No, I thank you. I *see* how they work already, and as I'm rather tired, I think I'll stay here."

"Very true, I forgot," replied the outlaw, laughing. "Nell, you may accompany us, and carry one of the guns, if you choose; but remember, if you hear the crow-call, you must start back to cover."

The maiden sprang with alacrity to avail herself of the permission, which was accorded more to shame Jones than for any other reason, yet her father scarcely apprehended the least immediate danger, or he would not have subjected one so dear to him to any unnecessary exposure.

Vrail was too polite to allow his fair companion to carry a heavy weapon, and he insisted on taking the burden of both guns, and the little party went forth, leaving Jones in a very uncomfortable state of mind in the cave.

"This is a pokerish kind of place to be left alone in," he said as they went out. "There's no telling what will come. Don't be gone long, and don't forget to come back."

"Oh, we shall come back," replied Johnson, still disposed to play upon the fears of his pusillanimous guest, "unless we get hard pressed, you know, and have to take to the boat."

"Oh, mercy on us!" exclaimed the terror-stricken man, half emerging from his hole. "What shall I do *then?* I guess I'd rather go with you, after all."

"Just as you please."

The agitator, now the agitated, in fact, followed his companions at a considerable distance, looking warily and rapidly on all sides, now starting violently at the sound of the rattling shells which the squirrel dropped from his feast of nuts, and now nearly fainting at the whir of the frightened partridge, as she darted from her covert at his side.

Johnson led the way over the hill to the southern part of the island, and soon came upon the traces of deer; but it was so easy a matter for these animals to pass from island to island, and their range was over so wide a territory, that he felt far from sanguine of catching a glimpse of one. There was abundance of smaller game, and he soon bagged a brace of partridges, a hare, and some large squirrels, with which trophies he was about to return, when his daughter called his attention to some fresh tracks of the nobler prey of which he had been in pursuit, and revived his sporting spirit. He followed the trail cautiously, and to his great delight he soon came in view of a herd of five deer, quietly browsing among some shrubbery near the water's edge. Making signs to his companions to remain stationary, he advanced cautiously to a favorable position, and selecting a fine stag for his victim, let fly his unerring missile.

The wounded animal bounded forward, and bearing the weapon plainly visible in his side, immediately took to the water, while the rest of the herd dashed off in another direction, with the speed of the wind. The hunter hurried eagerly to the beach, and fitting another shaft to his bow, waited for an opportunity to discharge it with effect, at the moment when the stag should rise from the water on the opposite side of the narrow channel which he was crossing. But the moment the animal's shoulders became visible, and while Johnson's fingers lingered upon the fatal string, he was startled by the report of a gun from a neighboring island, and he saw the deer fall mortally wounded. At the same instant, a signal from his son in the tree-top gave warning of danger, and the hunter drew back a little into the woods, where, without exposure, he could keep his eye on the opposite shore. Here he was at once joined by the rest of his party, all greatly alarmed, and anxious to know the nature of the danger which threatened them, but he replied to their inquiries only in pantomime, enjoining silence, and pointing to the body of the deer. It was observed, however, that he kept his arrow fitted to the string, and held the bow in position for immediate use, and Vrail did not doubt that if an enemy should appear to claim the carcass, he would share the fate of his prey.

In a whisper he expostulated with Johnson upon the rashness of thus disclosing his retreat, and courting an immediate attack from superior numbers, and that too while his children were yet with him.

"They saw the deer swim from the shore," was the reply, "and they will see the fresh wound and the arrow yet sticking in its side. How long can I remain unsought here, if I do not frighten them off. The boats are ready on the other side of the island, for instant flight, if flight becomes necessary."

"Oh, don't shoot, for mercy's sake, good Mr. Johnson," exclaimed a trembling voice, with a running accompaniment of chattering teeth, "for they can cross over here in half a minute, and shoot us all down."

The individual from whom this protest proceeded was not easily discerned at first, but on minuter examination, his pallid face was discovered peering down from an adjacent tree, among the boughs of which he was snugly ensconced.

"Can you see or hear anything of an enemy from where you are, Jones?" asked Johnson, after glancing contemptuously at him.

"I—I don't know, I have not looked; but there is a strange noise off in this direction, and oh, bless me! Yes, I certainly see somebody now peeping around a tree at us. There, there, Mr. Johnson."

"What! on *this* island, Jones?" asked the other earnestly, at the same time levelling his huge bow as near as possible in the direction indicated.

"Yes, right off here; I just saw his red cap, and listen now to that voice, he is going to shoot."

"Blast the fool!" exclaimed Johnson, catching a sight of the object which had excited the coward's fears. "He is frightened by a *woodpecker!*"

Scarcely, however, had the hunter resumed his watch, when a small boat hove in view, containing six armed men, and almost at the same moment the lad George came running up to announce that there was still another boat-load visible from the tree, and that the whole party were at least a dozen in number, and were the same which he had seen farther west a few days previous.

Imminent danger was evidently at hand, and the alarm was general.

"Is it certain they are in pursuit of you?" asked Vrail.

"Yes, what else could they seek here? They have supposed it a good time to watch for and intercept me on my return from Prescott."

"What will you do?"

"I cannot decide," replied the outlaw, manifesting an agitation and doubt entirely unusual for him. "I would fire upon them without a moment's hesitation, if these children were not here. I must wait a moment. Possibly we may not be discovered."

While he spoke, the boat had landed on the opposite island, immediately beside the fallen deer, and several of the party had leaped ashore and gathered around the carcass. The distance was so slight that all their movements were plainly visible, and although their conversation could not be distinguished, the sound of their voices was at times audible. The discovery of the arrow led, as had been anticipated, to a scene of excitement, and to much discussion. Gestures were made towards Rainbow Island, indicating that it must have come from there, and the weapon was finally held up and waved in the air as a signal for the approach of the other boat, which proved to be near at hand, and in which was the leader of the expedition.

"Let us fly," said Vrail; "we can do nothing against so many."

"It is too late," replied Johnson, for at that moment the other skiff came in view, and still nearer to the fugitives than were the party on shore, and the energetic commander, seeming fully to understand the gestures of his comrades, steered at once towards Rainbow Island, signalling the other vessel to follow.

Johnson had hesitated until this moment; but there was no longer time for indecision, for the direction of the enemy was one which would bring them to the beach almost at their very side.

"To the cave! to the cave!" he said, seizing his daughter by the arm, and springing forward. "Don't be alarmed Nell; we are safe enough, and I would not run from such an enemy as that but for thee."

Vrail and the lad George started with the guns at the moment that Johnson gave the order for flight, and simultaneously with him, and all four had proceeded well on their way before it was remembered that the half-dead Jones was left behind in the tree where he had taken refuge. Whether his alarm had so far stupefied him that he had not seen the flight of his companions, or whether he had thought his position safter than their companionship, they could not tell, but it was too late to return for him without the almost certainty of encountering the enemy.

With many vituperations upon their craven comrade, yet not without sympathy for his probable fate, Johnson hurried forward, and with his little party soon arrived at the cave, without being able to perceive any signs of pursuit, and not without hope that his hiding-place might remain undisturbed until the shades of night should afford an opportunity for a safe retreat.

CHAPTER XXIV.

A THOUSAND POUNDS FOR HIS HEAD.

NEARLY paralyzed with terror, Barak witnessed the landing of the two boats, and the disembarking of their crews at a point so near to him as to allow of his hearing the orders which were issued to the men, although the condition of his mental faculties scarcely admitted of his understanding their full import. That somebody was to be taken, dead or alive, and was to be shot down if he did not surrender upon the first summons, he very distinctly understood, and he scarcely knew for the time whether he himself were not the hunted outlaw whom a detachment of soldiers had been sent to seek. The very bough to which he clung shook with his agitation when he heard the sanguinary command; and greatly as he dreaded being captured by the British, he resolved not to be made a target for the balls of the soldiers for want of any readiness in yielding to the first demand for surrender. He stood ready, indeed, to drop into the arms of the foe at the first moment of discovery.

The pursuing party, meanwhile, separated into two divisions, and, leaving two men to guard the boats, started in opposite directions to traverse the island, keeping sufficiently near the beach to see any boat that might put off from the coast, while at the same time they could observe a considerable portion of the interior. After this circuit, and after securing any boats that might be found, it was contemplated to make a close examination of every part of the little territory, where there was so much reason to anticipate a successful termination to their expedition. Barak might have heard of these plans as they were informally discussed between Sergeant Ward and his men; but he did not. He soon comprehended, however, that the enemy were leaving him undisturbed, and his heart grew lighter as the sound of their voices died away in the distance. He even began to contemplate the daring feat of descending from his elevated quarters and seeking the cavern, where he did not doubt that his late companions were now concealed, but the fear of observation by the boatmen, and an uncertainty as to his ability to find his way to the cave, deterred him for a long time from making the attempt. An hour of irresolution, which might have procured safety, passed away, and in the meantime the enemy had completed the circuit of the island; they had found and taken possession of the two boats of Johnson, sending them to the place where their own skiffs remained under guard, and they had again set out for a second and more thorough search after the thousand pounds value of human flesh which was fully believed to lurk somewhere among the recesses of this *terra incognita*.

Unconscious of what had taken place, Barak decided to descend and attempt his transit to the cavern at the very moment when the experiment was most perilous, both for himself and his subterranean friends. He reached the ground, indeed, in safety and unobserved, and guessing his way as well as he could, he accomplished nearly half the distance without molestation, but on reaching the summit of the hill which it became necessary to cross, he found himself in full view of one of the divisions of the foe. Had he instantly drawn back or fallen to the ground, he might yet have escaped observation, but he hesitated one fatal moment, and in the next he was hailed, and called upon to surrender.

Barak had no weapon in his hands, nor could he have used it if he had. Trembling in every joint, he sank to the earth, where he sat, with his hands uplifted deprecatingly toward the half dozen men who were rushing upon him with levelled guns, and with shouts of exultation.

"Don't fire!" exclaimed a voice from the rear of the approaching party, and so the foremost man contented himself with knocking Barak over with the butt of his gun, and then asking him who he was.

"I—I—don't know," groaned Jones, regaining his sitting position, and again putting up his hands. "Don't fire—please don't let 'em fire, Mr. Captain!"

"This is not the man," said the sergeant, with a disappointed air; "but he may know something about him, notwithstanding. Who are you, and what are you doing here?"

"Oh, I was not doing anything, but looking around," replied Jones, quite wild with terror, yet instinctively withholding his name.

"Looking around, hey! Well, you had better look around now pretty sharp. You have a name, I suppose. Who and what are you?"

"I'm Mr.—Smith—Mr. Smith; that's my name, and I ain't a patriot at all."

"Oh, ho! we'll see about that by and by. But who is here with you on this island—whose boats are these that we have found, and where is the owner of them?"

"I don't know."

"Who shot the deer that swam across to the opposite island, with a large arrow in its side?"

"I don't know."

"Let some one fetch a rope from the boats, and we will see if the truth cannot be extracted from this fellow. I shall not waste time or words on you, my man, you may depend on that. You must answer these questions, or in five minutes you shall dangle from the bough above your head. Do you see it?"

"Oh, no," groaned Barak, "you won't hang me; it's against the law."

"There is no law here except the law of the strongest."

As he spoke, the report of a musket startled the group, and one of their number fell to the earth mortally wounded. Such a commentary upon his text was quite unexpected, and before the alarmed sergeant could issue an order, or could even ascertain from what direction the shot came, a second was sent with equally fatal effect. They might have fallen from the clouds for any clew that could be found to their origin, for neither blaze nor smoke was seen, and the echoes and reverberations were so rapid and so many as to baffle all conjecture as to the source of the original report.

Sergeant Ward gave orders to his men to withdraw over the brow of the hill, a command which was very hastily obeyed, but not without dragging the trembling prisoner along, who had begun to indulge some faint hope of a rescue by the chivalrous man whose favor he had done so little to deserve.

The party halted in a dense part of the wood, and the leader, who was a brave and determined officer, addressed his men, informing them that there could no longer be any doubt that they had entrapped the dangerous man, for whose capture so many and so great efforts had been made, and that they only required a little courage and coolness to secure the prize, and entitle themselves to the thanks and the bounty of government.

"We have his boats," he continued, "so that he cannot leave the island, and we will soon know his haunts, if there is any virtue in hemp."

The messenger, who had been sent to the boats, had returned, bringing with him one of the ropes which had been used as a cable, and at a signal from the sergeant, it was looped and thrown suddenly around Barak's neck, who had not observed the preparations for this ominous proceeding.

With a scream, a groan, and a shudder, with eyes starting from their sockets, and hands grasping convulsively at the tightening rope, Jones sputtered out his submission.

"Oh, don't—I'll tell all—I will! I will! Take it off! Take it off!"

"*Fasten it to the bough!*" shouted the sergeant, with a threatening look and a terrific voice; "if you have anything to say, you must be quick."

"Yes—yes—I will—I will! Take it off! take it off!"

"Who shot the deer?"

"Bill Johnson!"

Notwithstanding this answer was expected, a visible emotion passed through the group of listeners, at the mention of so formidable a name.

"How many men are with him on the island besides you?"

"Only one, and a boy."

"Where are they now?"

"In a cave, over that way," pointing in the direction of the cavern.

"Will you go with us, and show us the safest way to approach it, and tell us all that you know about it, without deceit or equivocation?"

"Yes—if—if you will let me go afterwards."

"It is a bargain. Help us to take Johnson, and you are free, but if you tell us one falsehood, or withhold anything from us, or in any way try to deceive or betray us, or to help the enemy, that moment you shall die. Do you understand?"

"Yes, yes—take it off! take it off!"

The rope which had inspired the craven with so much horror was removed, and no sooner was he free from it, than he sprang forward as if from the touch of a serpent.

Sergeant Ward immediately set his band in motion, guided by the treacherous Barak, and they were soon approaching the cavern from a direction in which they would not be visible to the concealed party until they were very near the entrance of their subterranean retreat. Ward did not expect to accomplish the enterprise without the loss of some men, but having questioned his prisoner, again and again, as to the strength of the foe, and becoming satisfied that the outlaw was almost entirely unsupported, he resolved to make a bold push for a victory, which was to prove at once brilliant and profitable. His men being equally sanguine and dauntless, he had no difficulty in leading them wherever he dared personally to venture, and the whole party were soon treading with cautious steps, and almost in Indian file, that rocky ledge which has been described, and beside which, hidden by shrubbery, was the entrance to the cavernous abode for which they sought.

Ward and one bold private led the way, keeping the guide between them, and when the latter earnestly assured them that they were but a few yards from the mouth of the cave, and pointed out the bushes which concealed it, the sergeant ordered his men to hug the hill-side closely, so that no shot could reach them, unless from an assailant who should expose himself in the act of firing. Personally pursuing this policy, the venturous leader advanced, with gun in rest, almost to the door of the cave, and then in a loud voice he summoned the inmates to surrender.

He knew full well that a forced entrance, however certain to eventuate in victory, must result fatally to the foremost of the attacking party, and brave as he was, he was not prepared to be the forlorn hope in such an enterprise, while other probable means of success were within his reach. His summons being unanswered, he loudly repeated it, stating his strength, and warning the enemy, that in case of non-compliance he should proceed at once to build a fire at the mouth of the cave, and either suffocate them in it, or drive them out to be shot down as they came forth.

Entire silence followed these formal demands, and notwithstanding Barak's repeated assurances to the contrary, Ward almost doubted that there was an enemy within hearing. Having waited a reasonable time for a reply to his summons, he ordered part of his men to gather a large quantity of the dryest boughs and underbrush, a task of no easy accomplishment, yet light compared with the more dangerous one of depositing the combustible material in the spot which was to render it efficacious. This, however was to be done by climbing the hill-side above the opening of the cave, and from this apparently unexposed position thrusting down at first ignited branches, and afterwards keeping the blaze supplied with fresh aliment from above, while a guard stood ready to fire upon any one who should emerge to remove the burning pile.

Savage as was this mode of attack, it had been decided upon without compunction by Ward, who had been maddened by the loss of his men, and who considered the enemy alone responsible for the extreme measures his contumacy rendered necessary. He could surrender at any moment, and thus avoid the threatened danger, and this was the result anticipated and hoped for by the sergeant, who did not know of the presence of a female in the fort thus barbarously attacked; for Barak, in naming the force which sustained Johnson, had not considered it necessary to speak of the outlaw's daughter.

CHAPTER XXV.

SUBTERRANEAN COUNCILS.

The condition of the besieged party was indeed one of great extremity, and indomitable as was the courage of Johnson, he could not but feel sensible of his great peril. There seemed to have been some fatality in the chain of circumstances which had frustrated all his remarkable vigilance and sagacity, and which seemed about to deliver him, like Samson, bound and helpless into the hands of his enemies. The unusual remissness of his sentinel son, in allowing the enemy to approach so near his retreat unobserved, the unfortunate flight of the wounded deer, bearing the betraying arrow in its side, and the craven conduct of Barak, had together woven a mesh which threatened to hold the strong man fast.

Yet did Johnson by no means lose hope or self possession. He had anticipated from the moment when he knew that Barak was captured, that he would be compelled to betray his hiding-place, and he was prepared for a vigorous defence against any ordinary attack; but he had not anticipated the savage mode of warfare to which he was to be subjected, until he heard it announced. Dismay and despair fell upon all his companions when the summons and warning were proclaimed, in a voice which rang distinctly through the cavern, and returned in mocking echoes from its far recesses. Johnson alone did not quail, nor intermit a moment his vigilant watch from a point where unseen from without, he could command a view of several rods in extent, on that side of the opening which the enemy had approached. He could not, however, see the main body of the assailants, while they continued to keep close to the hill-side, but he occasionally caught a glimpse of the leader, who in summoning the subterranean garrison had approached nearer than had any one of his men.

He had indeed, more than one opportunity to fire upon the sergeant with certain fatality, and his singular forbearance in this respect excited the wonder of Vrail, who watched his movements with painful solicitude.

"You have had him twice under your gun," said Thomas; "and even now half the width of his body is exposed. You could plant a ball in his breast this minute."

"I know it."

"Why, then, do you not fire?"

"There would be *nine* left. Wait a little and keep still. He will come nearer."

"And if he does?"——

"He will be. *alone* presently; his men are gathering brush. Look sharp, and be silent."

Vrail did not comprehend this remark. His anxiety was intense, and the horrors of his position were aggravated by the reflection that his safety had been so nearly secured. An unconditional surrender seemed to him almost unavoidable, in order to escape immediate death, and to save the helpless female who was under their protection, yet he refrained from counselling this course as long as Johnson himself seemed to have any resource. Submission would be death to the outlaw, and doubtless to Vrail also, as his abettor and accomplice; yet even this would be preferable to the present destruction of the whole party by means so dreadful as those which had been threatened. A silence of some minutes ensued, during which Johnson remained at his post in a crouching attitude, vigilantly watching the sergeant, who, in his turn, was watching and giving orders to his men, now separated from him at various short distances, gathering the material for the burning pile.

The private who had accompanied Ward, in advance of the band, went and came at short intervals, but both had been thrown off their guard by the entire silence which reigned in the cavern, and by the absence of all signs of hostilities, or even of life in that quarter. A suspicion that the enemy had escaped before their arrival was fast gaining ground in the mind of Ward, who began to wince in contemplation of the ridicule which might attach to his pompous summons for the surrender of an imaginary garrison. He did not, however, intermit his design, being resolved to put the question to a speedy proof, and he urged his men to increased activity in their work, no longer thinking of retaining any at his side, save Barak, who sat shaking on the ground before him.

"He is alone *now!*" whispered Johnson, laying down his gun, and advancing steathily a few paces, until his head protruded a little beyond the doorway. As the panther springs upon his prey, the outlaw, with the speed of thought, rushed upon his unwarned victim. The strength of that momentary energy which desperation or violent passion sometimes gives, and which is so nearly allied to that of madness, was upon him, as with glaring eyes and demoniac face he came flying like some terrific vision, upon the astonished sergeant. In a twinkling the soldier's musket was snatched from his grasp, and was flung into the ravine, while Ward himself clutched in the iron grasp of his adversary, was dragged rapidly to the cavern doorway, despite all resistance, and into its dark recesses.

Had Satan suddenly emerged from the bowels of the earth, and carried off one of their number bodily, the soldiers could not have been more astonished or terrified, and if there was time or opportunity to fire upon the strange assailant, they could not have done so without risk of killing their comrade and commander.

Placing his son on guard over the prostrate and unarmed man, with orders to fire upon him if he attempted to rise, Johnson hastily resumed his post at the doorway, where together with Vrail, he remained for some minutes prepared to repel any sudden attack that might follow his daring achievement. But there were no signs of pursuit, and whatever course the enemy might see fit to adopt in this new phase of affairs, it became pretty evident that they did not mean to follow their leader into the lion's den.

The stunned and frightened sergeant expected no mercy at the hands of a man of whose atrocities he had heard so many fabulous tales, and of whose prowess he had such convincing proof. Expecting each moment to be his last, he listened sullenly and at first without reply, to the questions of his captor.

"You meant to smoke us out, did you, young man?" said the outlaw, in a voice far from harsh; yet the question was repeated several times before it was answered.

"I meant to take you, if possible," replied Ward, at length; "I gave you fair warning."

"You did; and you see I have profited by it."

"I was a fool. You have conquered me, and will kill me, of course; but you need not taunt me."

"If I had wanted to kill you, I need not have taken such pains to bring you here. I covered your heart three times with my rifle."

"What then do you want?" asked the sergeant, eagerly. His mortifying discomfiture had at first scarcely left him the wish to live, but with the hope came back the strong desire of life which is natural to every human heart.

"What do you suppose? I want to be let alone. I want your men to retire from this island, and to permit me and my children to do the same."

"Let me go, and I will withdraw them instantly," said Ward, eagerly.

"I cannot trust you."

"On the honor of a soldier"——

"Say rather, a savage, who would have burned me and my children together, or would have shot us down as we fled from the flames and smoke of our dwelling. I cannot trust you."

"I only did what I thought justifiable towards an outlawed man."

"For whose head there was a large reward, part of which you expected to pocket, and you would do the same again if you were at liberty. I should be a fool to trust you."

"How can I convince you? What can I do?" asked the prisoner, in a tone of great anxiety.

"Call to your men, and bid them lay down their guns at the door of the cave. Let them also bring their muskets from the boats. Then they may depart, leaving me one boat, and one for you to follow them with. Tell them your life depends on their compliance, as it most certainly does."

Ward was ordinarily a brave man, and he hesitated long before he would consent to redeem his life by such means; but the ignominious personal defeat which he had already sustained prepared him for a descent to further disgrace. If he rejected the proposal of his captor, and suffered the death which such rejection was sure to bring upon him, there would be none to proclaim the heroism of the act; but living, he might in some degree vindicate his reputation, and explain his mortifying discomfiture.

"How can we trust *you*," he said, at length, "after surrendering all our weapons into your hands?"

"On the faith of a word which was never pledged and broken. If this is not sufficient, let your men see to their own safety by all taking to their boats, excepting one, before their arms are surrendered. Surely you must have some courageous friend among your men, who will venture to be the last man, and who will bring the arms to the cave."

"Davy Giles will do it, if I bid him. He is a daring fellow, and he owes me his life."

"He will risk nothing—not a hair of his head shall be harmed."

"But how shall I be able to communicate with my men? You will not trust me outside, and they dare not come here."

"My daughter has pen and ink and paper. Write your message, and it shall be passed out at the end of my longest fishing-rod. Doubtless your daring friend will approach near enough to take it."

Ward accepted the proposition, though with some misgivings as to his ability to bring about so dishonorable a submission of his company. He did not, indeed, doubt that they would be very anxious to save his life, but he feared they might prefer to attempt his rescue by other means, which would be certainly fatal to him, although redounding more to their credit as military men than the ignominious surrender and retreat which he was compelled to counsel.

He made, however, an earnest appeal to his men to comply with the proposition of the outlaw, and reminded them that, although a prisoner, his orders were still binding upon them, and would devolve all the responsibility of the act upon himself. They could not, he added, honorably desert him, nor could they in any way attempt his rescue with so little risk to themselves, or with any hope of benefit to him. He assured them, in conclusion, that his own death would be the immediate and certain consequence of their refusal to comply with his request.

This letter, when finished, was extended out of the cavern in the way suggested by Johnson, a white cloth being, at Ward's request, also attached to the rod, both as a means of attracting attention, and of signifying a desired truce.

The sergeant had not been mistaken in the fidelity and daring of his friend Giles, who immediately advanced, took the missive from the pole, and returned with it to his companions, all of whom, as well as himself, were greatly delighted to learn that their leader yet lived, and that there was a chance of procuring his release. They did not hesitate long about obeying a command which relieved them of any personal responsibility, and rid them of so disastrous and unpromising an enterprise.

They had lost two of their companions in some mysterious way, before even catching sight of an enemy, and now their commander had been suddenly spirited away from them, and would doubtless suffer some barbarous death if they did not rescue him in the only way which seemed possible. They agreed to the terms, and Giles volunteered to remain after the departure of his companions and surrender the arms.

He was to accompany them to the boats, and depositing all the guns in Johnson's skiff, was to row it around, after the embarkation of his comrades, to a part of the beach nearest the cave, and thence he was to carry the weapons to the invisible conqueror. These things being agreed upon, Giles advanced fearlessly to the mouth of the cave, where the white flag was still flying, and announced the decision of the men, greatly to the delight both of the besieged party and their prisoner.

The soldiers then withdrew, by a route which would enable them to take with them the bodies of their slain companions, and in a short time they reached their boats, and quitted the island, first designating a rendezvous where they would wait for the liberated sergeant and Giles to join them, if they should be fortunate enough to escape from the supposed monster, in whose power they were to be wholly left.

Giles was himself by no means free from apprehensions on this score. He felt, at times, as though he were relying on the faith of an ogre, but he was accustomed to danger, and he was animated by the noble principle of fidelity to a friend.

It need not be said that his fears were speedily dissipated. No sooner were the dozen weapons deposited at the door of the cave, than Johnson and his party emerged from their retreat, accompanied by their unharmed prisoner, who, like his friend, was still uncertain of the fate which awaited him.

But the mild aspect and deportment of their conqueror, and the frank, honest expression of his countenance, at once convinced them that they had nothing to fear, and the abashed sergeant, after expressing his obligations for the forbearance of his captor, took his departure, with greatly changed views of the man whose destruction he had so recently sought.

The fate of Barak was the next subject of inquiry, but a considerable time elapsed before any clew could be obtained to his whereabout, and the impression began to prevail that the soldiers had taken him with them; but he was discovered at length, in the ravine, where he was lying very still, awaiting the issue of the fearful events which had been transpiring around him. His descent into the valley had not been a voluntary movement, nor altogether a pleasant one. When Johnson made his sudden *sortie* from his subterranean fort, Barak, as has been stated, was seated on the ground near the sergeant, and in the impetuous rush of the outlaw, he was overturned and rolled over the cliff, without observation from either party to that violent struggle. Of course, he was at first greatly frightened, and fully believed that his end had at last come, as he went rolling, log-like, down the declivity; but when he found that, although much bruised, he was not seriously hurt, he rather rejoiced at an accident which had transported him to a place of comparative safety.

Although Johnson had learned from his prisoner, the treachery of Jones, he did not waste any reproaches or vituperations upon him. The man had sunk too low even for the reach of contempt.

"You are alive yet, Barak, I see," said the commodore, on meeting him.

"As much as ever, sir; sich a tumble as I had you never heord tell on, I guess, and then I felt all the worse, you see, because I thought you pitched me off on purpose. I didn't know that you captured the sergeant until just now Mr. Vrail has been telling me about it, and how you got rid of the rest. I'm glad you ain't killed—and I'm glad I ain't too. I never mean to go to war again."

"Not if all Canada rises and shakes off?"——

"No, *sir!*—I don't care *what* she shakes off—I'm going hum, just as soon as I can get there, and there I mean to stay."

"I think it will be the best thing you can do."

Rainbow Island was, of course, no longer a safe abode for Johnson, and he resolved to quit it with as little delay as possible. Forced to forego the hope that the triumph of the patriot cause would enable him to seek a home in his native land before the winter set in, he was yet resolved that his children should not partake of the perils and privations of an outlaw's life during that inclement season. He had secured a home for them in a farmer's family on the American shore, where they had already spent several months, and where, being entirely unknown, he was enabled to make them brief visits without much danger of detection. To this place he resolved to take them that very night, while at the same time he would afford Vrail and Jones an opportunity to set foot again on their native soil.

Barak was in ecstasies at this announcement, and Captain Vrail was scarcely less delighted, and both lent a willing hand to the preparatory steps for departure. The grotto being no longer a secret place, it became necessary to conceal whatever in it was of sufficient value to be protected, and everything was speedily stored away in a remote and obscure angle of the cave, which there was little danger of ever being explored by strangers. A portmanteau was filled with some articles of apparel, including various devices for effecting a complete disguise of the outlaw, who contemplated visiting Ogdensburgh and other places, on business connected with the patriot cause, before he returned to the islands.

The time of his return was, indeed, a matter of the greatest uncertainty, for he knew not what hope might yet remain for his friends, nor how soon another military expedition might be planned. No effort of his, he resolved, should be wanting to revive the hopes of the dispirited, and renew the contest.

The little party embarked in the evening, and reached the American shore without difficulty, where Johnson's first aim was to rid himself entirely of Barak, before going to the future home of his children, and before putting on his disguise, for he did not wish to place himself again in the power of so weak and craven a man. Yet, to do poor Jones justice, he was rather imbecile than vile, and he would by no means wantonly have injured the outlaw, whom he rightfully regarded as the preserver of his life.

There was no difficulty in effecting the object which Johnson had in view.

"You would like to land *here*, I suppose, Mr. Jones?" he said, as the bow of his boat touched the beach. "We are going some way further down the stream before we stop, but I suppose you are in a hurry to go ashore."

Barak was out of the boat before the other had done speaking.

"I am out, Commodore," he said; "I want to go no further down stream, nor up stream, nor on the islands, nor, least of all, back to Canada. I'm on American sile—I am. Hoo--rah!"

"Good-bye, Barak."

"Good-bye, all! Good-bye, Commodore! Look out that you don't get nabbed. I'm safe now—I am. Hoorah for the 'nited States of America!"

So saying, Jones marched off, and Johnson, pushing his boat a short distance from shore, resumed his route down the river about a mile, when he again landed in the vicinity of a small village. Here it was agreed that Vrail was to seek lodgings at an inn, where Johnson was to join him in the morning, after placing his children in their home, and they were to proceed together to Ogdensburgh. The house of Flynn was still further down the river, and thither the outlaw proceeded, readily finding admission at the friendly farmer's, although his arrival was at a late hour in the night.

CHAPTER XXVI.

SAMSON UNBOUND.

On the ensuing morning, while Captain Vrail sat reading an Ogdensburgh gazette, in a public room of the Eagle Tavern of ———ville, he was informed that a Mr. Miller was inquiring for, and wished to see him, and while wondering that he should have any acquaintances in a part of the world in which he had never before travelled, he was approached by a well dressed-man, apparently of about middle age, whose hair was very black and glossy, and whose whiskers, of the same hue, were very bushy and very abundant. The stranger wore spectacles and carried a light ratan, and when he offered his hand to Vrail, it was without removing its close-fitting beaver glove, and without speaking.

Tom was quite at a loss.

"Mr. *Miller?*" he said, inquiringly, as he took the proffered hand of his visitor.

"Yes," was the short reply.

"I do not know that I have the honor"——

"Captain Vrail forgets his friends quickly," replied the stranger, smiling.

"Oh, ho!" cried Tom, "what a dolt I am, or rather, what a genius you are, Mr. Miller—or rather, Mr. Wind-Miller," he added, sinking his voice. "Why, the transformation is complete. You might go to Canada, and dine with Sergeant Ward in safety."

"It was to try my disguise that I approached you thus," replied the outlaw; "and as to going to Canada, I have been there more than once in this character, and I may possibly receive tidings at Ogdensburgh, which will require my presence there again this very week, even at Kingston."

"Is it possible? And would you really take so great a risk?"

"If it would materially serve the cause, I would not hesitate. Our other leaders are venturing as much everywhere. How often has the great Mackenzie perilled his life! And think of poor Van Shoultz, our noble and gallant ally, and of your own unfortunate brother, both probably in the hands of a government, which, tottering to its fall, dares not, if it would, show mercy. I have but one life, and it is at the service of this cause and its friends. If our leaders on the other side can show a satisfactory reason for failing to join us at Windmill Point, and if my presence among them is necessary to concert and effect another joint attack which promises to be more successful, I shall certainly go, without counting the risk. I hope you do not think of throwing up your commission."

"I scarcely remembered that I had one. No; I do not wish to resign it, as long as there is any prospect of a well planned and successful expedition; but I shall never again be one of a few hundreds, to cross the St. Lawrence, and set myself up for a target for British muskets."

"You are quite right in that."

"I have been reading this journal in hopes of finding some tidings of the prisoners, but I can learn nothing, excepting that all who were taken were sent to Kingston. No names are mentioned, excepting of the principal officers."

"Have you really the news there so soon? How many of the enemy were killed? How many of our men were taken? How many escaped? Let me see it."

Johnson spoke eagerly and quickly, taking the offered journal from his companion, and perusing it hastily.

"The tidings are meagre, and probably unauthentic," said Vrail, "but they are correct enough in ascribing great deeds to the Hero of the Thousand Isles."

"Tut—tut—they are determined on making a lion of me, whether I roar or not. But I hope yet to do something worthy of the distinction they force upon me."

"The United States Marshal was at Ogdensburgh a few days since, and may be still there. Will it be prudent for you to go there?"

"Quite, there is not a person there who will know me in this guise, and there are dozens of hunters who would swear to me as Mr. Miller, for by that name I have mingled with them in their lodges, and have partaken of their deliberations. They know, indeed, that I often *see* Bill Johnson, and that I speak his views by authority, for when I visit them in my true character, I always fully endorse my supposed envoy."

"Is it possible that you can successfully keep up this twofold character?"

"Not only there, but in other places. My secret rests with you alone, and I do not fear that you will betray it."

"You need not, on the honor of a very poor soldier, who has run away from the only battle in which he was ever engaged," replied Tom, laughing.

"Yet who fought well while fighting was of any use. I wish your brave brother was with us."

Tom colored at the allusion to his brother, but a moment's reflection convinced him that no innuendo was designed, and that he had as yet only the reproaches of his own conscience to bear for his disgraceful desertion of so noble a friend.

The companions proceeded the same day, by public conveyance, to Ogdensburgh. Vrail carefully schooled himself to address the outlaw, at all times, by his assumed name, yet scarcely restraining his laughter at the dignified and eminently pacific deportment of the man whom he had so lately seen rushing, tiger-like, upon a British sergeant, and carrying him off bodily into a cave of the earth. They took lodgings at different hotels, the young man stopping at the most central and public house, where he would be most likely to gain the intelligence he sought, while Johnson chose the safer obscurity of a quiet and more retired inn.

CHAPTER XXVII.

THE EXPRESS TRAVELLERS—AN UNEXPECTED MEETING.

Several days passed, during which Captain Vrail heard no tidings of his brother, and he almost ceased longer to entertain a hope that Harry had escaped. How dreadful would probably be his fate, if a prisoner, he very well knew, and he felt, if not the pangs of affectionate regret, the stings of an accusing conscience, which pointed to himself as doubly the author of his brother's misfortunes. To rid himself of this remorse, and to avoid the censure of the world, if from no worthier motive, he would have done much to bring about his brother's liberation, but he lacked that bold energy of character, and that noble, disinterested affection, which prompts to great and self-sacrificing deeds.

While he hesitated in ignoble irresolution, he heard of the extreme severity of punishment which was decided by the Canadian government to be visited upon the foreign portion of their prisoners, and especially upon all who shared in any degree the responsibility of command. Rumors of summary trials and executions began already to prevail, and he trembled to think that he might at any hour hear of his brother's death.

While he sat on the piazza of his hotel, gloomily reflecting upon these things, his attention was arrested by an approaching stage-coach from the south, which was entering the village with most extraordinary rapidity, its four stout bays covered with sweat and foam, and their driver urging them with lash and voice to still greater speed.

"Here comes an extra, with a crazy driver or a drunken one," said the landlord of the inn, attracted to the door by the sound of the approaching vehicle, for it was not the regular hour for the arrival of the daily coach.

"Why do you drive into town at this mad rate?" he continued, addressing the Jehu as he drew up at the tavern door, and leapt, reins in hand, to the ground.

"I don't know—it's on the way-bill, to be put through by eleven o'clock this morning, and I've done it, and two minutes to spare."

"Better spared your horses," said the landlord, taking the offered way-bill, on which the driver pointed out the orders which justified his seemingly improper speed. "An exclusive extra, hey?" he continued, examining the paper more closely, and then turning to see who his new guests were, for by this time the coach door had been opened, and its inmates were alighting. Whatever may have been the inn-keeper's impression of the strangers, there was one person whose astonishment was unlimited at the sight of them.

"Gertrude Van Kleeck, by all that is wonderful!" exclaimed Captain Vrail, "and young Van Vrank, and I don't know who else. What can all this mean? She must be married, of course, and they are on their wedding trip. But how singular that they should come *here!* And to such a fellow as that, too!"

Tom uttered these words in soliloquy, finding a gleam of consolation for his rejection by Gertrude in the thought that it must have resulted from an engagement to her boorish cousin, and he was about to retire from observation, but he had already been discovered both by the lady and by Van Vrank, the latter of whom summarily left his companions and rushed up to him with extended hand, and with a broad smile of joy upon his good-natured countenance.

"Why Squire Tom," he said, shaking him painfully by the hand, "it *is you*, sure enough, isn't it? I'm right glad to see *you* safe out of the scrape, any way—that I am; and is Harry really here, too?"

Gertrude and Ruth had been left standing on the stoop but a few yards from Vrail, and he could do no less than instantly approach them, which he did before replying to the question of Van Vrank. He was startled by the pale face and anxious expression of Miss Van Kleeck, as he addressed her and inquired after her health, and by a similar look of alarm and distress in the countenance of the fair child at her side. If this were a bridal party he thought, it was the most doleful one he had ever seen.

"It has kind of frightened 'em both you see, to meet you here so unexpectedly," continued Garret; "and they are afraid of hearing bad news, I suppose. Let us go inside, where we shan't have everybody staring at us, and there you can tell us all about it."

From the moment Gertrude had caught sight of Vrail, her emotion had been almost overpowering. The blissful hope that Harry was also safe was accompanied by the dread of meeting him under such embarrassing circumstances, but these feelings were instantly followed by a harrowing fear that he was not saved, and an oblivion of all other considerations.

Again and again she strove to speak the simple words, "Is your brother safe?" but utterance was as impossible to her as to one untaught in articulation. They entered the ladies' public room, but they were alone.

"Now tell us about your brother, Squire Tom," said Garry. "I'm afraid he isn't here, or we should have seen him before this."

"Are *you* his *brother?*" exclaimed Ruth, now for the first time comprehending who was the stranger they had encountered. She sprang forward impulsively as she spoke, and laid a hand upon his arm. "Oh, he would have died for *you*," she continued; "he talked so much of you, and feared so much that you were taken and when he found the boat was gone which would have saved him, he laughed for joy to think that *you* had taken it."

Tom sank to a chair and covered his face with his hands.

"He is lost!" exclaimed Gertrude faintly.

"You may as well tell us the worst now, Mr. Vrail," said Garry; "it won't be worse than we are all thinking already. Sit down, Getty, before you *fall* down. If he is shot or hung, why, say so, Tom, and have done with it. It can't be helped now."

"I know nothing of his fate," replied Vrail, "excepting that he was not killed in battle. I have never heard of, or from him since."

"Thank God!" exclaimed a gentle voice, which the soldier did not hear.

"Well, come, now, it isn't so bad after all. I expected to hear worse news than that, and there may be some hope yet."

Tom shook his head, as if incredulous.

"If that is the last you have heard of Harry, we can tell *you* some news, or rather, Ruth here can, and I will leave her to do so, while I go and order breakfast, for we must be moving again soon, I suppose. *They* would go without eating, but I must have one good meal before I can go another mile, for I am hungry enough to eat my boots."

Garret went out, and Ruth, in reply to Tom's eager and rapid questions, told in few words the substance of her story, as far as related to Harry, and not deeming that there was any cause for the suppression of the whole truth, she concluded her statement by saying, that they were on their way to Kingston, to see if anything could be done to save him.

The young man was really affected at hearing the certainty of his brother's perilous position, but his concern yielded temporarily to surprise on learning of Miss Van Kleeck's extraordinary undertaking. He had never suspected the existence of any attachment between Harry and Gertrude, but the suspicion now flashed upon his mind that they were really plighted lovers, and that he had been deceived by Harry, and had been duped into making the proposal which had had so mortifying a termination. But a moment's reflection banished this idea, for he *knew* that Harry was in all things the soul of sincerity and frankness. They might, however, have become engaged since his own rejection by Gertrude, and this he concluded must have been the case, although he thought it strange that Harry should not have informed him of it. These changing thoughts had passed through his mind before the sound of Ruth's voice had died upon his ear, and he was impulsively about to say something to Gertrude expressive of his surprise, when, speaking for the first time, she anticipated his remark.

"You will think very strange of all this, I know," she said, hesitatingly; "but there was no one else to respond to your brother's appeal for help, which this poor child had travelled three hundred miles to bring to his friends. Your grandfather was too ill even to be allowed to hear the sad tidings, and cousin Garret, who met your brother's messenger in the village, brought her to me, at my request. Harry was my father's friend. I knew what *he* would have done, had he been living, and I am his representative. We may not be able to effect anything in your brother's behalf; perhaps it is presumptuous to to hope that we can; but if I had allowed any opportunity to pass, of assisting a friend in so great a peril, I should always feel in some degree chargeable with the consequences, which in this case may be so very terrible. No one at home knows of my undertaking, excepting my legal adviser, Mr. Gray, and he will disclose nothing. I shall rely also upon your perfect secrecy, and I have even hopes that, if we should succeed in our enterprise, it can be done without your brother ever knowing of my agency in obtaining his release. But gratifying as this would be to me, you may be assured no chance of benefiting him shall be sacrificed to a consideration so purely personal."

The events through which Thomas Vrail had been passing, and

the revelations of nobler natures than his own, which had been disclosed to him, were gradually working a favorable change in his own character.

"You are an angel, Getty," he said, "and that was what poor Harry always said of you. I will keep your secret; not only that which you have confided to me, but that which I can so easily guess. I should be a monster if I could do or say anything to annoy you."

Gertrude blushed scarlet at these words, but she extended her hand to meet the one offered by her late lover, in pledge of confidence and appreciating friendship.

"How soon shall you resume your journey?" he asked.

"I hope to be in Canada within an hour," replied Gertrude, and on the way to Kingston as soon as a conveyance can be procured. We have to wait here for breakfast."

An impatient look accompanied this remark. The young man mused a moment, apparently in perplexed and painful thought, and then said,

"It will be a perilous undertaking for me, but I will accompany you. I have risked my life once for fame; let me now do it for a nobler motive."

"I am glad for your sake to hear you make such a proposal," replied Miss Van Kleeck; "but you may be assured it is not the most prudent course even for your brother's interests, for your detection and arrest would greatly complicate matters, and would perhaps defeat the few chances we may have of success. Let me advise you rather to remain here, where a messenger can reach you in a short time from Kingston, if we find that your services can be rendered available there."

"If the case were reversed, I know that Harry would not be withheld from coming to me at all risks, but I shall never be as good as he. I will be guided by your advice, but do not hesitate to send for me if I can do anything for him. But a thought occurs to me this moment which may possibly be of importance, and yet—I do not know "——

Thomas hesitated, but in obedience to Gertrude's anxious look of inquiry, he continued,

"There is a man here of singular powers and resources, who, I believe, is about to proceed to Kingston, and who might be in some way serviceable to you there. I am not at liberty to say more of him, but I think it would be well for you to meet him here, and to let him know your errand in Canada."

"If there is the least probability of his aiding us, let us see him, of course, for we are going among entire strangers."

"I will go for him immediately, and if he has not already left town, I will bring him to you."

Vrail went at once in pursuit of Johnson, now known and spoken of only as Mr. Miller, whom, to his great joy, he found at his lodgings, but as yet undecided on making his hazardous journey. He manifested a great interest in the singular effort which was being made for Harry's release, and although he could see little prospect of its favorable issue, he immediately accompanied the young man to meet the travellers, and showed an earnest disposition to co-operate with them in their generous undertaking. He gave to Miss Van Kleeck letters to an influential and prominent member of the patriot cause at Kingston, instructed her at what hotel to stay, and hinted at the possibility of himself seeing her there within a few days.

For all this Gertrude returned the sincerest thanks, little suspecting the true character of her visitor, and hoping little from his alliance. Their interview was short, and within an hour after he had taken his leave, the travellers were in Canada, and were posting by express coach to Kingston, Gertrude being too impatient to wait for the steamboat, which was not to leave till late in the afternoon.

CHAPTER XXVIII.

THE PRISONER OF PRESCOTT.

OUR narrative returns to that memorable morning when Lieutenant Vrail was taken from his Prescott prison to be transferred, in company with eight or ten others, to Kingston, where the principal portion of the captured patriots had already been sent, and whence many of them were soon to depart on a longer journey, some to Van Dieman's land, and some to that land " from whose bourne no traveller returns."

Manacled, and tied together in pairs, they were attended to the place of embarkation, not only by a military guard, but by a rabble of men and boys, who jeered and derided the hapless band as they passed, and scarcely refrained from acts of violence towards them. It was probably intended as an indignity to Harry, who was suspected of being an officer, and who was, at least, known to be a gentleman, that the negro who had been taken in his company was pinioned to his side, instead of being mated with one of a lower class of the prisoners; but Harry did not regret this circumstance, nor manifest the least repugnance to it. The patience and good-nature with which he submitted himself in this, and in all respects, to the disposal of his captors, gained him some sympathy at their hands, but did not exempt him from the ridicule of the mob, to whom his position proved peculiarly attractive, and afforded a rich theme for derision.

Brom bore the scoffs of the crowd less patiently, and he did not feel the fetters upon his limbs as much as the restraint which his master had imposed upon his tongue. His large eyes glared fiercely, and he longed to give back taunt for taunt, and to dare his deriders to a three to one combat—nay, he would have singly assailed the whole rabble, if he had been unbound, so great was his rage against them.

The journey was performed by steamboat upon the same river (belonging to and dividing the two nations), which had so recently borne the invading band, full of hope and courage, to the place of their anticipated triumph. Over the same route, and in view of the same scenes which they had then beheld, did they now pass, bound and helpless, to partake of whatever doom their incensed conquerors might see fit to award. The shores of their native land stretched before them many a league as they were borne upon their sorrowful way; they could see its green fields and its waving forests; its quiet frontier towns came successively into view, and at times the sound of its village bells reached their ears. Alas! for them, they had forfeited their citizenship in that happy land—they had lost the protection of that powerful government, under whose benign and calm strength they had so long reposed in safety, and there was none to interpose for their rescue or relief.

As the day wore away, another and less welcome sight became visible to them in the distant spires and domes of that dreaded city in which their prison homes awaited them, and that afterdoom, the horrors of which they could only imagine. It was evening before they landed; but as the news of the arrival of a new lot of prisoners was soon disseminated throughout the town, they did not fail of another rabble escort, as they were marched in procession through the streets, to the music of drum and fife, and the more discordant sounds of fiendish merriment and exultation.

So galling was this exposure, and these continual insults, that the wearied and disheartened prisoners were glad when the grim walls of Fort Henry interposed between them and the mob, and received them within its dreadful shelter. They were all confined in one large room, which had already a number of occupants, undistinguished among whom Vrail was astonished and grieved to find his late commander, Colonel Van Shoultz, of whose escape he had until then ventured to indulge a faint hope.

Their instantaneous and mutual recognition was unfortunately followed by an unguarded utterance by the Polander of both the name and title of the young officer, and although Harry instantly checked his friend's words, it was too late to prevent the dreaded exposure.

"*Lieutenant Vrail!*" repeated a sergeant of the guard, who had conducted the prisoners to their quarters, at the same time taking out a pencil and paper from his pocket; "that's it, is it? We supposed he was a captain, at least, and probably something higher, but lieutenant is enough to hang him."

"Shay thought he was one of their sham generals, because he had a servant with him, and he expects a large reward for taking him," replied another.

These remarks were made in an undertone, which was not intended to reach the prisoner's ears, but Harry, who had been startled by his friend's salutation, and had watched to see if it had been observed, caught every word of a conversation which boded him so much evil.

The Polander, when at length the withdrawal of the soldiers permitted free conversation, bitterly reproached himself for his imprudence, but Harry fully exonerated him from censure, and reminded him that since suspicion had evidently been so strong against him as an officer, other means would doubtless have been found, and would still be found 'to prove it.

"Your words will not be evidence against me," he said; "other testimony will be needed to show that I was the bearer of a commission."

"You may be convicted as a private, yet without a private's

chance for mercy, if government believes you to have been an officer."

"That my captors have fully believed from the moment of my arrest; so I shall be in no additional jeopardy by reason of what you have said. But tell me now, my friend, about yourself, and what you can learn of your prospects."

"There is no hope for me," replied Col. Van Shoultz, solemnly. "Everything betokens that, too decidedly to admit of a doubt: The government is resolved on severe measures. They utterly ignore the existence of any war, revolutionary or otherwise, and while they will punish as traitors that portion of the prisoners who are their own subjects, they will prosecute us, who are foreigners, as brigands or murderers. So says their organ, and such, I learn from other quarters, is their determination."

"Let us hope for better things."

"I cannot hope. The defection of our original leaders has devolved the chief responsibility of this movement on me, and I must bear it. I assure you I feel a presentiment of my coming doom. But do not think I shall shrink from it. I have courted death too often on the battle-fields of my own country to quail before it, even on a British scaffold."

"If you will not hope, my dear friend, I will at least hope for you. Your foreign birth and education, and your more excusable misconception of the true state of the revolution in Canada (on which point we have all been deluded), entitle you to leniency, even more than others. Doubtless you will be allowed counsel on your trial."

"Oh, yes; we are to be furnished with a copy of our indictment a few days before the trial, and we are at liberty to employ counsel, if we can induce any one to defend us, which, considering the state of public sentiment, is not like to be an easy task. Failing in this, counsel will be assigned us, by the court, who will be sure to defend us with decorum, and who will do nothing in our behalf which can offend his lordship, the judge, or which shall displease the prosecuting attorney."

"How do you learn all this?"

"From one here who knows the full history of trials that have already taken place."

The picture which the Polander had drawn of their prospects was dismal enough, and, as Harry could not fail to perceive, was probably correct. Van Schoultz, he could scarcely doubt, would suffer death, and his own peril, imminent enough before, he knew would be increased by his intimate relations with that officer. The brave colonel was the first to point out this danger to his friend, and to urge a cessation of all intercourse between them; but Harry would not listen a moment to this proposition. He could not forget that his companion was a foreigner, without interest, or hope of influence from any quarter in his behalf, and he would not withdraw from him the slight chance of benefit, or, at least, of solace, which his friendship could bestow. Whenever or wherever his voice could be heard in his advocacy, he resolved he would not be silent, and in thus contemplating his efforts for another, he at times lost sight of his own danger.

But in this oblivion he was not long allowed to rest. When Colonel Van Schoultz was furnished with a copy of the indictment found against him, a similar document was served on Harry Vrail, and he was notified that his trial would take place, either jointly with that of his commanding officer, or immediately after its termination. This association of his case with that of the leader of the expedition was ominous enough to leave him little hope of escaping the same fate which was so evidently in store for the former.

Yet, desperate as their cases seemed, neither of the young men were willing to relinquish life without making as vigorous an effort for escape as circumstances would permit, and they resolved to employ counsel, if it were possible to procure a man of ability and standing in the province to undertake their cause. He might at least do something for them, if it were only, by his ingenuity or influence, to obtain time, until possibly milder counsels might prevail in high places. England was powerful enough to afford to be merciful, if she would, and they were even willing to ask for mercy. They learned, on inquiry, that an eminent lawyer of Kingston had been employed for the accused in several of the State trials which had taken place during the preceding summer, and that he had conducted his defences in a masterly manner, and in one instance to the entire acquittal of his client.

But this solitary instance of success in resisting the powerful influence of government had caused him to be besieged by applications from the unfortunate prisoners, not one in ten of whom he could defend, and not one in twenty of whom could remunerate him for his services. The natural result was, that Counsellor Strong was retained by the few only whose means would enable them to place a large retaining fee in his hands, and all others found the necessity of relying on less distinguished aid. To obtain this man's assistance had become an object of earnest desire, both on the part of Van Schoultz and Harry, but when they learned the formidable extent of his charges, they were forced to abandon their purpose.

But from the moment their project was seen to be impracticable, it became the more desirable in their estimation, until, as they discussed with increasing regret the lost opportunity, they became almost persuaded that it would have restored them to liberty.

To one of these conversations, Brom became an interested listener, and he heard with astonishment that so much might be hoped for, from the efforts of one man.

"Let's hab him for *you*, Massa Harry, of course," he said; " mebbe he'll get you off."

" I can't pay him, Brom. He won't defend any one for less

than forty pounds in advance, and a promise of I don't know how much more in case of success."

" Forty pounds of *what?*" asked the negro, in amazement.

" Forty pounds sterling, or two hundred dollars of our currency."

" Oh, is that all?" replied Brom, contemptuously; " send him along then—I'll hire him, and I'll pay him something extra, too, for puttin' in the fine touches."

" What do you mean, Brom? You certainly have not two hundred dollars with you?"

"Never you mind. You just send your big lawyer along to me; I'll 'tain him for you—but I don't believe he can make sich a speech as Squire Gray's clerk, Barney Blait, did in Jake Smith's pig suit last summer. You mout a heard *him* bellow half a mile for a whole hour, and he got his case, too, and only charged Jake half a dollar for it. Howsomever, I dare say this Mr. Strong is smart enough for a Britisher."

" But, Brom, if you really have so much money, I cannot consent to take it from you."

" I don't mean you shall, Massa Harry. I'll give it to Massa Strong."

" But it might do no good after all; I cannot let you throw away so much of your hard earnings, which I may never be able to repay you."

" It isn't hard earnings; I earned it mighty easy I 'clare to you. Besides, you can't stop me! I shall hire lawyer Strong."

" But you will want to be defended yourself, and you will want all your money for that."

" Nebber mind. Maybe I got money enough for that too; but they haven't summonsed me yet, and there'll be time enough to think of that by and by. One of them soldier fellows said I should have to be tried all alone, 'cause my *case* was *darker* than the rest. I don't see what he meant by that."

Harry smiled, but he did not explain the enigmatical words. He decided, after some hesitation, to acept the mysterious funds which were thus fairly forced upon him, believing that whatever might be his own fate, he could make provision for repayment to his sable benefactor, if the latter should be ever allowed to return to his native village.

Brom retired, as on a former occasion, to an obscure corner of his prison, to withdraw his golden store unobserved from its place of concealment, and he soon reappeared with each hand closed over more than it could conceal of the glittering coin, which peeped from between the insterstices of his fingers, like the yellow corn bursting from its husks. Whispering for Harry to hold his hat, he buried his hands within it before disgorging them of their precious contents, which were deposited as silently as possible, in order to avoid attracting the attention of their fellow prisoners. Vrail and Col. Van Shoultz looked on with astonishment, both being utterly ignorant of the source of supply; although the former had once before had a proof on a much smaller scale, of the negro's financial resources. They were amazed not only at the amount of treasure produced, but at the very apparent fact that its owner was entirely unable to compute its value.

"How much is dare, Massa Harry?" he asked, in a whisper. "Is dat enough to pay de big lawyer?"

"Yes, twice over, Brom."

"Den you get him for you and Colonel Van Shoots too—mebbe he clear you both," said the negro, rubbing his hands.

"But you, Brom, will have to be tried too, by and by."

"Nebber mind; they habn't *summonsed* me yet; and"—sinking his voice to a whisper, and pointing to the coin—"dere's a few more left."

Harry, after thanking the negro, and assuring him that he should make no arrangements with counsel which did not include him also in its provisions, pocketed the treasure, and at once applied for permission, which was readily accorded, to send a messenger to the legal Goliah from whom so much was hoped.

A fee of sufficient magnitude to ensure attention was enclosed in the application to the counsellor, and the return of their envoy brought them the gratifying assurance that the great man would wait upon them some time in the course of the ensuing evening.

How much will the angel Hope do for the human heart in every strait to which it can be reduced! How busily in the brief interval which elapsed before meeting their legal adviser, did the unfortunate prisoners imagine and discuss the ingenious theories of defences which were to be maintained in their behalf, perhaps to their triumphant and honorable acquittal.

But, alas! the arrival of their counsel rather dissipated than strengthened these bright anticipations. Mr. Strong was a matter-of-fact man, who knew what it was to oppose a prosecution which would be sustained by irrefragable proof, by the whole weight of popular sentiment, and by governmental sanction.

Having learned from the prisoners the particulars of their arrest, he at once advised Colonel Van Shoultz, when arraigned, to plead guilty to the charge of having been found in arms against the Canadian government, inasmuch as, having been taken in actual combat, there was no possibility of his evading a conviction.

"We will make the best use we can of the extenuating circumstances in your case, and we shall find both the court and the governor more ready to listen to these, if we make no useless contest on points which cannot be defended. I do not mean to say," he continued, "that there is much probability of mercy being shown; I fear there is not. But I think a slight chance of pardon would result from such a course."

The Polander's strong presentiment of his coming fate, of which his mind had become temporarily divested, returned to him with increased force on hearing the undisguised opinion of the lawyer, with whose views he fully concurred; but he chose to deliberate a day or two before deciding a matter of so great moment as that of pleading guilty to a capital crime.

"As to Mr. Vrail," continued the counsellor, "his case is somewhat different. His arrest was subsequent to the battle, several miles distant from its scene, and the proof of his having been engaged in it may possibly not be so certain as to ensure conviction. I would advise a defence in his case, although I must caution you against any sanguine hopes of acquittal. The prospect, I grieve to say, is all the other way. Proof will be raked from all possible quarters, and both court and jurors will be against you."

"The most formidable witness against me," said Harry, "will doubtless be the man Shay, who arrested me, and to whom I had made the unguarded avowal of which I have told you."

"Yet that is testimony that may be shaken," replied the counsellor, with a sudden flashing of his dark eyes, as if he felt himself already in the forensic arena, with some material for successful effort. "The man will be infamous by his own showing, besides which, the fact that your conviction will entitle him to a reward, will throw discredit upon his evidence of your confessions. I think the prosecution will have to produce other proof of your having been in the battle. Can they do it?"

"I think not, unless they can use my comrades as witnesses against me. Can this be done?"

"They cannot be compelled, of course, to testify against you; but may not some of them be induced to do so by a promise of pardon for themselves."

"Yes, if the prosecuting attorney will stoop to such means to procure my conviction, he will doubtless find some wretch willing to save his life at the expense of mine. There can be no hope for me, Mr. Strong, if such a course is to be pursued."

"Not so fast. There may not be much hope, and yet there may be some. Are there not extenuating circumstances in your case, even if your participation in this war should be clearly made out?"

"I do not know of any."

"Think again—you are very young."

"Yes; I am but twenty-three, but that is two years past the legal age of manhood, and it is a time of life when a man is fully accountable for his actions."

"Do not argue the case so strongly against yourself. Is there not something else that may be shown or said in your favor?"

"No."

"Yes," replied Colonel Van Shoultz; "something very important, if it can be proved."

"What is it?" asked the lawyer, eagerly.

"He was for a long time unwilling to engage in this war, strenuously resisting all arguments in its favor, until a younger brother's enlistment influenced him to join us, more for the protection of that brother, than for any other cause."

"Is this true?" asked the legal adviser.

"Yes, substantially. I did, however, become a convert to the cause, before joining it, and I have frequently avowed and advocated the doctrines of the patriots and revolutionists since."

"Never mind—*we* don't want to prove that, and if you go on n this way, you will be rising and making a speech against yourself in court, when your trial comes on. The facts mentioned by your friend may have some weight, if we can prove them."

"Which we certainly cannot do; I have not a witness to produce."

"Where is this brother?"

"Alas, I know nothing of his fate. If he has escaped, which may Heaven grant, I would not for worlds that he should come here to testify in my behalf, for his danger would be even greater than mine."

Counsellor Strong was perplexed. He had become deeply interested in both his unfortunate clients, and he thought he saw a glimmer of hope for the younger of the two, which influenced him to vigorous efforts in his behalf. As to the leader of the expedition, he clearly foresaw his fate, and though he tried to argue himself into the belief that there was a remote chance of his escape from death, a contrary conviction clung to his mind. He resolved, however, to do all that was in his power for both parties, and after making a few memoranda of the leading facts which had been furnished him by the prisoners, he departed with a promise of seeing them on the ensuing day.

Within the few days which elapsed before the sitting of the court, the prisoners were visited daily by their zealous advocate, but alas, with an increased air of concern as the time passed away without bringing any accession of strength to his cause, and without, as far as he could read the signs of the hour, diminishing the ferocity of pursuit with which it had too evidently been decided that his clients were to be hunted down.

The Polander observed his generous grief, and begged him not to be distressed on his behalf.

"I see it all," he said; "they cannot spare me, if they intend to convict any. The principal must be punished, or the accessories must all be acquitted, and England is not generous enough for that."

"I fear you are right; but we will try."

"Try, but do not fear; at least, not for me. I shall not tremble before my judges, and if they send me to the scaffold, I do not think I shall tremble there."

It would be a painful task, and one which the progress of our history does not demand, to dwell upon the details of a trial which was destined to result, as the most hopeful could not fail to foresee, in a sentence of death. Trial it could scarcely be called, for the defendant had pleaded guilty to being found in arms against the government, leaving it to his counsel to establish if possible his position, that the contest was of such a character as to entitle any foreigners who had been engaged in it to all the immunities of prisoners of war, or that, if any crime had been committed, it was not of a capital nature. In all this, of course, he failed, and in every appeal, either to court or jury, for a recommendation to the mercy of the sovereign.

Stony hearts decided his doom, and stony eyes, from which no pity gleamed, rested on the friendless foreigner, as his dreadful sentence was pronounced. How nobly he bore it all, how manfully he met his fate when the dreadful day of doom arrived; what countless tears fell on Freedom's shores at the recital of his sad story, history has told, and future ages will know.

He was executed in Fort Henry soon after his trial, at the age of thirty-one, leaving, say his historians, "a proud name to be handed down to posterity with those of Steuben, De Kalb and Kosciusko."

CHAPTER XXIX.

LIGHT IN A DUNGEON.

VRAIL did not see his friend again after the trial of the latter They had parted like brothers on the morning of that sad day, each exhorting the other to good courage, and each almost as solicitous for the other's safety as for his own; but after conviction Van Shoultz was removed to other quarters until his execution, and Harry, plunged in the deepest dejection by the tidings of his doom, awaited without hope the summons to his own trial.

This event did not, however, immediately occur. Col. Abbey, Col. Woodruff, and some other gallant men, were first tried, convicted, and sentenced to the same doom with their leader, and all like him suffered death on the scaffold, meeting their fate with a dignity and fortitude which proclaimed the native heroism of their hearts.

Many of the prisoners, including Harry, and his inseparable companion, Brom, were, in the meanwhile, removed from the fort to the city prison, a large stone building which stands in a central part of the town, and which is provided with a permanent gallows accessible from an upper story, and of a capacity to do a threefold work of death.

Seated in his cell, within this dreadful abode, a few evenings preceding the day for which his trial was finally appointed, Harry was startled from a gloomy revery by the approach of a turnkey accompanied by a stranger, who, being conducted to the door of his cell, was informed by the officer, as he turned away, that he would call for him in half an hour. Vrail could not distinguish the visitor by the dim light, but supposing him to be some messenger from his counsel, he awaited without much curiosity the announcement of his errand.

"You don't know me, I s'pose, Harry Vrail," said a voice of friendly cadence, while the speaker's face was pressed almost against the bars of the cell door.

The prisoner came quickly forward, and peered closely at the half-visible countenance, on which a faint light from the hall rested.

"I cannot see you," was the quick reply; "but the voice is like one I have heard in H——. Tell me quickly if this is so."

"Yes, I am your neighbor, Garret Van Vrank."

"Garry Van Vrank! Is it possible? What good angel has sent *you* here, Garry; but before you answer this, or any other question, tell me whether you know anything of poor Tom's fate?"

"Yes, I know all about him. He is perfectly safe and well, and is now at Ogdensburgh."

"Thank Heaven for that! Thank Heaven for that!" exclaimed the prisoner, drawing a long free breath, for his inhalation had been suspended while he awaited, in great anxiety, the answer to his question. "Safe and well! You really remove a mountain from my heart, my dear friend, by bringing me such news as this. Tom is safe—*safe*—SAFE; thank Heaven for this great mercy! Fortified by the knowledge of this fact, I almost feel as if I could defy my judges to do their worst."

"You mustn't talk so, Mr. Vrail; that won't make matters any better, you know, and your life is worth as much as Tom's—rather more, I should say."

"Than Tom's! Why, bless you, my dear fellow, you don't

know Tom. He is worth a dozen such as me. Thank Heaven, again, that he is free!"

"But *you* are not," replied Van Vrank, designedly rattling the grated door of his cell, to awaken the unselfish man to a sense of his own condition.

"No," answered Harry, "and I am not like to be; but let me ask you, friend Garret, how is it that you, on whom I have no claims, have come to see me in my adversity?"

"Well, never mind about that, Mr. Vrail. I am here, prepared to do anything for you that I can, which, I fear, isn't much, but what I am come for to-night, mostly, is to let you know that you have friends at hand, who are ready and anxious to help you."

"Friends, Garry? Who are they? Who besides you? My grandfather is certainly not here?"

"No—but do you know a young girl by the name of Ruth Shay?"

"Yes, I know almost an angel of light by that name. Is that dear child with you?"

"Yes, she is in the city. She brought the news of your capture to H——, and I have come with her to see if we could do anything for you."

Harry's heart sunk within him as he thought of the utter inutility of any such aid, but he was too generous to allow his disappointment to appear.

"I am certainly very grateful for this kindness, both yours and hers," he said; "and if there is any way that you can serve me, I will be sure to let you know. I can think of nothing better now, than that you should both go and see my counsel, Mr. Strong, and tell him all that you know about me. He can tell better than I whether you can be of service, or not."

"That is part of my errand here to-night, to learn whether you have a lawyer engaged, and who he is. *She* wants to see him."

"What, Ruth does? What can she have to say to him?"

Van Vrank hesitated and stammered, and finally added,

"I should say, *we* want to see him; so you will please to give me his name and number on a slip of paper, and we will go and find him early to-morrow morning, or perhaps this evening."

"It is not yet too late, and there is but little time to spare. You can easily see Mr. Strong this evening, if you will."

Garry said he would certainly make the attempt, and in order to lose nothing by delay, he would depart at once. A few hurried questions of Vrail, in relation to his grandfather, and some other friends at H——, including Miss Van Kleeck, were as hastily answered by the visitor, who was about to depart in search of the warder who had admitted him, when he was accosted by a voice from an adjoining cell.

"Massa Van Vrank! Massa Van Vrank! please to step dis a-way a minute. I'se here, too; you don't ax no questions about me; but I 'clare I'm very glad to see you."

"Well, Brom, I should be very glad to see you too, but I can't," said Garret, peering into his cell, where the few rays of light which entered, found nothing to reflect them, and the negro might be said to be quite invisible. "I forgot that you were here," continued the visitor, talking in the direction whence the other's voice proceeded, "though I now remember hearing that you went to the war."

"Yes, I did, Massa Van Vrank; but I wish I hadn't, nor Massa Harry too. You see, it hasn't turned out just as we 'spected, and now I am very afraid it will go hard with Massa Harry, for dey'se hanging 'em up here every few days, like strings of onions, three at a time, right back of the jail here."

"Is it possible, Brom?"

"Yes, Massa Garret; only dis mornin' dey turned off three, two colonels and a captain: they walked right past here, and nodded good-bye to Massa Harry as they went along. Dey never flinched, only one on 'em shivered a little when he first saw the gallows—but he only said, 'It is a cold morning,' and went on."

"It is very horrible; but where is the gallows you speak of?"

"Right dere, at the end of that long hall you is in now."

"What! in the house; and up here in this story?"

"No, no, Massa Van Vrank, at the end of this long hall is a large door, opens out-doors. Jes s'pose you going to be hung, now. You walk right out of that door on to a little platform, big enough to 'commodate three men; that platform is a trap door; you all three stand on it; den dere is three ropes hang down from a beam over head; den"——

"That's enough, Brom. I understand it. I don't want to hear any more about it."

"Den you"——

"Never mind."

"Dey put the rope on you"——

"That will do."

"And knock de bottom out of de trap-door," continued the pertinacious negro; "and you drop down great ways—partly behind a stone wall which is built up outside, so dat de crowd can't see nothin' but your head and shoulders. One of de jailers told me all about it, to 'muse me, one mornin' when I felt bad."

"Does Mr. Vrail know all this?"

"I tink he does."

"And yet he does not seem much frightened."

"Massa Harry is a berry brave man, and he is berry good man too. He tell me to trust in the Lord, and if I fear him, I needn't fear anybody else, and dat's what I'm going to do—but I 'fraid for Massa Harry, 'cause he was an officer, and they hang all de officers."

Leaving the African to his clouded faith, and promising to see him again on the morrow, Garret stepped back to the cell of Vrail, and thrusting a purse through the bars, which fell heavily to the floor, he whispered—

"There is what may possibly, be useful to you, and if you want twenty times that sum, or more, it will be ready for you to-morrow. It is not my gift, but it comes from one who makes you as welcome to it as you are to the air you breathe."

Before the astonished listener could ask any questions, his visitor was gone, and he remained lost in wonder as to who could be the mysterious benefactor who was willing to contribute so freely to his necessities, but the question admitted of no approach to a solution. He raised the heavy purse, and from such examination as he could give it, he became satisfied that its contents must be very valuable, and again he fell to wondering who among all his friends would be willing to sacrifice even that large amount for his sake, to say nothing of that greater sum, of which this was but an earnest. His grandfather and his brother, he knew, were entirely unable to command any such sums, and besides, there could be no reasons for secrecy in imparting anything they had to offer for his assistance. He could not indeed imagine why any one who was willing to befriend him so nobly, should not do so openly, but supposing that the mystery was only a temporary one, which would soon be disclosed, he checked his curiosity as best he could, and began to reflect whether he could make any use of the means so liberally provided. He could think of no mode of applying it, except by more largely feeing his counsel, and by empowering him to employ additional aid among the most eminent of his legal brethren, and this he resolved to do on the morrow. For the present hour, he determined to provide for the comfort of himself and his sable attendant, beyond the bare necessaries which had been furnished them, and thus prepare for a better physical endurance of their approaching trials, for although Brom's means were not exhausted, he prudently reserved them for emergencies, never dreaming of bestowing anything on luxuries, and least of all, for himself. His fund was a sacred one, pledged for Harry's benefit, and for that alone he was resolved it should go.

When, therefore, the warder next came his rounds, he was startled not a little by a request from a prisoner who had before accepted ungrumblingly the coarse fare of felons, for a substantial supper of such viands as gentlemen are accustomed to order at the best hotels, and this, not only for himself, but for the humble African in the adjoining cell. "Could this be done?" he inquired.

"Yes, if it was paid for," was the curt reply; "but it won't be cheap."

"I suppose not. I can pay for all I order, and, also, for your trouble. Next, we want clean, comfortable beds and bedding in both cells. Will you be allowed to furnish us with these things?"

"There is no rule to prevent your having such accommodations, if, as I said before"——

"I understand. Here is money enough to pay for it all, and to pay yourself, and you shall have more if my orders are faithfully executed."

The turnkey stepped back a few paces, and held up towards the light the two gold-pieces which had been put in his hands, and having become satisfied of their genuineness, he returned with a smile of very evident satisfaction on his lips.

"It shall all be done as you wish," he said. "Is there anything else? Would you and the colored gentleman like to have your supper together?"

"We should; but there is not sufficient room in either cell—we must remain as we are."

"To-morrow, perhaps, you can be better accommodated. There is a larger room, which is now occupied by two, but which will be vacant in the morning," said the turnkey, glancing expressively towards that end of the Hall which might be said to open into eternity. "If you would like to have your servant with you, I think I could manage to procure that room for you."

"I would like it, and I will pay your price for it," replied Harry.

"There is no *price*, of course, for this kind of lodgings," said the other, smiling; "and whatever you may choose to give me, of course you won't say anything about it to *him*, if he should come to see you."

By *him*, Harry understood the man to mean his principal, and he readily gave the required promise of secrecy, after which the turnkey withdrew. The promised change of rooms was never effected, but in other respects the warder fulfilled his engagements. In due time the viands for which Harry had stipulated were brought up, greatly to the delight of Brom, whose appetite was in no way impaired by his imprisonment, and who had grumbled much at the coarse fare to which he had before been confined. Knowing nothing of his master's private arrangements with the turnkey, he looked upon this change of treatment as a favorable omen, indicating a merciful feeling on the part of government, which would doubtless result in their release. This hope was increased into something like certainty, when a servant came to replace the folded blanket, which had been the only bed on his cold cot, by a substantial mattress, and to cover this, in turn, with real sheets and comforters, not omitting even the luxury of a pillow.

"Tank you very much," he said; "if ever you come my way, I'll do as much for you. Tank you, dat will be soft and warm, and please to take dem old bed-clothes away—I tink dere is sometin' in dem wid teeth. Tank you, good night, and please to bring me jis such a breakfast to-morrow mornin' as dis I jis had."

Gratified, but not surprised at being informed that his morning meal should be as good as his supper, and having satisfied himself that his master was faring in every respect as well as himself, Brom retired peacefully to bed, more with the exultation of a liberated man, than with the forebodings of a prisoner in jeopardy of death.

With less hope, yet without despair, Vrail sought his couch, after committing himself trustfully to His care to whom prison gates and bars are like " the spider's most attenuated thread," and whose holy will alone, he knew, must control his fate.

CHAPTER XXX.

A' MYSTERIOUS CLIENT.

On that same evening, Counsellor Strong, while seated in the midst of his family circle, endeavoring to divest his mind of professional cares, yet unable to banish from his thoughts the important trial in which he was so soon to take a conspicuous part, was informed by a domestic that a gentleman and two ladies desired to see him on business. The visitors had been shown into the library of the lawyer, and thither he immediately repaired, wondering not a little at so untimely a call, and still more surprised when he perceived that the parties awaiting his entrance were all entire strangers to him.

Gertrude Van Kleeck, notwithstanding the energy and resolution which had enabled her to do so much, was continually embarrassed and agitated by each new step in her great enterprise, and when she found herself in the presence of the learned advocate whom she had so longed to meet, and whose deportment, though mild, was dignified in the extreme, she was at an utter loss how to introduce the painful subject of her mission. She looked at Garret, but he was biting his glove in still greater embarrassment than herself; she looked at Ruth, and she, with flushed face and flashing eye, sat leaning forward on her chair, as if scarcely restrained from springing toward the lawyer to implore his powerful aid.

"You desired to see me, I believe," said the barrister, addressing the gentleman of the party."

"Y–yes—sir," said Van Vrank, " this young lady wishes to see you."

"Yes, sir," said Gertrude, but she could not fix upon the next word.

"Yes, sir," exclaimed Ruth, impatiently, rising as she spoke, and advancing close to the counsellor's side, " we have come to see you about poor Harry Vrail; we have come hundreds of miles—we want you to save him—you *must* save him!" she said, looking tearfully into the lawyer's eyes; " we all want to do all we can for him, and we want you to tell us what we can do. Now, Miss Van Kleeck, you please to speak to him—you can tell him so much better than I."

"I believe, sir," said Gertrude, emboldened at length to speak, "that I cannot better explain the object of our visit to you than this child has already done. We are friends of Mr. Vrail, and are most anxious to serve him, and having heard that you were acting as his counsel, we have taken the liberty of calling on you at this unseasonable hour. I hope, sir," and Gertrude's voice sank almost to a whisper, " that you do not consider him in very great danger."

"I am very sorry to say," replied the lawyer, looking compassionately upon his beautiful visitor, " that I entertain the most serious fears in his behalf. I have been told to-day that the proof with which the prosecuting attorney is furnished in his case is very clear and positive, and that it will show, not only that he was engaged in the battle at Windmill Point, but that he was a commissioned officer. I hope there may be some mistake about this."

Mr. Strong saw that the young lady turned very pale as he spoke, and he added the last sentence by way of a restorative.

"But if all this should be proven," asked Gertrude, desperately, "it does not surely follow that there is no hope for him?"

"If these facts should be fully proven, there would be no possibility of avoiding a *conviction*, and all further hope must be in the mercy of the queen, who might pardon him, or commute the death penalty to transportation."

"But the queen would surely be merciful, for she is a woman," exclaimed Ruth. "I would go to her myself; I would tell her all about him, and I would bring back the pardon. I *know* she would give it to me."

Gertrude did not speak, but with a hope, something like Ruth's, in the mercy of the sovereign, she anxiously awaited the lawyer's opinion.

"I think it highly probable," replied Mr. Strong, "that her majesty would have listened favorably to petitions in behalf of many of those who have already suffered, if they could have reached her ears, but the great misfortune in these cases is that, unless the jury or the court recommend the prisoner to mercy, or unless the governor of the province interferes to suspend the sentence, there will be no time to apply to a monarch living three thousand miles distant."

"Then we will go to the governor," said Miss Van Kleeck, in a low voice, "and wherever else there is the least hope of doing anything. We are prepared to make every effort that it is possible to make."

"And every effort will be perfectly useless," thought the lawyer, as he reflected on the character of the jurors and the judge who were to try the accused, and on the fate which all similar applications to the governor had hitherto met with; but he did not utter these sentiments, and he tried not to show them in his countenance.

"You are right," he said to Miss Van Kleeck; "but the first step is to prepare for the trial. I should be glad if there were means to procure the aid of additional counsel, which might possibly increase our slight chances of success."

"We are fully prepared on that point," replied Gertrude,

quickly; "we can amply remunerate both yourself, and all whom you see fit to call to your aid."

"I fear you speak without a full knowledge of the weight of such expenses. I should, indeed, be relieved if we could command means sufficient to bring Counsellor H——, of Toronto, to our aid. He is a man of the highest talent and influence, and he has had much experience in these State trials in his own city, and always, of course, on the defence."

Gertrude had deposited one of her large bills of exchange in a bank at Kingston, since her arrival, and she was entitled to draw upon that institution for the amount of it, at such times and in such sums as she chose. Without further reply to Mr. Strong's doubts, she asked him for a blank check, and it having been furnished, she requested him to fill it with whatever sum he could in any way make serviceable in the cause he had undertaken. Amazed at so extraordinary a *carte blanche*, the lawyer sportively filled the draft with an order for a thousand pounds, and handed it to the lady, closely watching her countenance as he did so. Gertrude glanced at the sum without any signs of surprise, and really with no emotion but that of pleasure, for she thought if so large an amount could be properly used on the trial, by a man of whose integrity she had the strongest assurance, it must be with *some* prospect of success. Seating herself composedly at the writing-desk of the barrister, she signed the check without speaking, and handed it to him.

"Is it possible?" exclaimed the counsellor, gazing at the paper a moment, with a smile. "Did you really mean to place this large sum of money at my disposal?"

He tore the check into fragments as he spoke, and threw them into the grate. Gertrude now looked surprised in turn.

"A fifth of this sum," he continued, "will abundantly repay all the professional aid we can bring to your friend's cause, and I am very happy, both for your sake and his, that you have the means to make so great an effort in his behalf. I shall be able to add Mr. Solicitor M——, also, to our legal team, and also to procure a few professional *claqueurs*, for out-door work; for we must sometimes resort to means like these in the cause of humanity.

"I do not quite understand you, but I have all confidence in your discretion and ability."

"Why, you must know that it is sometimes possible to *create* a little public sentiment in relation to an approaching or pending trial, and if such means are ever justifiable, they certainly must be so in combating the very violent and fierce spirit which prevails, in some classes of our community, towards the unfortunate American prisoners."

"Is there really so much hostility against them?" asked Gertrude, shudderingly.

"Yes; but we must admit that the provocation has not been slight. Let us hope, however, that the government and the people have become satisfied with victims, and that a milder spirit may begin to prevail. I must warn you, however, not to indulge in anything like sanguine expectations of the success of our efforts. A very moderate amount of hope is the utmost that I dare to encourage."

A heavy sigh was Gertrude's only response to this remark, and it did not escape the observing eye of the barrister that a tear stood upon the cheek that was half averted from his gaze. He proceeded to question her at some length with a view of ascertaining whether there were any point on which she, or either of her companions, could give any useful testimony for the prisoner, but unfortunately there was nothing to which they could testify which would be pertinent to the defence, and Mr. Strong became convinced that the only hope of evading a conviction must be in the possible insufficiency of the government testimony against the prisoner. Every effort was to be made to assail and break down this evidence, or, at least, to cast enough of doubt around it, to enable a jury, whose hearts should first be awakened to some touch of compassion, to acquit the prisoner if they would.

There might, indeed, be some strong legal points made for the accused in relation to the nature of the offence, if proved, but on all such grounds, he knew from experience, that there was almost nothing to be hoped from the court with which he should have to deal.

Having taken the address of his visitors, and promised to call and see them the next morning, for further consultation, they took their leave, but not before Miss Van Kleeck had placed in his hand another check for the smaller, but still considerable amount, which he had named.

With alternating hope and fear, Gertrude retired that night to a sleep in which there was no repose. Frightful dreams haunted her pillow, dreams of every variety of wildness and incoherence, yet all agreeing in presenting to her distracted mind the figure of a chained prisoner, whose pale and boding face was ever the same, and whose only words were those of sad farewell which she had last heard in her own home, and the accents of which a faithful memory had preserved to be the instruments of her torture now.

CHAPTER XXXI.

AN UNLUCKY WALK.

DAYLIGHT dispelled the horrors of distempered dreams, only to supplant them with more dreadful realities. It was a day of military executions, and Gertrude did not escape the knowledge of the appalling deeds which were taking place around her, and which were reflected in painful significance from every face she encountered.

The streets were thronged with a mob of the lower classes, gathering to witness the fearful tragedy which was soon to be enacted, and, alas! how often yet to be repeated!

She understood now why it was that Mr. Strong had proposed to call upon her, on that morning, for further conference, instead of requesting her to visit him at his place of business, which for a lady would have been almost an impossible undertaking, and she appreciated, too, the kind consideration which had foreborne to allude to the cause of so marked a departure from professional habits.

He came to find Gertrude prostrated with painful excitement, yet rallying at his approach, and stimulated to fresh exertion for her friend by the very terrors she had been obliged to contemplate.

There was little in the interview that needs to be narrated. The lawyer had some further inquiries and some suggestions to make, but he dealt out as sparingly as ever to his distressed client the precious medicine of Hope. How Gertrude dwelt upon his words to catch the meaning of each oracular sentence, and how skillfully she extracted from them the most auspicious interpretation they could be made to bear! How, when he was gone, she tried to recall the exact words in which his views had been expressed, and the very tone and look which had given them significance, ingeniously arguing herself into the belief that he entertained a greater hope than he revealed to her!

The day wore heavily away, for having wisely confided all preparations for the trial to the able barrister, there was nothing that she could do, excepting to await in painful inaction that great event.

Van Vrank paid a second visit to the prisoner in the afternoon, and during his absence, which was unexpectedly prolonged, Gertrude remembered that she had omitted to make a certain suggestion to Mr. Strong which she thought it might be important to bring early to his mind, and she looked anxiously and often for Garret's return, in order that he might accompany her to the lawyer's office. The streets had become comparatively quiet, although there were still many passing, but there was no throng that could prevent them being easily traversed by a lady under the escort of a gentleman. But Garret did not come, and Getty grew more and more impatient. As she went again and again to the window to watch for his approach, she observed that the number of passers still diminished in the streets, that there were more well dressed people, and occasionally a pair of ladies unaccompanied by a gentleman, and she began to contemplate venturing out with no other attendant than Ruth. She would have engaged a carriage, but she could not brook the delay which she had learned by experience that such a step would occasion. It was not a long walk to the barrister's office, which adjoined his house, and they both were familiar with the way; and while Gertrude yet hesitated, Ruth herself proposed that they should go, and with her usual impulsive action, was almost instantly arrayed to start.

"We shall meet Mr. Van Vrank, I know," she said; "and if we don't, it is no matter. The sun is an hour high."

They went, and so slight was the obstruction in the streets that Gertrude soon forgot her apprehensions, and under the refreshing effects of a walk in the open air, she even obtained a momentary respite from her more absorbing grief. When however, they had turned into another street, she became uneasy at observing that it was less quiet than the one they had left, and that occasional sounds of wassail and revelling were to be heard from some of the lower inns and drinking-shops which they were compelled to pass. Groups of men of rough exterior were standing on grocery stoops, and at the corners of the streets, noisily discussing the revolting scenes of the day, and others whom they met, in boisterous parties of two or three, gave similar evidence of having been witnesses of the same fearful spectacle.

Gertrude and Ruth quickened their steps, for having accomplished more than half their journey, it was easier to proceed than to return, and the evil neighborhood seemed to be of but brief extent. A little further on, the street bore a more respectable aspect, and it improved in the distance into a genteel and fashionable vicinity, but before attaining these promising precints, there were several blocks to be passed, and a vacant lot of considerable extent. While hastening to get past these dreaded localities, Gertrude's alarm was greatly increased by observing that they were followed by two men, who, without attempting to overtake them, seemed to keep at a uniform distance in their rear. It might be accident, she knew; indeed she believed it was, and rapidly as she and Ruth had been walking, they still increased their speed, but only to find, to their great alarm, that their followers also walked faster than before.

Miss Van Kleeck looked in every direction for some one to whom she could appeal for help in case of necessity, but she saw no one near them in the garb of gentlemen, and she was just trying to argue herself into the belief that her apprehensions were groundless, when the elder and shorter of their pursuers stepped suddenly in front of them, and peered into the face of Ruth. Screaming and springing backwards, the terrified child attempted to run, yet clinging to Gertrude, whom she tried to drag with her.

"Tain't no use to scream, nor to run, Ruth," said the man, rushing up, and seizing the girl by the wrist with a vice-like grasp. "I've found you at last, and pretty company I've found you in, too—I know how all these fine clothes come. Ha! ha! ha!"

Ruth was so utterly overcome with fright at the sight of the abhorred man who had so long been her master and tyrant, under the name of relative, and her mind so readily fell back into its accustomed thraldom, that she could not articulate a word. In any other presence or power, however great, she could have said something in self-vindication, but here was the man who from her earliest infancy had controlled and subjugated her will, and whose very voice and eye seemed to have power to re-impose upon her those mental fetters which she had temporarily thrown off.

Gertrude, indeed, spoke for her friend, as soon as her great terror permitted, but her faint voice was lost amid the jeers of a mob which had gathered quickly around to witness the unusual sport.

"*You* can go, if you want to," said Shay; "I don't want nothin' of *you;* though you ought to be took up, if rights was done."

Placing Ruth between himself and his companion as he spoke, they attempted to march off with her, but the poor child having recovered a little vitality, struggled violently, and called piteously on Gertrude for aid.

"Oh, will no one help us?" exclaimed Miss Van Kleeck, flitting around the outside of the circle of men and boys interposed between her and her late companion; "is there no good man here to save the child?"

"What's the row?" inquired one of a pair of shabby-genteel young men, with cigars in their mouths, who came up at the moment and stopped near to Gertrude.

"Oh, sir, they are carrying off a little girl; they have no right to her, I assure you. Won't you please to stop them?"

"Hallo there!" shouted one of the men, "let that girl alone, won't you? Joe run around to the station and call a police officer —we'll see about this"

"It's all right, Jem," said another, addressing the would-be philanthropist; "it's his daughter, and she ran away, and this one is"——

A wink finished the sentence, and the man, after staring a few seconds rudely at Gertrude, passed on heedless of her protestations."

Shay and his assistant, in the meantime, had succeeded in starting with their prisoner, whom they half dragged, half carried a few steps, followed by the rabble, and by the almost swooning young lady.

"Bring her in here," said a burly, red-faced man, who had stood in the doorway of his own grocery, watching the fracas, and who now thought he could turn it to his own account, by getting the crowd into his shop; "bring her in here, and let's have the whole story."

The mob poured into the groggery, nothing loth, completely filling it, and Shay at once began to explain his conduct, which was in substance as follows: The girl, he said, was his niece, but that she in fact had always been the same as his daughter, as she had lived with him since her infancy, and her parents were both dead. She had been enticed away from his house by one of those piratical Yankees who was to be tried and hung in a few days. How she came here, he did not know, but he supposed after the man's arrest she had fallen in with bad women, who had brought her here.

"Tain't no use to scream, nor to run, Ruth," said the man, rushing up, and seizing the girl by the wrist with a vice-like grasp. "I've found you at last, and pretty company I've found you in, too—I know how all these fine clothes come. Ha! ha! ha!"—PAGE 239.

UNIV. OF
CALIFORNIA

The grocery keeper said she ought to be ashamed of herself, and a dozen others said the same, and whatever Ruth had to say was lost in the clinking of glasses and decanters which followed. Shay and his companions treated pretty freely, and altogether a Bedlamite confusion was soon produced, during which the child became mute, despairing, and motionless.

Gertrude had not waited to hear the speech of Shay, for she saw that she could neither get into the room, nor be listened to if she did. As a last hope, therefore, she ran up the street with great rapidity towards the residence of Mr. Strong, hoping she might get there in time to bring him to the rescue of her friend.

From the moment that Ruth found herself in the power of her *soi-disant* uncle, and deserted by Miss Van Kleeck, utter despair took possession of her mind, benumbing all her faculties, and rendering her incapable of any serious resistance to her persecutor's designs. She felt certain that she was doomed to a return to her former dreadful state of bondage, the horrors of which she shuddered to contemplate, and that the late magical change in her condition, with all its dazzling hopes for the future, was to pass away like a dream forever. Without a struggle, for struggles she had seen to be useless, she accompanied Shay to his lodgings at a second-rate hotel in an obscure quarter of the town, and she heard without reply the harsh invectives which he bestowed upon her by the way. It was even with something like a sense of guilt that she listened to her tyrant, so great was his influence over her, and so accustomed had she been to be told, from her infancy, that she was perverse and wicked. He told her now, what he had often said before, and what she feared was true, that she had been given to him by her parents before their death, and that he had the same lawful power over her until she came of age, which her own father would have had, if living. There was no law, he said, which could take her from him, and certainly no one, and, least of all, any rascally Yankee, ever should be allowed to do it without the help of the law.

The case looked too strong for hope, and so Ruth gave it up, and thought the sooner it was all over, and she was back again to feel the worst of what she had to endure, the better.

She soon learned there was to be no delay in sending her home. Shay could not, indeed, himself leave the city, because he was compelled to remain as a witness in the approaching trial of Vrail. But Hull, the man who had assisted in capturing the child, was a neighbor of his, who having come to town on business of his own, had been induced to take part in the rare sport which had resulted so successfully, and was now made willing, by a slight compensation, to hasten his departure for home, in order to secure the trophy of his own and his friend's valor. For Shay had had a glimpse of Ruth's late protector, the heavy-fisted Garret, and notwithstanding his assumed confidence of retaining his prize, he preferred not to come in conflict with the young man. It had been, indeed, while Ruth was walking with him and Gertrude on the previous day, that Shay had first discovered and recognized her, and he had been carefully watching, with his ally, ever since for an opportunity to meet her unaccompanied by so formidable a champion. Gertrude's presence alone had almost deterred him from his design, for guilt is always cowardly; but he feared so good an opportunity might not again occur, and trusting to the favorable locality in which he was enabled to encounter his victim, and to the promptness of his measures for removing her beyond reach, he resolved on the attempt.

The inn at which he had taken lodgings, and to which he had conducted Ruth, was not many rods distant from the steamboat landing, and he remained with his friend and their trembling prisoner in his room until a little before five o'clock in the afternoon, which was the stated time for the vessel to start, when they set out together for the boat. Ruth, of course, had no baggage, and Hull had only a light portmanteau, which he was about to take in his hand, when the more wary Shay, beckoning to a stout, broad-shouldered porter at the door, placed the box in his charge.

"It is to go to the steamboat," he said, "and we want you to keep close by us until we get on board. I will see you paid."

He added something in a low tone, which did not reach Ruth's ear.

"Oh, if that's the case," said the porter, "you had better let me call Joe, the ostler; he's a jolly fellow for a row, and he'll be glad to go."

"Let him come along, though I don't think there'll be any trouble, for they'll be safe aboard in five minutes, and in ten more the steamer will be under way."

Joe was called, however, and grinning with satisfaction at the implied compliment to his prowess, he took hold of one end of the small trunk, of which the porter held the other, and the two, carrying their light load like some plaything between them, followed close on the steps of the travellers. Ruth did not suspect that they were a guard for her, and having no longer any hope, their presence, fortunately, gave her no additional apprehension. She submitted passively to all the requirements of her master, walking faster or slower, as directed by him, and even trying to remember some messages which he bade her deliver to his wife when she arrived at home. But the hated vision of that home rose before her as he spoke, and with it came the sweet remembrance of all which she had lost, renewing her agitation, and increasing it almost to madness; but she was hurried rapidly along, amidst a crowd which thickened as they approached the wharf, among carriages, and carts, and porters staggering under heavy loads, all hastening to the landing, where the ready vessel was adding to and outsounding all the din with the noise of discharging steam.

CHAPTER XXXII.

JACK SHAY AND HIS GANG.

WHEN the distracted Gertrude fled from the scene of her young friend's capture to seek for aid, she ran, as has already been narrated, with great rapidity towards the residence of Mr. Strong, but soon exhausted by excitement, and by the violence of her exertions, she was obliged to abate her speed to a fast walk. Even this velocity her failing strength compelled her to diminish, until her progression became like that of one who, in a dream, attempts to fly from danger, and finds each step more difficult than the last, until his limbs seem chained by some viewless power to the earth. Compelled to pause, she looked back to see if the kidnappers had yet emerged from the shop with their prisoner, but seeing nothing of the crowd, she took courage, and with recovered breath again darted forward, heedless of the wondering gaze with which she was followed, and of the hasty questions of sympathy as she passed, for she had now reached the more genteel portion of the street, but she dared not again trust to the championship of strangers.

She did not see that doors were thrown open, and that windows of stately dwellings were thronged with fair faces to behold her flight; she did not heed that a gust of wind snatched the rich tippet from her neck, and sent it whirling down the street; she only saw the near residence of the friend whose aid she sought, and into whose office, panting, but speechless, she burst.

The amazed lawyer rose hastily from his book-strewn table; the pens of half a dozen clerks became suddenly stationary, and all eyes were turned upon the fair client, who stood supporting herself by the open door, vainly essaying to speak.

"Why, Miss Van Kleeck," exclaimed the barrister, advancing quickly to her, and placing a chair at her side; "pray be seated, and tell me what is the matter. A glass of water here, George! and Edwards, please to step into the house and bring some wine."

Gertrude shook her head, and pushed aside the proffered water, without thanks.

"You must go with me quickly," she said; "I will tell you as we go along."

"We shall lose nothing by knowing our business before we start," replied the lawyer, coolly taking his hat and cane as he spoke, but waiting for further information.

Gertrude was obliged to explain, but it was far from a lucid statement which her agitation permitted her to make, yet by a few rapid questions the barrister obtained all the facts which he deemed it necessary to know.

"I can do nothing without process," he said; "but I will."——

"Oh, no, no; I cannot wait for that; they will take her away; I must seek help elsewhere."

"I will accompany you instantly; but let me first leave directions which will render my interference of service to you."

He quickly wrote on a slip of paper the names of the necessary parties, and handed it to his most advanced student.

"A *habeas corpus*, Mr. Jones," he said, "as quick as pen can draw it—Edwards will go for an officer while the writ is being prepared, and one of the young men will be on the watch to tell you as nearly as possible where to follow us; I only know that it is somewhere down this street. Mr. Thompson, you and Mr. Smith may accompany us, if you choose."

This permission, which was equivalent to a command, was accepted with great alacrity by the individuals named, who, Gertrude did not fail to observe, were two of the stoutest young men in the room, and who became at once the objects of envy to their less favored companions.

"I say, Tom," said Thompson, lingering at the door a moment until the lady and the barrister had passed out of hearing, "don't hurry with that writ, you know; give us a chance, and we'll do it up without the sheriff. Here, Sam, give us that other shillelah; that stupid Smith has actually gone with nothing but his fists."

The students, each swinging a heavy cane, quickly overtook their companions, and the whole party proceeded on a very rapid walk down the street—the impatient Gertrude fairly dragging the lawyer, whose offered arm she had accepted.

"Faster! faster! they will be gone," she said, "and then I know I shall never see dear Ruth again—and he would be so grieved if she were lost."

"You mean Mr. Vrail, I presume."

"Yes; a little quicker—we are almost there now."

"We cannot go quicker without positively running," replied the panting barrister, "and I really do not like to do that."

The young lady gave a slight scream at this instant, exclaiming, "Oh, there is Garry!" and slipping her arm from that of her grave companion, she darted across the street to meet her cousin, and inform him of the great disaster.

The story was quickly told, and in another instant the alarmed young man had joined the pursuers, or, rather, had preceded them, and was the first to reach the shop designated by Gertrude as that where she had left Ruth in charge of her kidnappers.

But here all was now quiet. The red-faced proprietor stood behind his counter, leaning his elbows upon it, and watching a game of draughts between two of his customers, who were seated on a bench, while a third was lazily lingering over the remains of a glass of ale at the bar, and looking wishfully at the inaccessible decanters behind it.

"No one else was there, and Garret, who thought he had mistaken the place, waited for the remainder of the party to come up, which they did very quickly.

"They are gone! they are gone!" exclaimed Gertrude in despairing accents. "Oh, why did I leave her?"

"Are you quite certain that this is the place, Miss Van Kleeck!" asked the barrister.

"Yes, certain; that is the very man who asked them to come in."

Mr. Strong stepped into the shop, and questioned the grocer, who affected much ignorance on the subject.

There had been a great many people in his shop, he said, and he had heard something about a young girl who had run away, but he had been too busy waiting upon his customers to pay much attention to the matter.

"Which way did they go with the girl?"

"I did not rightly notice, but I think in that direction," he said, pointing down a street in which he knew they did not go.

"He said the girl would be a hundred miles from here to-morrow morning," said one of the draught-players, "and he would see that she did not get away again. He was a-going to send her home with one of his neighbors to-night—that man, I suppose, that helped to catch her."

"To the steamboat! to the steamboat!—it leaves at five o'clock!" shouted Garret, leaping from the shop, and coursing the streets like a greyhound on the chase.

The clerks followed at a less rapid pace, but still running, and Mr. Strong, having the good fortune to catch sight of an unemployed hackney coach, immediately engaged it for himself and Gertrude, giving orders to drive with speed to the steamboat landing. There was need of haste, for it lacked scarcely a quarter of an hour of the stated time for the vessel's departure.

The hackman did not spare his horses, but they did not overtake the fleet Van Vrank, whose desperate efforts were caused by the painful reflection that if Ruth were lost it would be through his remissness. Never for a moment abating his headlong velocity, and seeming by intuition to select the shortest routes, he arrived, panting, at the crowded pier, long in advance of the impeded vehicle, and of his pedestrian followers. He was none too soon. Scarcely had he stationed himself beside the passage-plank which stretched from the wharf to the boat, where with flashing eyes, he peered closely into the approaching throng of passengers, when, to his great joy, he discovered Ruth among them, closely surrounded by her escort, and evidently quite submissive to them.

Fortunately, he was not seen, or, at least, was not recognized by Shay or his friend, who, having accomplished so much of their way without interruption, seemed no longer to anticipate trouble; and as they came to the plank they fell, for the first time, into single file, for the purpose of more easily passing the return current of porters, draymen, and others who were going out.

It was at this critical moment that Ruth felt an arm passed gently around her waist, and found herself lifted up and borne quickly in a lateral direction from the crowded gangway, where she was set down in a comparatively open space.

She half uttered a scream, but catching a glimpse of her friend, and hearing his well-known voice, she became silent, and with quick perception and ready tact she obeyed him when he directed her to stand behind him, for she saw her captors rushing furiously after her.

Shay, although in front of the child at the time of her seizure, had retained hold of her hand, and when she was snatched away, he, of course, became aware of it, while Hull and the porters, who were close behind, saw the whole transaction, which was too quickly done to admit of their interference. But they now rushed pell-mell upon the daring intruder, and without a word of parley, three of them assailed him at once, while the fourth, Shay himself, dodged around the combatants, seeking to seize upon and regain his prize.

Garret, nothing daunted, succeeded, by a few well directed and ponderous blows, in speedily grounding two of his enemies, but the pugilistic ostler, who was, unfortunately, a well-trained boxer, proved a more serious antagonist, dealing him some heavy hits, and affording little opportunity for any effective return.

A crowd, of course, gathered around them, some greatly enjoying the sport, and some seeking to terminate the combat, but the absence of police force, as usual on such occasions, prevented any effectual interference with the affray. Van Vrank was impeded by the necessity of retaining a position which should shield Ruth from her watchful adversary, who was too wary to come within the sweep of his long arms, and who resorted to invective as a substitute for valor. He denounced Garret as a scoundrel Yankee, who had stolen his niece, and wanted to carry her off to the States, and he asked the people if they would stand by and see it done.

"Shame! shame! do you want more than four to one?" shouted a porter, who stood, with a heavy trunk on his shoulder, watching the combat, and a laugh among the crowd indicated a sympathy with the weaker party.

"She isn't his niece, gentlemen," said Garry, knocking down the venturous Hull, for the second time, as he spoke, and then continuing his remarks, with a watchful eye upon the ostler, and apparently without much fatigue; "he stole the child himself, and I am her friend and protector."

A shriek from Ruth at this moment indicated some new danger, and, at the same instant, Garret felt himself grasped from behind by the resuscitated porter, while the two other assailants at once grappled with him in front, and despite the most Herculean efforts, he was borne to the ground.

"Now's your time!" shouted Hull; and Shay, who seemed to be of the same opinion, improved the moment to rush forward and grasp the trembling girl's arm, and by some threatening words, in that voice so sure to subdue her, he compelled her silence, (who was there now to appeal to?) and half led, half dragged her onward. Hull followed, leaving the prostrate man to the care of the two menials, for the boat's bell was ringing for the last time, and there was but a few remaining minutes to secure their passage.

But at that instant other actors came upon the stage. The students, Thompson and Smith, made their appearance, panting, in the crowd, and confronted the luckless Shay, at the moment that he was about to step for the second time upon the vessel.

"Stand back here, if you please!" shouted Thompson; "I have a writ for you, sir!" (The writ was half a mile behind.) "No kidnapping here, if you please!"

"Not on British soil," interposed Smith, bluffly, taking hold of one arm of the bewildered girl, while his companion grasped the other. "Please to consider yourself in our custody, and follow us."

The air of authority with which the young men spoke, and their genteel dress and bearing, had an effect for a moment, but the cunning Shay, after an instant's reflection, demanded to see the process by virtue of which they assumed to act.

"Oh, you'll see it soon enough; come along, sir!" said Thompson, who was quite willing that his orders should be disregarded, if they could succeed in getting off with Ruth, with whom they had begun to retreat through the crowd.

"All ashore that's going!" shouted a voice from the boat, and the amazed Shay, who saw himself so nearly foiled by what he began to believe a mere trick, rushed desperately after the young men, accompanied by Hull, and calling loudly also upon his other allies for help.

They were quite at liberty, for Garret had shaken them off, and regained his feet, and was at the side of Ruth and her new protectors, quite willing and ready to encounter them afresh when they came up, but fortunately the tardy arrival of a pair of police officers prevented a new collision.

Shay appealed vociferously to the men in authority to restore to him his niece, who, he assured them, was being forcibly taken away from his rightful control, and as his companion Hull and the two porters seconded his assertions, he seemed likely to prove successful.

"Ask the girl herself whether we are taking her against her will," said Thompson to the officer.

"Oh, no, no," cried Ruth; "don't let him get me again," and she clung close to the side of the protecting student, as Shay advanced towards her.

"It's no matter what *she* says, you know," added Hull; "she is but a child, and he is her uncle and lawful guardian. She wants to run away with them chaps. Be quick, now, my men, or the boat will be off."

"Don't hurry," said Garry, laughing; "here comes a man who can tell you the whole story, gentlemen, and who can tell you what you ought to do. Here's 'Squire Strong."

The lawyer's carriage, which had been long impeded by the throng of vehicles on the wharf, stopped at their side as he spoke, and Gertrude gave a shout of joy as she saw Ruth so near her.

Mr. Strong leaped out, and speedily learning how affairs stood, he said to the officials, who knew him well—

"You perceive that there is no proof of any kind that this man is what he claims to be, a relation and guardian of the child. Let her, therefore, decide for herself with whom she will go. It with me, I will be responsible for her appearance, whenever legally called upon."

"All right, sir; we know you; let the girl choose," replied one of the officers.

"Who will you go with, Ruth ?"

"With Gertrude! with Gertrude!" she exclaimed, giving a frightened look at Shay, and then darting to the carriage, the door of which had been left open, and springing in, she threw herself sobbing into the arms of her delighted friend.

Utterly baffled and discomfited, and conscious that he had not even a pretext for any proceedings to recover his lost slave, for she was nothing more to him, the enraged Shay muttered some idle threats, and turned away, accompanied by his coadjutors, while a very decided cheer arose from a portion of the crowd who had been interested spectators of the scene.

Garry, bruised, soiled, and with torn habiliments, was compelled to accompany his friends in the carriage, but he was too much delighted with the successful result of his championship, and with the very evident gratitude of Ruth, to think of the sorry figure which he made.

As to the students, it would be difficult to say, whether they best enjoyed their own share in the exploit, or the great chagrin of their colleague, Young, who came up, with his dilatory writ and a pair of sheriff's officers, just at the moment when all parties were starting for home.

CHAPTER XXXIII.

A TRIAL—AN UNEXPECTED WITNESS.

The delight which Gertrude experienced at the recovery of her young friend, for whom her attachment had daily increased, alleviated for awhile the intensity of that suffering which had arisen from her apprehensions for Harry.

Success of any kind always strengthens the faculty of hope, and Gertrude willingly allowed her joy to become an augury of that greater happiness which, with almost sanguine expectation, she dared to anticipate as near at hand. But ere the following day had passed—that day which preceded the one on which Harry's trial was to take place—her heart again failed, and she looked forward to the great event of the morrow as one too terrible in its possible results to contemplate.

She could not forget that her own friend, and the friend and counsel of Harry, with every disposition to encourage them both, had warned her again and again that there was the greatest danger of his conviction, despite every effort that could be made in his behalf; and in her last interview with the lawyer on that very day, the sad earnestness of his look and of his voice had impressed her with all the overwhelming depth of his own apprehensions.

Mr. Strong had advised both her and Ruth to be present at the trial, though not informing her of his reasons for such a course, and with great effort she resolved to comply with his request, for, after all that she had undergone, she was unwilling to risk anything for want of further endurance. Harry, indeed, would probably see her, and suspect her agency in his defence, but the crisis was too great, and the events which depended on the morrow's doings were too momentous to admit of being counterpoised by any scruples on these points, however commendable the sentiment from which they sprung. Let him know all, if he must. She asked nothing but to save him. Let the world deride, if it would. She could bear even that, but she could not bear the reproaches of her own conscience, or the bitter grief of her heart, if Harry were lost, and she had withheld any effort in his behalf.

Ruth was eager to go. With her usually sanguine heart, she believed that she could do something, she knew not what, to assist the prisoner; and her confident anticipations strengthened the heart of Gertrude, and emboldened her for the performance of her passive, but painful task.

Van Vrank had continued to pay daily visits to the prisoners, and contributed in every practicable way to their comfort, and had given them what encouragement he dared to offer of a safe deliverance; but Harry did not allow his mind to be dazzled by a hope which he knew might prove entirely illusive. Yet life had become doubly dear to him since he had suspected—for something had awakened the suspicion—that his unavowed but powerful benefactor was she to whom his heart had so long paid its secret homage. Not that he by any means supposed his affection to be reciprocated by Gertrude, for with his knowledge of her generous and compassionate nature, he could account for her conduct without resort to so pleasing a hypothesis. He did not indeed suspect half that she had done and was doing for him— he did not dream that she was in Canada, that she was near him, that she had personally employed and consulted counsel in his behalf, and, least of all, that she was to be in attendance upon his trial; but if he had known all these things, he would still have looked upon them as the results of a noble philanthropy alone.

The day and the hour so long anticipated came at last, and Harry Vrail was taken from prison and conducted to the place of trial. Though he went forth with sad forebodings of his return in perhaps a few short hours as a condemned and doomed man, yet he went with firm and elastic tread, and his face, radiant with the fresh light of youth, was free from all trace of the anxiety which, despite the trustful and resigned tenor of his contemplative moments, now forced itself upon his mind. He saw with a shudder the dread instrument of death as he passed it, but at the next instant his eye rested tranquilly upon the calm blue sky, from which it had been so long excluded, seeming to imbibe its serenity and to reflect its radiance.

Apparelled with care for the occasion, yet without any approach to gaudiness, the unconscious elegance and refinement of his appearance, and his youthful and innocent look, seemed to impress all beholders as he entered a crowded court-room, between two grim custodians, and took his seat in the prisoner's box, while his vigilant guards ranged themselves carefully on either side.

Remote from him, heavily veiled, and with eyes veiled yet more by streaming tears, two trembling females sat, amidst many others of their sex, in a portion of the room allotted to ladies, and which, as now, was often crowded during trials of great interest, or when any distinguished forensic display was anticipated.

Everything was ready for the opening of the trial, and the process of empanelling the jury was at once commenced, but was greatly protracted by a free use on the part of Mr. Strong of the prisoner's right of peremptory challenge.

Many were set aside whom the lawyer happened to recognize as violent partisans of the government, and as vindictive opponents of the revolutionists, and many more with whom he was not personally acquainted, were refused on the advice of his secret agents at hand, who knew or fancied some cause of distrust.

Some, again, the astute counsellor rejected without a question, solely on account of their appearance, and before the panel was finally filled, he had exhausted nearly the whole privilege, extensive as it is, which the law humanely allows to every man who is on trial for his life.

The prosecuting attorney, a harsh, severe man, of a very pompous air, who had been accustomed to do up his work on these state trials with very little opposition, and with every facility from a willing court, was surprised to find, on the present occasion, an array of the most eminent talent engaged for the prisoner, numbering not less than four of the very *élite* of the profession.

This circumstance, and the vigilance used in empanelling the jury, convinced him, as he said in his opening address, that a great effort was to be made to rob justice of a victim, which attempt he should trust to the good sense and loyalty of the jurors to defeat.

The prisoner, although young, he said, had been an influential and leading officer of the brigand band which had invaded the province, and although they might not be able to prove positively that he bore a commission in the army, they would at least show that he was an intimate and confidential friend of the chief of the banditti, who, thanks to the intelligence of a Canadian jury, had already paid the forfeit of his crimes.

The irascible attorney grew excited as he proceeded in his remarks, seeming to wax wroth at the bare contemplation of the prisoner's escape.

Why so unusual an effort was to be made in his behalf, he said, glancing at the silent but powerful legal army opposed to him, he could not imagine, and he would not trouble the jury by conjecturing. It at least showed that the prisoner was a man of means and influence, and, therefore, one of whom it was the more necessary to make a striking example. The Fourth of July heroes of Yankeedom, he said, had boasted over their wine cups how their fathers had whipped the British, until some of them had grown courageous enough to make an experiment of their valor on Canadian soil. "Our soldiers," he concluded, "have done *their* duty in conquering and capturing them; it remains for us to do *ours*."

With great majesty of air, and with as much seeming confidence in the success of the prosecution as if he were already listening to the death-sentence from the court, the attorney sat down and called, as his first witness, John Shay, by whom, he said, he should prove the prisoner's confession, while taking refuge in his house, that he was a member of the patriot army.

The circumstances of that confession, and the deceit and treachery of Shay, which will be remembered by the reader, were all well known to the defendant's counsel, who still hoped to make a strong point on the non-identification of the accused as one of the invaders. On merely legal exceptions, although prepared to interpose a perfect net-work of these, they placed but little reliance, for the court had again and again, in former trials, broken down all these flimsy barriers. There was the less chance of technical objections, because the indictment had been framed under a new law, passed since the border troubles began, expressly for the trial of citizens of the United States who had taken up arms against Canada, and who had entered the province with hostile intent. Shay testified positively and with great alacrity to all which the prosecuting officer had expected. He fully identified the prisoner as the man who had come to his house in the evening, a few hours after the battle at Windmill Point, in company with a negro, both being armed. Their fatigue, their hunger, their anxiety to be rowed across the river, and, finally, Vrail's confession to him that they were patriots, escaped from the defeated army, were all positively and distinctly narrated, while thousands of eager listeners held their breath to catch the fatal testimony which fell from the witness.

He next proceeded to give the particulars of the arrest. He left, he said, the defendant and the negro in his house, and went to the "Point" for assistance. When he returned, accompanied by soldiers, they fled, were pursued several miles, and were arrested in the very act of launching a boat in which to cross the river to the States. "If we had been three minutes later," he added, exultingly, "we should have lost them."

The witness said nothing about his own pretence of friendship for the fugitives, and for the patriot cause, by which he had won their confidence, nor of his violated promise to aid in their escape; nothing, in short, which could fasten upon himself the merited charge of falsehood and treachery. He found it, indeed, an easy and gratifying task to tell his story on its first direct recital, and had begun to fancy himself quite a hero in the estimation of the audience; but when the poor knave fell into the hands of Mr. Strong on the cross-examination, both himself and his evidence assumed a very different aspect.

Forced to testify to his own perfidy, and to his violated hospitality, and driven, in the attempt to evade the truth, to a series of contradictory and irreconcilable answers, the miserable man soon found himself so thoroughly self-impeached, that even the prosecuting attorney angrily dismissed him from the stand.

A gleam of hope electrified the heart of the prisoner and his friends at this result, but other witnesses were at once brought forward. The soldiers who had assisted at the capture of Vrail successively came upon the stand, and swore to all the particulars of the arrest, but the utter darkness of the night had prevented any of them from seeing his face at the time so as to fully identify it now. On reaching Prescott they had only seen his features indistinctly as he passed into the jail, and on the ensuing morning, when the prisoners were brought out, this man now on trial, they said, was among them, and was pointed out to them as the individual they had captured on the previous evening. This was the extent of their testimony, and the evident wrath and chagrin of the prosecutor showed very plainly that he considered it of no value. It left everything uncertain. Even if the jury would believe that the defendant was the person arrested by Shay and his companions, there was no positive proof of his having been in the battle. He had acknowledged nothing to the soldiers, and Shay's testimony of his confession, on which so great reliance had been placed, was shaken beyond all hope of reparation.

When the court, showing some impatience, asked the prosecutor who was his next witness, and when that baffled gentleman replied, with a very disconcerted air, that he did not know, the exultant expression of Counsellor Strong and his associates showed plainly that they considered the battle won. A breath of relief, long suspended, went up from the heaving breast of the excited prisoner, and Gertrude, straining eye and ear to catch every favorable indication, almost swooned with the tumultuous emotions of her heart.

At this moment the figure of the repudiated Shay, gliding through the crowd, approached the chair of the attorney general; his long arm, and his malign and cunning countenance were stretched out towards that officer, and he whispered loud enough to be heard half across the silent court room—

"*Call Ruth Shay!*"

Counsellor Strong started as if electrified by the words—he glanced at Vrail and saw that his countenance suddenly changed to an expression of alarm—he looked at Gertrude, and he saw her head droop slowly to the rail before her.

"Who is she, and what does she know?" asked the prosecutor, impatiently.

"She is my niece—she was present—she knows all."

"Are you certain?" was the quick, earnest response of the eager lawyer.

"Certain."

"Did she hear the confession you speak of?"

"Yes—yes, everything—everything."

With all the exultation of look which the prisoner's counsel had so lately exhibited, but had now, alas! lost, their opponent passed the name of the new witness to the crier of the court, and at the next moment the arches of the building were ringing with the words—

"Ruth Shay!"

Again and again was the summons repeated without response.

All eyes were turned towards the quarter where the ladies were assembled, and many saw a trembling child hiding her face in the lap of an older, but equally terrified companion, who was idly trying to shield her from view.

CHAPTER XXXIV.

HEROISM.

The attorney-general immediately made out the necessary legal process to enable him to enforce the attendance of the reluctant witness, caused it to be served upon her, and informed her, in as mild a tone as his habitual harshness could be softened into, that she must come upon the stand.

She paid no heed to him, nor to the severer voice in which the judge informed her that she must obey; and when the sheriff, in obedience to the mandate of the court, advanced and laid his hand upon her arm, she gave utterance to a scream and partially swooned.

In that condition she was brought forward, and placed upon a chair on the witness stand, and when a glass of water had been put to her pale lips, and a draught of air had been admitted from an adjacent window, she revived and looked wildly around, seeming yet scarcely conscious of her position.

The prosecutor being convinced that so reluctant a witness must have decisive evidence to give, eagerly proceeded to his examination. The oath was recited to her inattentive ears, the Bible was pressed against her unresisting lips, and a thousand heads bent forward to catch the first tones of that voice which few doubted must prove fatal to the hapless prisoner.

Ruth saw them not. She saw only the saddened face of Harry Vrail, and the alarmed expression of Counsellor Strong, each of whom was gazing intently at her. At that moment a marked change came over her countenance, a sudden color suffused her fair, pale cheeks, her eye kindled with unusual light, and rested with a proud, defiant look upon the lawyer, whose first questions, in a conciliatory tone, had just fallen upon her ear.

" Ruth, do you know the prisoner at the bar ? Have you ever seen him before, and if so, please to tell the jury when, and where ?"

Such were the questions to which, amidst the profoundest silence, all ears awaited an answer. But no answer came ; and after allowing time for the child to recover from her embarrassment, the question was repeated in a yet milder tone. Still there was no reply, nor did Ruth's countenance give any indication of embarrassment or hesitation.

Again and again were the interrogations repeated with slight variations in terms, but soon with a decided change of tone. Severity took the place of gentleness, and wrath flashed from the lawyer's eyes, as, in a loud voice, he *commanded* a reply, warning her, at the same time, to remember her oath.

Ruth remained silent. Her countenance did not change. Her eye, unquailing, met the fierce gaze of her questioner, and her compressed lips spoke the firmness of her resolution. Only the silent heaving of her chest evinced her deep emotion.

The attorney-general now informed the witness that she would be compelled to testify, and that it was in his power to send her immediately to prison if she continued refractory.

His threats and persuasions proving unavailing, the judge next addressed her, with great dignity, yet with a kind air. He informed her that it was the duty of every good and loyal citizen to give evidence against crime ; that she had no legal 'or moral right to withhold her testimony out of regard for the prisoner, and that her plain and only duty was to tell the truth, regardless of consequences.

" Did she understand this ?" he asked.

Ruth gazed on him as she had at the attorney-general, with the same fixed look, and in the same imperturbable silence.

"It is no idle threat," the judge continued, "which the prosecuting attorney has made. He has full power to commit you to jail, and I am sorry to say it will become his duty to do so, if you do not answer."

There was an increased color in the child's cheeks, but no voice issued from her lips, which might have been marble for any sign of opening which they gave.

"It would be a sad thing," continued his lordship, "to place a young, fair girl, like you, within the stone walls of a solitary cell, to remain night and day alone, to live on felon's fare, and sleep on a felon's cot. Do you not think so?"

No answer.

"This is no jest, Ruth! The laws must be sustained, and to jail you will certainly go, if you do not testify. Do not think, either, that your imprisonment will be brief. It may last for months, aye, years, and this trial can be postponed to await the end of your contumacy. What do you say to this?"

Ruth said to this exactly what she had said to all the rest—nothing.

"We are talking to a statue," said the judge. "The attorney-general must do his duty."

That officer had made out the necessary process for committing the witness, while the judge was addressing her, and now placed it in the sheriff's hands, still believing that it would not become necessary to execute it, and that she would yield at the last.

He was mistaken. Ruth trembled, indeed, when the sheriff approached her and informed her that she must accompany him, but she obeyed in silence. Sobs were heard from every part of the ladies' quarter of the room, and almost every man rose to catch a more distinct view of the heroic girl as she passed from the apartment.

"Who is your next witness, Mr. Gale?" said the Judge, as soon as quiet was restored; and the prisoner's counsel, whose late hopes had been revived and increased, were surprised to see that the prosecuting officer appeared by no means disconcerted at the question of his lordship; but that, on the contrary, there was an unusual determination expressed in his face as he rose to reply.

"If it please your lordship," he said, "I now propose to take a step which I had by no means anticipated could become necessary in a case like this, where the guilt of the accused is so certain and ought to have been so easily susceptible of proof. But the enormity of the offence with which he stands charged, and a due regard for the vindication of the law, and the safety of the province, seem to me to justify a resort to those extreme measures for procuring evidence which such emergencies require. There is now lying in the city prison, a colored man who was arrested in company with the prisoner, and who, like him, was a fugitive from the brigand army. He is, I am told, an intelligent person, and in every respect a competent witness, and, with your permission, I shall call him to the stand."

"You are aware that he must be discharged from custody, if we make use of him as a witness?"

"Most certainly. I am prepared to enter a *nolle prosequi* upon the indictment against him. The ends of justice scarcely require such a victim, and no harm can result from his release. He has evidently been the dupe of wiser heads, or rather of whiter ones, for there seems to have been no wisdom in the affair at all."

"Let him be sent for, if you desire it, Mr. Gale. The court has no disposition to interfere with your management of the case."

"The sheriff will then please to dispatch a messenger at once for the witness, and I hope the court will instruct the officer to see that no individual is allowed to have speech with the negro until he is placed upon the stand."

Gale gave an angry glance at Mr. Strong as he made this

remark, as if he would insinuate that the contumacy of Ruth had been the result of his advice or procurement.

"That is very proper," replied his lordship; "the sheriff will see to it."

Strong smiled quietly, and drummed with his fingers upon the table, without reply.

Three minutes sooner, at the very instant that Gale had broached his project of making black Brom a *Queen's evidence*, the vigilant barrister had turned partly round upon his chair, and fixed his expressive eye upon one of his agents, an ex-bailiff, named Welton, a small, slim man, with a very wide-awake look, who immediately comprehended that something was expected of him in connection with the proposed movement. He returned the gaze of the lawyer with an earnest and intelligent look, and the latter, as soon as he saw that the attention of his agent was fully arrested, slowly turned his eyes toward the door of the court-room, and then glanced in the direction of the city prison, at the same time resting a finger a moment on his lips.

Welton fully understood this pantomime, and taking his hat, he slowly sauntered out of the room, but no sooner was the door closed behind him than he started with the speed of the race-course for the jail. His former official capacity had made him well acquainted with the jailer and wardens, and he had no difficulty in obtaining immediate access to the cell of Brom, whom he found partaking leisurely of a choice dinner.

"You are Brom, Mr. Vrail's man," said Welton, breathlessly, as he approached the bars, "ain't you?"

"Yes," exclaimed the negro, jumping up and coming eagerly forward; "is Massa Harry free? is he got off?"

"No—but he will be, unless they can get you to be a witness against him. They are coming for you now, and they will be here in a few minutes. They want to make you swear that he was in the battle, for they can't prove it by any one else."

"Guy!" exclaimed the negro, snapping his fingers, and cutting as much of a caper as his narrow quarters would permit; "don't be afraid of me. I won't swear—I swear I won't."

"But they will offer you your freedom."

"Nebber mind what they offer me—jis don't you be afraid of Brom. Brom knows. Won't Massa Harry be right there before him, and Missa Gertrude, too? Do you think dey goin' to make Brom swear away Massa Harry's life? No, *sir*, not if dey should hang me twenty times over, and den twenty times more on top of that, and *then* I wouldn't."

The negro was so energetic in his protestations that he had well-nigh upset his dinner-table, and Welton became satisfied that nothing was to be feared from his want of loyalty to his master, however much might be apprehended from his want of discretion.

"But they may get something out of you unawares," he added. "Lawyer Strong thinks the safest course is for you not to say a word when they question you. If you begin to speak, you may let something slip out that will hang your master, after all."

Brom promised the utmost discretion; and Welton, who did not wish to be found there by the sheriff when he came after the witness, hastened away.

CHAPTER XXXV.

BLACK BROM AND THE ATTORNEY-GENERAL.

But a short time elapsed before the sheriff's messenger arrived, and the negro, guarded by that functionary and two assistants, set out for the court-house, revolving, meanwhile, some strange thoughts in his mind.

The law which, both in England and America, authorizes the employment of one criminal as a witness against his colleagues in guilt, and rewards the traitor with his freedom, is the most unjust and dangerous feature of the criminal code, and ought not longer to disgrace the jurisprudence of any civilized country. No more powerful incentive to perjury can be imagined than that which it offers, and the rights of an accused party can never be safe under the operation of so unjust a principle. It is but a weak argument in its favor to say that this mode of procuring evidence is but seldom resorted to, and that in the hands of a discreet and just prosecuting officer, the power conferred by such a law may usually prove conducive to the ends of justice. A right so liable to abuse, and so possibly fatal in its results to a single innocent party, can find no justification in any principle of State policy, especially in lands where the laws are professedly tempered with the spirit of that sacred book, which says it is better that ten guilty men escape, than that one innocent man should suffer.

Brom was informed on his passage to the place of trial, that he was to be called as a witness against Mr. Vrail, and that if he consented to testify, he would be set at liberty, and he was made aware, by his custodians, that such was the universal practice in relation to those favored criminals who were selected as "Queen's evidence." It was true he was not advised, nor required, either then, or when he came upon the stand, to swear to anything more or less than the simple truth, nor was his own release even to be contingent upon the conviction of his master. But testify he must, if he would hope to be set at liberty, and he knew very well that he could not say a word in evidence without convicting Harry Vrail.

We have said that Brom was revolving strange thoughts in his mind; what they were will presently appear.

He entered the court-room between his guards, and was conducted to the witness stand, where he at once became an object of general curiosity and attention, and there were many whispered words of indignation against the prosecution for bringing a negro accomplice to swear away the life of the prisoner.

Brom was briefly informed by the attorney-general why he had been sent for, and the clerk undertook to administer to him the usual oath, but the negro drew hastily back, and pushed the Bible from his lips.

"Dey said I was to be *free*," he said, nodding his head towards the men who had conducted him from the jail, and who still stood near him. "Where's my pardon?"

"You must swear first," said the prosecution.

"No, no; I must be free first—I 'fraid to trust strangers."

"I can only say to you, that if you will swear to the whole truth, nothing more or less, you may expect to be set at liberty. We do not want you to say a word that is not strictly true."

"I shan't swear to a word that is not true, after you let me off—I must be let off first."

"It cannot be."

"Den let me go back to de jail," said the negro, with great dignity, at the same time stepping down from the stand.

"And to the gallows!" said Gale, looking sternly at him, with an angry air.

"Yes, to the gallows!" returned Brom, excitedly. "How do I know that I shouldn't go to the gallows after I had swore?"

"You have my word for it, and the court's."

"I don't know you, nor the court. You mout change your mind about it. I want a receipt first."

A smile passed round the bar at the singular voucher required by the negro, and even the grim Gale seemed to be moved by merriment into a milder mood.

"It really matters very little to the government," he said, rising and addressing the court, "how soon this man is discharged. Occupying so humble a station, and having been so evidently the dupe of others, he would, if convicted have a strong claim upon the executive-clemency. He seems honest, and willing to tell the whole truth, and as it is only the fault of his ignorance that he does not understand the security afforded him by my promise, I shall move the court for the privilege of entering a *nolle prosequi* at once upon his indictment."

Both Harry Vrail and his counsel exhibited some uneasiness at the singular course which events were taking, and especially when the attorney-general asserted so decidedly that the witness was willing to tell the whole truth; for they did not know but he might possibly have some assurances on that point which they had not heard.

The judge replied, by reminding the prosecutor that he had power to cancel the indictment without an order of the court—a fact which Gale very well knew, but he had preferred to make the judge share with him any censure that might attach to the act.

He immediately drew out from his green bag a bundle of papers, and selecting from them the indictment against the negro, he seized his pen and hastily dashed across it the magical endorsement which was to render it a dead letter.

"You are *free* now, Brom," he said; "if you have any counsel of any kind, let him come forward and examine the record and convince you."

"Massa Strong is my lawyer," replied Brom, with great dignity.

Strong, in the meantime, quietly reached his arm across the table, receiving the quashed indictment from the hands of the prosecutor, and having barely glanced at it, he said,

"It's all right, Brom—you are free."

"Are you certain, Massa Strong?" asked the negro, with a look of delight.

"Quite certain. You are free *this instant*," said the counsellor, with marked emphasis, and bestowing a meaning look upon the witness.

"Tank you — much obliged," said Brom, nodding to the attorney-general; "I tank you very much."

"Very well—now then," said Gale, hastily, "the clerk will please to administer the oath."

The clerk rose to do so; but at that instant the attention of the court and the jury, and the excited auditory, was diverted from the witness, upon whom every eye had been earnestly fixed, by a rustling movement in the ladies' quarter of the house, where many had risen to allow one deeply veiled young lady to pass. Gertrude had been in agony ever since the moment that she had heard the proposition to use Brom as a witness against Harry; for, although she well knew his fidelity in ordinary circumstances, it was more than she dared hope, that either his courage or his affection would be proof against the gallows and all its horrible accompaniments. With death staring him in the face, on the one hand, and an unconditional release offered upon the other, it was too much to hope that so humble and ignorant a man would resist a temptation appealing to what is often called the first law of human nature, self-preservation.

But if she had been terrified by the bare proposition of sending for Brom, his appearance in court, and all that had taken place since he stepped upon the witness' stand, had added confirmation to her dreadful suspicions that the wretched man was really about to sacrifice his master. She had listened in speechless torture until now, when, oblivious of everything but the great peril of the moment, she arose with desperate energy, and, although trembling from head to foot, she rapidly crossed the court-room, stationed herself behind Mr. Strong, placed her hand upon his chair for support, and throwing aside her veil, fastened an appealing gaze upon the face of the witness.

Several of the lawyers immediately arose, and offered chairs. She accepted one, without acknowledgment of the courtesy, and without removing her eyes from the face of the negro.

Her striking beauty, her extreme pallor, and the sudden and singular nature of her movement, had arrested every eye, and it was some moments before the consequent stir and bustle had subsided into the perfect quiet which had before prevailed.

Brom saw her, and smiled, and when the clerk again presented to him the Bible, he once more put it aside, and said,

"Massa Gale, I told you that after I was let off I wouldn't swear to nothin' but the truth. Dat was all I promised—dat was all."

The negro spoke in an excited manner, and seemed anxious to vindicate himself in the step he was about to take.

"Very well," replied the prosecutor; "that is all we require—we certainly don't want you to swear to a syllable that is not true."

"I said I wouldn't swear to nothin' but the truth—didn't I, Massa Gale?"

"I believe you did."

"Well, I'll keep my word—I shan't swear to nothin' at all. I'll go to jail, like Missa Roof, but you can't hang me."

Much commotion followed this singular announcement, which had not been unexpected by some who had carefully watched the negro's manner, but which the prosecutor, in his blind and eager pursuit of his victim, had not anticipated. His wrath was without bounds, but nothing could move Brom from the position he he had taken, and he was accordingly committed to prison, like the previous witness, for contempt of court.

Many hours had been consumed by these various proceedings, and it being now past the middle of the afternoon, the court, on the motion of the attorney-general, adjourned until the next morning, thus affording a long and dangerous interval for the procurement of additional testimony against the unfortunate prisoner.

CHAPTER XXXVI.

THE "QUEEN'S EVIDENCE."

It is not necessary to impute any peculiar inhumanity t. the "attorney-general," to account for the seeming ferocity with which he pursued his prey on this and similar occasions He had been incited in this case to extra exertions, by the very force of the opposition which he had encountered, until he had come to regard the issue as a matter deeply affecting his reputation as a barrister and as a legal tactician.

He must triumph by some means, and in doing so, he doubted not to serve the government and the ends of justice; and as for the accused, tortured by the harrowing suspense of that long night of doubt, no thought of commiseration for him interfered with the plans of the learned man and his zealous agents.

Most active among his employees was the repudiated Shay, who was incited to strenuous exertion by the fear of losing the coveted reward, which had been unofficially promised him for the capture of the prisoner, and which now threatened to elude his grasp, from the want of sufficient evidence to insure a conviction. He obtained access to many of the prisoners who had been privates in the invading army, in the hope of finding some craven who could fully identify Vrail as a fellow-soldier, and who would be willing to appear against him. It is sad to say, that after many indignant refusals, he found a man ready to listen to his proposals, he being the same individual who had pusillanimously led the way in laying down arms, and asking quarter, in Col. Allen's division of the army, and who had been trembling ever since with the direful apprehension of his coming fate.

He unfortunately knew Vrail well, and in order to substantiate his own credibility, he undertook to describe the accused in court, if desired, before seeing him. He knew, also, that he was addressed as lieutenant by the other officers of the army, and that he was on the most intimate terms, both with his own commanding officer, and with Col. Van Shoultz, the leader of the expedition. To this latter point there was also other testimony, which the prosecutor had withheld until the main charge was proven, and when Gale came into court on the ensuing day, it was with a confident and blustering air, which alarmed the friends of the prisoner, and gave them sad forebodings as to the result of the night's researches.

Alas! their worst apprehensions were destined to a sad realization. The recreant soldier testified in the clearest and most positive manner to Vrail's presence and active participation in the battle at Windmill Point, and no legal ingenuity, on the cross-examination, could make him gainsay or controvert his position.

Point by point, through long and weary hours, the hopeless contest was maintained by the prisoner's counsel, until every question of law was decided by a predetermined court against them, and until the main question of fact was considered legally proven by the prosecutor, and was so announced by his ally on the bench, in his charge to an obedient and loyal jury.

No gleam of hope illumined the countenance of Counsellor Strong, when the jury, who had listened apathetically to his most eloquent and fervent harangue, retired to deliberate upon the verdict; and the despairing Gertrude, who had occupied through the day her first position in the court-room, saw plainly, and with an agony no language can express, the look of dismay which had gradually settled upon the faces of her legal friends. At Harry Vrail she dared not look, but if she had done so, she would have seen but little evidence of the anguish he was enduring, for, amidst it all, the habitual serenity of his features remained nearly undisturbed. The young and vigorous cannot easily divest themselves of that strong love of life which is ever incident to human nature, even in decrepitude and misery, but the experiences of the past few days, and the hopes which they had revived, had given a new charm to existence in the mind of the unfortunate prisoner.

The sight of Gertrude, and the knowledge of her extraordinary exertions in his behalf, had awakened a thousand agitating surmises as to the real nature of her regard for him. Had he been mistaken in supposing her indifferent to him, and was there something more than friendship and woman's pity influencing her present conduct, the sacrifices of which he computed far less by expended toil and treasure, than by the wounds to which it must expose a delicate and sensitive nature ?

These hopes, though slight and unpresumptuous, had taken shape in his mind, and with them were mingling the bright anticipations of restoration to freedom and home, when the changed aspect of the evidence against him compelled him to contemplate another future, alas ! how appallingly different.

No sooner had the jury retired than Mr. Strong, who well knew that their absence would not be protracted, hastened to join Miss Van Kleeck, and advised her to withdraw to her hotel, where he promised to transmit to her the earliest intelligence of the result of the trial.

" Is there any hope ?" asked Gertrude, faintly.

" You had better prepare your mind for the worst, Miss Van Kleeck," said the lawyer, sorrowfully, and with these words sounding like a knell in her ears, Gertrude, leaning heavily upon the arm of her cousin, Van Vrank, passed out of the court-room. A carriage was summoned to convey them to their hotel, and there, in an agony of dread, she awaited the terrible tidings, which were soon brought by the humane lawyer himself, for he dared to trust no messenger with the news, to be, perhaps, abruptly and harshly disclosed.

"It is all over!" she exclaimed, trembling violently, and speaking with choked and indistinct utterance, as Mr. Strong entered her apartment. "It is all over. I see it in your face. You have come to tell me that he is found guilty."

The strong man bent his head in silence.

"But they have recommended him to mercy? You said they could do this. Oh! tell me that it is so."

A dreary negative was indicated by a gesture.

"Oh, merciful heaven! Is there, then, no help for us?"

"The governor, Sir George Arthur," replied Strong, speaking with hesitation, "has the power to suspend the sentence, or its execution, if he thinks there is good cause, until a petition can be forwarded to the queen, and an answer received."

"But will he do it?" cried Gertrude, frantically. "Alas! I have heard that he listens to no such petitions—that he will not even read them."

"If the jury had tempered their verdict with the slightest qualification," replied Strong, whose whole air and manner were expressive of hopelessness, "if it had contained any suggestion of mercy, however slight, our case would have been less perplexing. But we can try. I will at once write a brief history of the case, to be signed by myself and my fellow-counsel, together with a petition, and I will forward them to Toronto to-morrow."

"You will *forward* them, do you say? No! You must go with them yourself, and so will I—and oh, if Ruth were but at liberty!"

"She will be released at once, as the trial is at an end, and there is no longer a pretence for her confinement as a witness. My clerk shall procure her discharge, while I am engaged on the petition."

Gertrude would have made an exclamation of delight, if her oppressed heart could have given utterance to joy, for the prospect of a reunion with Ruth, and of her companionship and assistance in her new undertaking, added something to her faint hope of success, and detracted something from her sense of desolation and wretchedness.

She had found time very soon after her heroic young friend's incarceration, to send a messenger to her with words of encouragement, and also to provide as abundantly for her comfort as her position would admit; nor had the faithful negro been neglected in these gentle ministrations of Gertrude. Both were set at liberty before evening; and Ruth, terrified by the tidings of the sad event to which she owed her release, hastened to mingle her tears with those of the wretched Gertrude, and to devise with her (alas! less sanguinely now) new efforts for arresting the dreadful doom of their friend.

Indefatigable in his labors, although so nearly hopeless of any favorable result, the lawyer was occupied with his colleagues until a late hour at night, in making the statement and petition which he designed to present to the executive officer of the province, and on the next day he succeeded in procuring the signatures of a few prominent citizens of Kingston, whose sympathies had been awakened for the prisoner. There was no time to be lost, for despite his most vigorous effort for a postponement of the sentence, it was pronounced on the morning after the trial, and left but a week's interval before the day of execution. These facts he vainly strove to conceal from Gertrude, who insisted on knowing the worst, and who braced her gentle spirit to the shock by the most resolute determination not to let despair paralyze her energies at so important a crisis.

Her courage and perseverance, and the impetuous ardor of Ruth, induced the lawyer to hope that their personal intercession might possibly be of some avail with the governor, and he was determined, at least, to afford them every facility in his power in the furtherance of their merciful errand. He took passage with them for Toronto on the afternoon of Friday, the day on which Vrail received his sentence, leaving Garret and the negro to await their return to Kingston, the former being enjoined by Gertrude to visit Harry daily, and keep him informed of all the efforts which were being made in his behalf, and also to write at once to his brother at Ogdensburgh, and impart to him the dreadful intelligence of the result of the trial. Brom, who by no means felt sure of retaining his new liberty, and who was unable to divest himself of apprehension while on British soil, would gladly have returned to his native shores, but for his extreme solicitude for his young master, whom, although he could not aid he would not desert. He accompanied Van Vrank daily to the prison, where, at a certain hour, they were permitted to see and converse with the unfortunate man, through the bars of his cell.

CHAPTER XXXVII.

SIR GEORGE ARTHUR.

COUNSELLOR STRONG took immediate steps, on the arrival of himself and his fair comrades at the capital of Upper Canada, to ascertain the most suitable time for waiting upon the governor and laying his petition before him; and when the proper hour, fraught with so momentous an interest, arrived, he proceeded to the executive mansion accompanied by both Gertrude and Ruth.

It was by their earnest desire, as well as by the advice of the lawyer, that Miss Van Kleeck and her young friend appeared personally as petitioners for the condemned man, yet the extreme excitement produced by alternating hope and fear had so nearly overcome Gertrude, that when their carriage stopped in front of the governor's residence, she was, momentarily, almost deprived of the power of speech and motion.

"I fear I can say nothing to him," she whispered, to the lawyer.

"You will be more composed soon," replied the latter. "Do not be alarmed—there may be no necessity for you to speak."

As Strong looked at the trembling form and the beautiful face before him, so pale with alarm and anxiety, he thought the mute appeal of so much loveliness in distress, might be more potent than any eloquence of language. He resolved that the governor should know all that this fair being had done and sacrificed for her friend, and he hoped, slightly, it is true, that the knowledge of these facts, together with such extenuating circumstances as he had set forth in the petition, might successfully combat, in Sir George's mind, the cold, stern dictates of governmental policy.

But if the timid, yet persevering girl was exhausted with fatigue and fear, there seemed to be a well-spring of energy and bold resolution in the heart of Ruth, who sought earnestly, and not without a degree of success, to infuse into her friend's breast a portion of her own courage and enthusiasm.

"I *know* that he will hear us, dear Gertrude," she said; "we will tell him how good and kind and noble poor Harry is, and how everybody loves him. Oh, I *know* he will be merciful, Gertrude. He cannot refuse *you*."

It was a child's argument, but if it had been weaker, the earnest, confident tone in which it was uttered would have done something towards re-animating the expiring hope of the wretched young lady.

Leaning heavily, and necessarily, on the arm of Counsellor Strong, she passed from the carriage to the house, where the little party of petitioners were at once conducted to the room in which the governor, at that hour of the day, was accustomed to receive visitors on official business, and which at other times served as his study. They were fortunate enough to find Sir George alone and unoccupied, though the lawyer did not fail to observe that in an adjoining room, a door to which stood partly open, there were several individuals, who, if they chose, could freely hear what passed in the executive chamber.

The governor of Upper Canada was a middle-aged, intelligent-looking man, of stern, cold aspect, whose countenance might have denoted him to be a fit person to hold the reins of government in troublous times, and who would scarcely be suspected of holding them with a lax or uncertain grasp.

There was little in his face or demeanor to impress the beholder with a hope of leniency to an offender, and there was a chilling effect in his first glance at Mr. Strong, whom he personally knew, and whose errand he suspected, which at once congealed the little hope that gentleman had ventured to entertain.

Rigidly polite and ceremonious, however, to his visitors, and especially to Gertrude and Ruth, he conversed for a few minutes on common topics, and then waited, with expressive silence, for the introduction of the subject which he evidently anticipated.

The lawyer at once produced his memorial and the accompanying statement, and handing the papers to Sir George, remarked at the same time that there were some peculiar features in the case which had emboldened him to make personal application in behalf of the prisoner.

"I have labored to be very brief," he said, "both in my history of the case, and in the petition, and if your excellency will do me the great favor to give these documents a present perusal, I shall be able to answer any questions which they may suggest."

"You have been very prompt, not to say hasty in this application," replied Sir George, coldly, after glancing over the first few lines of the petition; "I have only this morning received intelligence of Lieutenant Vrail's conviction and sentence, and I have yet to hear (if it is necessary to re-judge the case at all) the public prosecutor's opinion of the circumstances which are supposed to warrant my interference."

The governor laid an emphasis, not strong, but decided, on the word "Lieutenant," in the foregoing sentence, which did not escape Counsellor Strong's notice.

"Your excellency will excuse me," he said, "for suggesting that there was no proof adduced on the trial, showing that the prisoner held a commission of any kind in the invading army. He is entitled to be regarded as a private, and as such has a claim upon your excellency's clemency."

"The loyal and intelligent jury who convicted him do not

seem to have been impressed with the force of this claim," replied Sir George, continuing to read the papers in his hand as he spoke; "their verdict contains no recommendation to mercy."

"It is unfortunately true—though I cannot help believing that this severity was induced in part by the fierce and excessive loyalty (if I may so speak) of the attorney-general and chief justice, who were equally bent on a full conviction. Your excellency will perceive that our petition contains the names of several citizens of the highest standing, who agree with me in thinking "——

"It would be a singular community where a few weak-minded men of high standing could not be found, whose sensibilities should outweigh their judgment. I can see nothing in this case which can justify my interference, or which requires me to trouble the attorney-general for his opinion. The public safety, Mr. Strong, will not permit of a weak or vacillating course in administering the laws at such a crisis as this. The war which has been checked by the gallantry of our troops at Windmill Point, is still waging in other parts. Invasion and insurrection are alike threatening us, and there is not an hour's security for our government until this war is effectually quelled. Is this, then, a time for leniency to leaders and influential members of an invading army, who have crossed our borders to incite the discontented subjects of her majesty to rebellion? You tell me that this Mr. Vrail is a gentleman of education and refinement, but this fact but aggravates his offence, and renders the necessity of his punishment more imperative. Doubtless, he is also a man of wealth and influence, since he is able to command the most extraordinary services of distinguished counsel."

The lawyer's eye turned to Gertrude, as if he hoped her to reply to this question, for although he could easily have answered it himself, he thought it a good opportunity for her to speak, and he despaired of producing any effect by argument upon the stoical governor, whose words, disheartening as they were, were still less so than the tone in which they were uttered, and the expression of eye which accompanied them.

Gertrude saw and comprehended the silent appeal of her adviser, and thrice she essayed in vain to speak, her colorless lips moving, without giving utterance to any sound.

Overwhelmed by the words which she had heard, and which seemed to her like the voice of Fate, she forgot for a moment her high trust in that Power which rules the hearts of princes, and which overrules at its pleasure the decrees of earth's highest sovereigns.

Whiter than the wall at her side, whiter than the marble table upon which her hand was resting, she sat, statue like, her eyes, from which the lustre was fading, fixed upon the stern representative of majesty, her ears still ringing with the dismal echo of words which seemed to her like the knell of doom. But while Gertrude was thus so near passing into a state of insensibility, Ruth, at her side, exhibited a picture of very different emotion. The excitement of the moment had added to the color of *her* cheek and to the lustre of *her* eye. Her breath came rapidly, like one who pants from fatigue, and in her face there was a rapt, glowing, ardent expression, which betokened an utter forgetfulness of everything but the weighty interests which hung on the decision of the hour. For a few moments she gazed earnestly into the face of Gertrude in silence, but when she saw her utter inability to speak, she rose suddenly, and fixing her flashing, but tearless eyes upon the governor, she advanced hastily to within a few feet of his chair.

"No, no, no," she said, clasping her hands as she spoke, "he is not rich, nor influential. He has no friends, but her,"—pointing to Gertrude—"and his poor old dying grandfather, and one brother. It was to protect *him*—that younger brother—that he came to the war, and not out of any ill-will to you, or to the queen. He is a good, kind, dear, noble gentleman, and oh, if you will but save him, we will love you and pray for you as long as we live."

Sir George listened unmoved to the child, and when she paused, he glanced angrily at the lawyer, and said,

"If it is by design that I am treated to this exhibition, I must beg you to reserve such artifices hereafter for the jury-room. They are certainly powerless here. I should poorly requite the confidence placed in me by her majesty if I could allow the tears of a child to jeopard the safety of her government in these provinces."

"Her majesty would not answer us so," replied Ruth, boldly. "She has a woman's heart, and is merciful. She would not frown upon us thus, when we came to beg the life of our dearest friend—I know she would not. Oh, give us time to go to her—dear, good Sir George—give us time! we ask for nothing more. Oh, think how much depends upon it! It is not one life alone—for if you refuse us, *she* too will die, and I shall be left without a friend in the wide, wide world."

It was not in the words that the chief force of Ruth's appeal consisted—it was in the wild, impassioned tone of her voice, in the strange light which flashed from her now tearful eyes, and in the trembling cadence with which the last few words were spoken, and the unrestrained hysterical sobbing with which they were followed.

Impelled by the painful interest of the scene, both Gertrude and Mr. Strong had risen and advanced nearer to the governor, closely watching his countenance for some change of expression which might betoken mercy.

Other spectators, too, were added to the scene, for two occupants of the adjoining room, a lady and a gentleman, attracted by the earnest petitions of Ruth, had drawn near the door, and although but indistinctly visible to those within, they were able to observe all that passed in the presence of the governor. Doubtless they were members or relations of his family, for their presence, which could not be unknown to Sir George, did not seem to disturb him. Perhaps it was in part to justify, in their estimation, the extreme inflexibility with which he adhered to his original position, that he had condescended to use so much of argument, and that he now again replied, not directly to Ruth, but to the legal gentleman, to whom all his remarks had been addressed.

"This very print," he said, laying his hand upon the morning journal, and continuing his remarks in his former tone, "contains authentic accounts of a new gathering of freebooters in a frontier town of New York, prepared to cross our borders the moment there is a sufficient rising among the disaffected here to give them any hopes of making a successful stand against our armies. Nay, they count on a portion of those very armies joining them against the government, and are widely issuing their wicked manifestoes among our people, to incite them to rebellion and treason. Doubtless there are among these some as gentlemanly and as well educated as this Mr. Vrail. Shall we invite them to come by our clemency to *him*, or shall we show them, distinctly, that every officer, and every leading member of their band of conspirators who falls into our hands forfeits his life, and that the forfeit will surely be claimed? Self-preservation, Mr. Strong, is said to be the first law of nature, and when both our lives and our government are endangered by faction at home, and by invasion from abroad, be assured that we shall do what we can to protect ourselves."

Sir George handed back the petition and the accompanying paper to the lawyer, and rose from his chair, as if to signify that the conference was ended, and when the despairing Gertrude at this moment found power to speak, and commenced an earnest, tearful appeal to him, he hastily interrupted her.

"On this topic I can bear nothing more," he said. "It would but prolong a suspense which must terminate unfavorably to your happiness. I honor the feelings and motives which actuate you, and be assured I sympathize deeply with your distress, but I cannot allow these feelings to influence my official actions."

Gertrude sank into a chair, and but for the timely support of Mr. Strong, she would have fallen to the floor. But she did not swoon. Wine was brought by order of Sir George, which she tasted, and after a few moments, being convinced that all further importunity would be useless, she took the offered arm of her legal friend, and slightly bending her head, in reply to the ceremonious adieu of Sir George, she withdrew from the room.

Ruth went less quietly. Checking her convulsive sobs, as she reached the doorway, she turned to the governor, who remained standing in the centre of the apartment, and said,

"Oh, Sir George Arthur, you will not listen to me—you do not care what I say—but if our good queen stood where you stand, we should not go away so wretched. She would not be afraid to pardon one poor, weak young man, lest he should overturn the government! She would take compassion on that dear young lady, who is now going home to die."

While Ruth was speaking, a young gentleman, apparently about twenty-two years of age, remarkably tall and slender, yet of the most graceful and easy deportment, entered the executive room from the adjoining parlor. After nodding familiarly to the governor, he stood listening to the fair speaker until she became silent, and then, with a pleasant smile playing upon his handsome features, and exhibiting a set of dazzling teeth, he addressed her, as she was about to withdraw.

"Will you please to tell me how it is that you, who are an American, speak of her majesty as *our* queen?"

"I am not an American, sir. I am a subject of the queen; but my home is in America now with this young lady," and Ruth pointed towards Miss Van Kleeck, who, with the lawyer, were waiting for her in the hall.

"And if Sir George had granted your petition, and had postponed the execution of this young man, would you really have gone in person across the ocean to see the queen, and to try to get a pardon for him?"

"Yes, sir, we should have gone, Gertrude and I; we had long ago decided upon that."

"Alone?"

"Yes, sir."

"Had you not considered that it would be a dangerous and very costly journey, and that probably you would never even be allowed to see the queen after you had arrived there?"

"We feel sure, oh! very sure, that we should see her, and that she would give us a pardon for Harry, and we do not fear the dangers of the journey. *She* would die to save him."

"Is she a sister?"

"No, sir."

"A relative?"

"No, sir, only a friend. But everybody loves Harry. Can you do anything for us, sir?"

This question was put with such a sweet simplicity, and so mournful a cadence of voice, that it quite drove the smile from the handsome face of the youth, and had nearly brought a tear into his sparkling eye.

He gave a hasty glance at the governor, whose eyes were fixed upon him, and then replied to the question by shaking his head.

"Then good-bye," quickly replied Ruth, who seemed indisposed to waste words upon one who could not assist the cause she had at heart, and hastening to rejoin her friends, they proceeded together to the carriage, and, in silence, returned to their hotel. Not a word was spoken—hope was annihilated, and grief was too great for words.

CHAPTER XXXVIII.

A NEW ADVOCATE.

"This seems rather hard, Sir George. Don't you think it might do to unbend a little in a case like this, and give these people a chance to try their fortunes with the queen's ministers?"

This remark was addressed to the governor by the young gentleman who has been described, immediately on the withdrawal of the despairing petitioners, and it was spoken in the familiar tone in which a man addresses his equal.

The governor started in surprise, and gazed a moment at his young companion, without reply, and when he spoke, it was no longer in the official tone in which he had addressed his late auditors.

"No, Hadley, there certainly is no other course for me to pursue than the one I have adopted. If you had been present during the last half hour, you would have heard sufficient reasons to convince you of this."

"I have heard everything in the next room, and am not convinced," replied the young man, smiling. "I really cannot believe it necessary to sacrifice these people to a question of state policy, because I do not think the stability of her majesty's government in these provinces is endangered by all these Quixotic enterprises. Pray, Sir George, let me beg you to reconsider this matter. I will wager fifty guineas that if these fair creatures should have the good fortune to obtain a direct audience of the queen, they will gain their ends."

"I am sorry to say they will never have that good fortune, Hadley, happy as I should be to gratify you"——

"In anything else," replied the youth, smiling broadly; "that is the usual formula, I believe, when you intend to deny a person the only favor he is like to ask of you."

"Yes, in anything else. This affair is *res adjudicata*. I am convinced, too, that a different decision on my part would be of no avail to the petitioners, excepting to prolong their suspense and subject them to a long and dangerous journey, ending in disappointment. They would never see the queen, and I should be blamed for permitting her ministers to be annoyed by their importunities."

"But I think the very fact that they had travelled so far alone and unfriended, on such an errand of mercy, would ensure them an audience."

"If that fact could be made known to her majesty, it possibly might; but she would never know it; and even then, the utmost she would do would be to refer the question to her council, who are much too frightened about the state of affairs over here to recommend a pardon which was not asked for either by the court, the jury, or myself."

"But you *can* ask it."

"I can *not*, consistently with the rules I have laid down for my official actions, and a little experience in my place, Hadley would make you of the same mind. If you had heard as many earnest petitions for pardon as I have heard (for not a man suffers death in this province who has not some hopeful and sanguine friend to importune for him), you would learn the necessity of disregarding all which are not founded on some substantial claims."

"By Hercules! Sir George, I wish you would try me for a week. Go on a visit to Sir John Colborne, in the lower province, and make me your lieutenant until next Monday."

"You had better swear by Phæton than by Hercules," replied

the governor, laughing, "if you ask me to place the reins of government in your hands. I think you would pilot the ship of state about as skillfully as he guided the chariot of the sun."

"I might rival his achievements," replied the young man, "but it would not be in granting a three months' respite to this unfortunate youth, nor even in recommending his pardon. I really do not know how to abandon this request, Sir George. Is there nothing in our relative positions, or in our family alliance, upon which I can found so trifling a claim."

"Much, certainly, on which you can base far weightier demands, so that they do not trench upon my official prerogatives. I am surprised, Hadley, at the pertinacity with which you cling to this boy-like fancy. Your father, Lord B., would certainly take an entirely opposite view of the case, and should I yield to you, no one, I am convinced, would censure me quicker or more severely than he."

The Honorable Edward Hadley B—— could not deny the truth of this statement, nor the force of the argument. He recalled to mind how often he had heard his father speak of the American leaders in this war in terms of the harshest censure and vituperation, and he knew that his verdict against them would be unpitying and unsparing. His own benevolent instincts revolted against the opinions of both father and governor; but he felt persuaded that further argument or importunity would be, useless. After a few moments' reflection, he walked silently from the room, nor did Sir George seek to stay his departure.

Young B—— was only a visitor in Canada, having come from England a few weeks before the time now spoken of, and proposing to return to London after a short sojourn in the provinces. He was distantly related to the governor, and upon that affinity, and upon his own high social position, he had based the intercession, which he had so reluctantly abandoned. Yet he did not readily relinquish any enterprise in which he had once embarked.

At home, in not much younger years, he had borne the reputation of a reckless and daring youth, who was wont to indulge his caprices at almost any risk, and with small regard to personal reputation. He was called thoughtless, wild, hare-brained, fool-hardy, and sometimes unprincipled, yet all his many faults had been mingled with so much that was amiable, high-minded and generous, that he seldom became the subject of severe and not often even of just rebuke. Such as his character was, we are not his apologist, but simply the historian of that episode in his life which briefly connects him with the personages and events of, our story.

CHAPTER XXXIX.

A PHYSICIAN DISAPPOINTED.

Gertrude and her friends had left the governor's mansion, where the rejection of their petition had been so peremptory and so positive, in silent and hopeless gloom, and they had returned to their hotel as mourners return from the grave. It was only when they had reached the private parlor which had been assigned to their use, that some faint, formal words of condolence and resignation were uttered, but not a syllable was said that breathed of hope.

Gertrude's grief was of that alarming type which finds no outward manifestation, and Ruth restrained her propensity to a more violent sorrow out of regard to her silent and suffering friend. Miss Van Kleeck's condition was such as to forbid the thought of an immediate return to Kingston, and Mr. Strong, although unsolicited, thought it advisable to seek medical aid in her behalf.

While he was absent on this errand, and while the young ladies were alone in their room, Gertrude was surprised by receiving the card of Edward Hadley B——, who was waiting, she was told, in the ladies' parlor to see her. Who the visitor was, she was utterly unable to imagine; nor could Ruth assist her conjectures, for she had not heard the name of the young gentleman who conversed with her at the governor's house, and to whose inquiries she had attached no consideration, because she regarded them only as the promptings of a casual curiosity.

Gertrude's first inclination was to deny herself to this unknown visitor, but with her second thought came a faint gleam of hope, so faint that it only served to render the depth of her despair discernible, that he might be some messenger from the relenting governor, and she resolved to see him. Ruth had not been inquired for, and she descended alone, tremblingly, into the ladies' public parlor, which she found unoccupied, excepting by the gentleman who was awaiting her appearance, and who immediately introduced himself with that air of graceful politeness which seemed to be his natural demeanor. Conducting her to a sofa, he took a seat at her side, and said hastily, as if anxious to remove what he knew must be a painful curiosity,

"I was present, Miss Van Kleeck, this morning, at governor Arthur's, and was a witness of the rejection of your petition. I have since added my own entreaties to yours, without avail; and I have now called upon you not merely to express an idle sympathy for your sufferings, but"——

Hadley hesitated, and Gertrude, who had listened with breathless attention, said, with sudden energy,

"But what? Can anything more be done? Is there yet any hope?"

"Speak lower, that we may not be overheard. I will not say that there is much ground for hope, but I think there may be some—if"——

Again the young man hesitated, but this time with a smiling air, and Gertrude again impatiently interposed—

"If what? There is no obstacle so great that we will not attempt to surmount it to save our friend. Pray do not keep me in a moment's longer suspense. If you knew all that I have suffered, you certainly would not."

"I will not keep you in suspense any longer than to impose strict secrecy upon you in regard to what I am about to say; secrecy from every one, even from the friends who are co-workers with you here in this cause, until the time comes when I will consent to disclosure."

"I promise everything faithfully, earnestly. I will swear to it, if you wish."

"I ask nothing but your promise. To be brief, then, it is useless longer to indulge the faintest expectation of the governor's relenting, and there remains but one chance for your friend, a slight one I grant, and yet a chance, if you can command a few brave hearts and hands, as I do not doubt you can. You must attempt his rescue!"

"His *rescue!*" echoed Gertrude, in a tone of sad disappointment. "Ah, what hope is there of that, from a prison as strong as his—aye, from a cell with walls of stone, with iron doors, doubly locked, and he chained within it. No, this is *no* hope—it is *impossible*," and the wretched girl gave way to sobs of irrepressible anguish.

"Listen to me. I have no object in deceiving you, and none in assisting you, excepting your happiness and that of your friends. Suppose that I could remove some of these obstacles of which you speak—that I could knock these fetters from your friend—could remove him to a more accessible room; and, in short, suppose that I had power to afford other facilities for such an attempt as I speak of—what then?"

There was something so expressive in the tone and look of Hadley as he said these words, that Gertrude's hopes again revived.

"Can you do this?" she asked, eagerly; "who and what are you, that you should be able and willing to do so much for us?"

"That is a question of no moment," replied Hadley, smiling; "I am a young man, as you see, somewhat accustomed to odd adventures, and taking particular delight in difficult ones. I want to serve you, because I have seen your great distress and that of your young friend. If I desire also to gratify my own whims, by baffling my obstinate cousin, the governor, that is an affair of my own."

"Governor Arthur your cousin!" exclaimed Gertrude, in a half whisper, and with an animated expression; "then, indeed, you can help us!"

"Don't be too sure of that. You fly, lady-like, from one extreme to another. But I think, as I said before, I can put you in a way of helping yourself, if you can command aid of the right sort. Not such men as your friend, Counsellor Strong. He must not receive any intimation of it, for it would ruin him to be suspected of the least cognizance of the affair."

"And *you*—are not you afraid for yourself?"

"I have outlived worse suspicions," returned Hadley, smiling; "and if you are as discreet as I hope, there will be nothing stronger than suspicion against me. Besides, my home is across the ocean, and I care for nothing, as long as the governor does not hear of it."

"Sir George will be sure to suspect"——

"Oh, I don't mean the governor of Upper Canada, but *my* governor, Lord B."

Gertrude was again astonished to learn that she was conversing with the son of a lord, perhaps a prospective lord himself, but she had been too much won by his unaffected kindness, and by his graceful and playful manners, to admit of feeling any embarrassment at this new discovery.

"I could not express my gratitude to you if I should attempt it," she said; "and now I can speak of nothing but this new hope. Yes, I have friends here, who will do and dare very much for me, and I can, perhaps, bring more aid from the American shore. I must have time to reflect. I may not even consult with Mr. Strong?"

"Most certainly not—nor even with your eloquent child-friend. Let me be your only counsellor at present; and first, I must warn you that you will need a sagacious and able man to take the management of the enterprise; and next you will require subordinates, who are strong and bold, and who are willing to incur some risk, for it need scarcely be said that the undertaking will be a dangerous one.

"Of course it must be so. I have with me a friend and servant, on both of whom I can rely in any emergency, and I can doubtless procure other assistants from the other side; but for such a leader as you describe I do not know where to look. Will there be time for me to go to Ogdensburgh and return ?"

"Abundant time. The a—affair is not to take place until next Friday."

Gertrude shuddered, but did not reply.

"You will not have any child's play in this matter, you know, and if you undertake it you must be prepared to make the most vigorous and determined efforts for a successful result. It will of course involve some heavy outlay, which, I hope, you are prepared to meet."

"Yes, money shall not be wanting nor any efforts that I can make. I must return at once to Ogdensburgh, where a brother of the prisoner awaits advices from us. There money will procure men, and, possibly, a leader competent to this great achievement. At all events, I assure you my whole fortune, if needed, shall not be wanting to reward the successful actors in this humane effort."

"I see that I shall have no cause to complain of you, if my pretty scheme falls through. You certainly deserve success, and I almost think I could find the man on Canadian soil, who would become your vicegerent, if I dared to risk my secret here."

"But when I go to my friends, I must be allowed to inform them of the nature of the aid they are to receive."

"Yes but only in general terms. Let them select a rendezvous upon some island near to Kingston where you can communicate with them at night by means of trusty messengers, and when the proper time arrives, let the details of my plan be communicated to their leader. With him I would like to confer personally, although, of course, my name must not be known to him."

Hadley proceeded to impart to the young lady more minute instructions and advice in relation to the part she was to act, and he also disclosed to her some further particulars of his proposed plan of rescue. What else should become necessary for her to know he would inform her of, he said, after her return from Ogdensburgh to Kingston, to which latter place he himself was to proceed within two or three days. He spoke in a cheerful and lively tone, and succeeded in inspiring Gertrude with a portion of his own sanguine expectation of success. He bade her keep up good courage, and assured her that he believed nothing was wanting but skill and boldness on the part of her friends, aided by the facilities which he would be able to offer them, to ensure a triumphant result.

But oh, how widely different were the emotions with which the two individuals contemplated the momentous project under discussion. To one it was the last faint hope of a long series, all of which had as yet ended in disappointment, and if this also failed, nothing remained to her but the submission of despair.

To the other, it was but an exciting and boyish exploit, prompted indeed in the first instance by humane feelings, but carried out in the spirit of adventure, and with that cherished oppugnation to authority which had ever characterized the young scion of nobility.

There was just enough of personal danger attending the attempt, danger of censure from high sources, and of amenability to violated laws, to add a zest to the undertaking. There was something to be eluded by skill, or to be borne with heroism.

The friends, for such a brief interview and a community of interest had made them, parted with a full understanding of their respective designs, and with an appointment of the time and place when they should again meet at Kingston, after Gertrude had visited and conferred with her friends on the American side.

When Miss Van Kleeck returned to her apartment, Ruth was greatly surprised at her changed demeanor, but still more at the secrecy which her friend was compelled to observe in relation to the visit she had received.

"Do not ask me now, dear Ruth," she said; "all that is proper for you to know, I will tell you hereafter. It is enough that there is something more to be done for Harry, and that there is *some*, oh, how little, I fear it is yet! *some* hope remaining."

Not less was the astonishment of Mr. Strong, who returned to his hotel, accompanied by a medical man, prepared to restore Gertrude from a state of syncope, and who found her already revived by a more powerful medicine than any described in his pharmacopœia, and making active preparations for departure in the evening steamboat, on her return to Kingston.

He did not seek to dissuade her, for he had no longer the least hope that any change could be wrought in the views of the governor, and he thought that the sooner the friends of the prisoner could reconcile their minds to his approaching and inevitable fate, the better it would be both for them and him.

He did not question Gertrude in regard to her change of deportment, supposing that she had resolved to devote the few remaining days of her friend's life to solacing him with her sympathy and with those lofty and glorious hopes of immortality, in the light of which all earthly joys and sufferings alike dwindle into insignificance. They left the capital that night and arrived the next day in Kingston where the humane lawyer, after conducting the ladies to their hotel, parted with them with many expressions of kindness, and with a promise to call upon them daily during the remainder of their stay in the city.

Garret and Brom were awaiting their arrival with great anxiety, and with no little hope that they were to bring a full pardon for the prisoner, whom they had encouraged to look for such a result.

"Has she got the pardon, Missa Roof?" the negro eagerly inquired, while Van Vrank sought similar information from his cousin.

"Oh! I know she has," he added, with delight, "because she does not cry. Let me go quick and tell him."

Ruth commenced weeping, and this was the negro's answer, confirmed the next instant by the voice of Gertrude herself, who turned from her sorrowful cousin to her faithful servant, and said, while large tears coursed down her cheeks,

"No, Brom, the governor will do nothing for us. Yet let us hope still in the Great Governor of all. We must have faith."

"Yes!" replied the negro, with a very frightened look and a very earnest manner, "we must hab faith; but Massa Harry has been *tried*, and *convicted*, and *sentenced*, and if the gubernor don't *pardon* him, dey will sartinly *hang* him, Missa Getty, you may 'pend upon it."

"Not unless it is God's will," replied the young lady, sighing deeply.

"I don't tink dey care any ting 'bout dat," replied Brom, who utterly failed to comprehend the strength and simplicity of his young mistress' reliance upon Omnipotence.

"Let no one announce this news to him excepting myself," continued Gertrude. "Garret, you will go with me to the prison in about half an hour; but remember that I must talk with Harry alone."

"I wouldn't tell him for a tousand dollars," said the affectionate negro. "I bin telling him all along how sartin sure you would bring a pardon, 'cause Massa Strong went with you hissef; but he would not believe it, and he said he knew this new risin' over on t'other side would make the gubernor so angry, he would not listen to you. See, he was right—poor Massa Harry!"

CHAPTER XL.

A SAD INTERVIEW.

It was with much trepidation that Gertrude anticipated her approaching interview with Harry, whom as yet she had not spoken with since the hour that he bade her farewell in her own quiet home on the banks of the Hudson—that oft-regretted hour, when a word of kind and earnest dissuasion from her might have kept him away from this disastrous war and all its awful consequences. Had she not then been too anxious to conceal the one great secret of her life, her pure and blameless affection for him, what long and bitter hours of anguish might she not have been spared, and what a fearful fate might have been averted from him.

Could it yet be averted? Ah! she would not count the cost now, whatever might be the wounds her sensitive heart must feel, whatever censure an ill-natured world might heap upon her—she would bear it all to atone for that one moment's remissness, and bring him back to life and happiness, even although not to her.

Let us not attempt to depict her emotions when, sustained by the manly Van Vrank, she entered the gloomy precincts of that prison-house, whence so many of her countrymen had passed to the unknown world, and where Harry Vrail was that moment looking forward with hopeless expectation to a similar fate. The massive doors opening and closing with terrific clangor around her, the long, dark corridors, echoing with the sound of her own footfall upon the floor of stone, the checkered light of heaven entering through the iron-barred windows—all was new to her, and terrible in its novelty.

Clinging to her cousin, she approached the cell in which Vrail was confined, and when near it, Garret left her for a moment, by her own request, that he might apprise Harry of her coming. He then conducted her to the door, and leaving her again, he paced the hall, at a distance where he might watch over her safety, and yet not overhear the conversation. It was early in the day, yet the light which found entrance into the cell was, fortunately for Harry, not sufficient to reveal either his pallor or his great agitation at this dismal meeting.

Poor Gertrude thrust her little hand between the bars of the door without an effort to speak, and yet without the possibility of restraining either her tears or her sobs.

"Do not weep for me, dear Gertrude," he said, at length; "the worst of my suffering is already past. May the Almighty Father bless you for all that you have done for me; for the noble heroism with which you have befriended me, and for this last act of kindness, which you need not tell me has been unavailing. I knew that it would be so. I am fully prepared to hear that the governor has refused to listen even to your intercession."

"I did not intercede—I could not speak to him," sobbed Gertrude; "but oh, Harry, if you could have heard that dear child Ruth, plead for you! His heart must be iron to resist her."

"Poor Ruth. I know, dear Gertrude, you will ever be her friend."

"She is my sister forever—but let us not talk of her now. Listen to me, for I must speak lower, and on a different theme."

Gertrude gazed earnestly around, to see that no one could hear what she was about to utter, and then she hastened to impart sparingly to Harry her new hope; for, while she was unwilling to leave him a moment in ignorance of it, she was also fearful that he might seize upon it with too much avidity.

She did not disclose to him all the particulars of the proposed rescue, for there were some details which, for reasons that will become obvious, it was designed to conceal even from him; but she told him of the great confidence expressed by their new friend in the success of his scheme.

Harry listened to her with a mournful silence, which gave no token of too sanguine expectation.

"For your sake, dear Gertrude," he said, "I will consent to have these dead hopes revived, even though they must in part distract my mind from those higher interests to which it should be given; but I cannot conceal from myself that success in such an undertaking as this would be most extraordinary, and is not to be anticipated."

"Not more extraordinary, Harry, than that Heaven should raise up such a friend to aid us, when all other help fails. Be at least hopeful enough to use all necessary means for making this last effort."

"I will—and if I cannot look upon what seems to me as the rash scheme of a sanguine boy, as a token of Providential interference, I will, at least, accept your unfaltering goodness and perseverance, dear Gertrude, as such an intimation. I will hope, and I will leave nothing undone on my part."

"You give me new courage now, Harry, and I shall go about my task with energy."

"But I must exact one promise from you—dear Tom must not come here. I will not have him incur any risk of taking my place in these horrid quarters. Promise me this."

"I certainly promise it, as far as it is under my control. But is there not danger that if your own brother stands aloof, others will refuse to come to your aid?"

"Not at all, for his would be a double risk, since, as an officer of the patriot army, his life would be regarded as already forfeited, and, if taken in this attempt, there could be no hope for him. No—I will never consent to his coming, even if the plan must be abandoned without him."

"He shall know all you say."

"But, Gertrude, there is one man, if he can be found, and can be induced to take part in this enterprise, who will be a host in himself; a brave, sagacious, wise man, who will find his own coadjutors, and will lead them. Let him but be convinced that there is any probable ground of success, and he will gladly undertake it, although less out of regard for me, than for the glory of the achievement, and from hatred to this government."

"Oh, tell me his name. I will find him—I will find him. He shall surely come and save you."

"Ah! Gertrude, restrain these too confident hopes. Weeks might be spent in the vain search for him of whom I speak, or if he were to be found, it might only be to assure you of the impracticability of all your plans. He knows too well the strength of British prisons, and the vigilance of British guards, to count lightly on the prospect of wresting any one from their keeping. Of all men, I fear he would be most likely to take a common-sense view of the enterprise, and to declare it impossible."

"No, no, no! not when he knows all that I can tell him."

"If he could but see Hadley"——

"He shall—he shall. I will in some way bring about an interview. They shall certainly meet. I have been told that there are islands very near to us on this mighty river, which do not belong to the British crown, but which form a part of our own country; and, better still, that some of these are uninhabited. He shall come to one of these, and Hadley will meet him there.

I know he will, for whatever may be his motive, he is fully in earnest in helping us."

"Your cheerful hopes are infectious, dear Gertrude, and I catch a portion of your sanguine spirit; but I fear the time is too short to accomplish so much."

"There is abundant time, with the means that I shall use; but it must not be wasted in words. The name—tell me the name of this powerful ally!"

"Come nearer, if you can, for it is one which I scarcely dare to utter on Canadian soil."

Gertrude pressed closer to the bars, and heard the faintly whispered name, long familiar to her ears, of "*William Johnson.*"

"With Thomas' aid you may possibly be able to find him," continued Harry, "but if you fail to do so, you must accept the next best assistance you can obtain. Your cousin Van Vrank, I suppose, is in the secret of this undertaking?"

"Not yet, but at the proper time both he and Brom will know all, and I count upon them both for efficient aid. Brom, I really believe, would lay down his life to save you; and Garret, although not quite so loyal, is brave and strong, and will be willing to encounter great risks in your service. If you have but few friends, they are all faithful."

"Ah! how undeserving am I of all this kindness."

"Before you see me again," interrupted Gertrude, "you will have seen Hadley, and he will have made known to you all the particulars of his scheme. Do not mistrust him, nor fear to be fully guided by his instructions. And now, farewell."

"Farewell, dear Gertrude. Do not hope too much, nor fear that my sufferings will be aggravated by failure, if we are destined again to disappointment. I shall hope sparingly, and whether my days be few or many, they will all be brightened by the remembrance of your kindness. If I perish, forget me, and do not idly mourn my fate, which you will have done all in your power to avert."

Gertrude did not reply; but beckoning Garret to approach, she took his arm, and departed in silence.

CHAPTER XLI.

AN INQUISITIVE MAN.

WITHIN a few hours after her visit to Vrail, Gertrude was on her way to Ogdensburgh, accompanied by her cousin, who was as yet ignorant of the object of her journey, and who was contented to be her escort and protector, without inquiring into any secrets which she chose to withhold.

Leaving the gentle girl to pursue her heroic mission, let us return to take a brief view of the doings of another actor in this eventful drama.

During nearly two days after the rejection of the petition for the pardon of Vrail, the governor's young guest remained at his house and to the surprise of Sir George, he did not again allude to a subject in which he had at first manifested so great an interest. Nor was there any change in his usual deportment, excepting in an increased vivacity of manner, and at times in even an extraordinary hilarity of spirits. In truth, the young man, partly from constitutional tendency, and partly from satiety of enjoyment, was the frequent victim of *ennui*, that bane of the happiness of the great; and it was only by some exciting occupation that this evil spirit could be fully exorcised. The topic which now occupied his mind was chiefly fascinating to him, because there were obstacles to overcome, and triumphs to achieve; yet the gratification of his naturally humane feelings was still a prominent element in the motives which actuated him, as it had originally been the only cause of his interference. But it would be useless to seek to fully analyze the secret spring which move a heart like his, accustomed to wild and irregular impulses, prone to strange and daring deeds because they *are* strange and daring, and unaccustomed to feel, although perhaps to acknowledge, any real fealty or fear for governmental authority.

On the second morning after the departure of Gertrude and her friends from the capital, Hadley announced his intention of immediately visiting the Lower Province, which he had for some time contemplated, and he would stop a few days at Kingston, he said, to see that city and its military works, and to make the acquaintance of some of the army officers to whom he had brought letters of introduction from England.

"I shall want to see all the lions while I am there, and one of them will doubtless be this young and handsome American lieutenant, so soon to be executed," he said, alluding for the first time to Vrail since his signal discomfiture (as Sir George complacently regarded it) in the argument about the propriety of his pardon. "If you can give me a brief line to the sheriff, or to the keeper of the prison, it will afford me an easy access to him, and save me the necessity of any personal solicitation."

Sir George was too polite to refuse so small a request, and being in a very self-satisfied mood in regard to the final disposition of this question, he wrote a very potent passport for his young friend, requesting that every facility might be afforded him to view the prison, and to see and converse, if he chose, with any of the inmates.

"I do not think it will be necessary," he said, handing the folded note to Hadley, "as your name itself would secure you admission, which, indeed, is very freely granted to the friends of prisoners under sentence of death. If you should have any curiosity to witness his execution"——

"Not the least, I assure you," replied B——, with an involuntary shrug of the shoulders.

"I dare say the jailer could give you a private box," said Sir George, smiling, "and it might be worth while to see how these men, who boast so much of their valor, can meet death."

"It is not worth *my* while, nor would I jeopard my night's sleep by such a sight," replied Hadley, who immediately changed the subject of conversation, lest some chance word or look of his should betray to the astute governor, the strange, deep interest which he felt in the fate of Vrail.

The next day he was in Kingston; but strange to say, he delivered no letters of introduction and sought no acquaintances, but entering his untitled name upon the register of the hotel at which he stopped, he remained unrecognized as a traveller of distinction, or as a man of noble family. He did not, indeed, expect or desire to remain *incognito* during the whole of his stay at Kingston, but he wished to avoid attracting any present attention which might impede his actions in the project he had at heart. His servant was dispatched to another inn, with instructions to take no notice of him, and not to disclose his station; and although the fellow entertained not the least suspicion of his master's design, he was too well used to similar disguises, for less worthy objects, to admit of much surprise or curiosity. At all events, he was faithful and trustworthy, and B——'s secret, if known, would have been inviolable with him.

Hadley did not deliver the governor's letter to the sheriff. He chose, for obvious reasons, to present it to the keeper of the city prison, on whom he correctly expected that both it and his own rank, which the letter disclosed, would make a profounder impression.

Early in the evening of the day on which he arrived in the city, he drove to the jail, and made known his errand to the keeper, whom he transformed at once, by virtue of the governor's note, and his own revealed rank, from a somewhat dignified official, to a very obsequious attendant upon his requests.

"It was late," the warder said, "and the halls were locked for the night, but if Mr. B—— wished to see any of the prisoners that evening, he should be gratified, certainly."

"You have an American officer here?"

"Oh, yes, quite a number of them, sir; they are thinning out, however—three were *turned off* last week, and one more will go soon."

"What! released?"

"Oh, no, sir! Oh, bless you, no, sir!"

"Ah! yes, I understand. Do you witness the executions?"

"Always, sir—always. I usually stand very near, and "——

"Let me ask you how they deport themselves. My cousin, the governor, is quite curious on this point."

"Well, sir," replied the officer, who hesitated between his regard for truth and his desire to please his auditor and Sir George, "I must say that they go through it very handsomely, sir—that is to say, sir, they continue stubborn to the last; they don't flinch."

"Yes, I understand; they conduct themselves in a way that you would call courageous, if it were in a better cause."

"They do, sir—they certainly do! They are really brave men sir, whatever else they may be."

"There is a young lieutenant here, by the name of Vrail, I believe?"

"Yes, he is to be hung next Friday. He is a harmless-looking fellow enough, though he is said to have been a desperate fellow among those brigands, as we call them. I dare say he richly deserves his fate."

"Ah! indeed. Now, Mr. ——, as I am an idle traveller in the provinces, and curious to see and learn all that I can, I should really like to converse a while with one of the leading men in this strange invasion, which excites so much interest at home. It will be something to tell of there, you know, when the Canadian troubles are discussed."

"Certainly, sir, certainly; you are, of course, quite welcome to see any of the men, or all of them, as much as you please."

"I think I should like to see this Mr. Vrail, of whom so much is said."

"Yes, sir. Do you wish to see him this evening?"

"Yes, at once, if he is disengaged," replied Hadley.

"Oh, as to that, he has not many engagements," replied the turnkey, jocosely, "and he is pretty sure to be at home to visitors."

"Of whom he has not many, I presume?"

"No, not many, sir. He has one friend, a sort of Dutch Yankee, who comes every day to see him, and there is a negro comes occasionally, who was his servant in the war, and who was in prison here with him awhile, but who got clear by some hocus pocus, I don't exactly know how—probably because he was not considered worth hanging. We allow them each to come once a day, if they choose."

"Are these all the friends he sees?"

"No; there was a young woman here, day before yesterday, quite a handsome girl, indeed, and very well-behaved, who talked with him for half an hour or more, at the cell door. I quite pitied the poor thing, who, I suppose, is his sweetheart; but she did not look so very much distressed when she went out, either. Probably she has other strings to her bow."

"Probably she has," replied Hadley, significantly.

"If you want to see Vrail, I will go with you to his cell directly."

"Ah! I do not like cells," said the young man, drawing out a scented handkerchief, and applying it to his face with a pretty air of affectation; "there is always a bad odor about them. As I may want to converse with this—brigand for some time, and possibly more than once, is there not some convenient room of your own in which you could allow me to see him?"

"I should be really happy to accommodate you," replied the keeper, with rather a frightened air, "if it can be done safely—but he is said to be a desperate fellow."

"Is he very large and strong?"

"Oh, no, sir—quite slight and delicate-like."

"Is he not chained?"

"Yes, he has chains upon his ankles, but he can take very short steps."

"And do you really think there is danger of such a man, so situated, getting away from us?"

"Well, I suppose not. I will tell you what I will do. Here is a room," he continued, leading the way to a good-sized apartment, which opened into the main lower hall of the building, a few feet from the front door; "here is a room which has sometimes been occupied by prisoners whom we wished to deal lightly with, a kind of gentlemen, you know, and which is tolerably safe. It is used by my family now, and is, as you see, comfortably furnished; but the windows are as strongly barred as any in the building, and if you choose to see the prisoner here, I will have him removed to this room for an hour or so, and will merely place a man on guard at the door."

"Outside?"

"Oh, yes, outside, of course."

"Very well, I will be much obliged to you, and I will mention your politeness to the governor."

The gratified officer summoned some of his men, and in a short time effected the desired change in Vrail's quarters, without at all taking pains to explain to the prisoner the cause of his removal or the exceedingly brief period which it was designed to permit him to enjoy his new and comparatively comfortable apartment.

CHAPTER XLII.

A VISIT TO A DESPERATE BRIGAND.

It was not until Hadley entered the room of the condemned man, and the key was turned upon them alone, that the latter suspected who his visitor was, and what was the nature of his errand.

It was a strange, sad meeting between two young and educated men, of refined minds and manners, whose ages were nearly equal, whose natural graces of person were not dissimilar, but whose present condition and prospects were, alas! how widely, how fearfully diverse! If Hadley had been so deeply interested in the fate of his companion before seeing him, how much was that interest enhanced by his first glance at the pale, intellectual features of the imprisoned youth, whose clanking chains, as he rose gracefully to return the salutation of his visitor, proclaimed the whole sad story of his fate.

Hadley advanced unhesitatingly, and offered his hand, saying, with his kindest smile,

"We shall need no introduction, I believe, Mr. Vrail; you have been informed both of my name, and of my object in calling to see you."

"I have certainly heard the whole story of your extraordinary kindness, if, as I cannot doubt, your name is"——

Harry paused with instinctive caution. He dared not supply the name, lest he might be mistaken in his visitor. The sentence was, however, finished by his companion.

"Edward Hadley B———. You have heard it from one who has your welfare deeply at heart, and whose distress has enlisted my services for you."

"She is an angel," exclaimed Harry, enthusiastically, "and if it were only for the few days more of hope which your aid and efforts must give her, I shall thank you with my latest breath."

"I hope to render you more efficient service than that," replied Hadley, smiling; "indeed, I may say, I feel confident of so doing, if Miss Van Kleeck succeeds in her part of the undertaking."

"But I cannot understand how a few, or many men are to obtain access to me, even if they should obtain peaceable entrance into the main building. There will still be two doors to be forced, and that in the presence of several guards."

"I do not intend they shall undertake any such miracles. This room, I think, will afford better facilities for your rescue, and I have already taken the initiatory step in my scheme, by having you brought here to-night."

"But I shall not be allowed to remain in this apartment."

"Certainly not. Yet you will be brought here again to meet me, and again, if my present designs succeed, when I shall *not* be here, and when your friends, concealed about the building, shall have an opportunity to rush in and bear you off, chained as you are. This door, if necessary, must be quickly forced. Used thus only for a temporary purpose, it is but singly locked, and these heavy bolts, as you see, are not turned.

"But the outer door?"

"Will be opened to give exit to one who is to visit you here. That is the critical moment which must be seized by those outside, and on that everything depends. Remember, too, at that particular instant the door of this room will probably be unlocked, as they will be in the act of removing you to your cell. If otherwise, it must, as I said, be forced, or the turnkeys must be overpowered, though of course not harmed, and their keys taken from them. These at least, are the chances on which we must calculate. Everything, of course, is liable to be defeated by unforeseen events, but I have not the least doubt," added the young man, with flashing eyes, which spoke his delight in daring deeds, " that I could accomplish this successfully, with three strong followers, and one able coadjutor inside. But, of course, I cannot compromise myself so far; indeed, it is even my intention, to be out of the city on the evening when the rescue takes place."

"Or is attempted," added Vrail, sadly.

"I cannot look upon it as a failure," was the reply; " and I should be deeply chagrined and grieved at such a result."

The pretext, under which Hadley intended to introduce a confederate into the prisoner's room, he did not disclose to the latter, for he had been warned by Gertrude that, however readily Vrail might consent to, or take part in a forcible rescue, he would perhaps refuse, in the solemn prospect of death, to be a party to any scheme of deception. Gertrude's own scruples on this point had not been light, but uncertain of her duty, she had not dared to jeopard the momentous interests at stake, by urging objections which she thought might be misplaced, and which her gay confederate laughed at as the merest puerilities.

An assumed lawyer, from "the States," was to be the prisoner's visitor, for the pretended purpose of drawing the will of the doomed man, who had the reputation of wealth, owing to the large sums of money which had been expended on his defence. This story Hadley believed would excite no suspicion, and he had decided upon it as the best of many schemes which he had contemplated.

"It will be painful to me," said Vrail, after a pause, "to be compelled to be an inactive witness of the struggle which must take place, as I can do nothing with my limbs thus hampered. If your interest could release me from these chains, I am sure I should be equal to any two opponents in a contest in which my life was at stake."

"I expected this suggestion from you, but I have already decided, after the most mature deliberation, against attempting it for two reasons. One of them is the very great danger of exciting suspicion of our plan, and thus defeating all hope of success, and the other is purely selfish and personal with me. It would almost convict me of being an accomplice in your escape, of which I shall be tolerably sure to be suspected at the best."

"Doubtless you are right. I must be content to be an idle spectator of my own rescue, or to do what little my bonds will permit."

"You will find enough to do in exercising a vigilant supervision of the scene, when the critical moment arrives, so as to take instant advantage of every favorable contingency. Accident, or what we call so, often favors the best laid schemes more than all the wisdom that is bestowed upon them, and, I need not say, it sometimes frustrates them. Your business will be to watch."

"This attempt must of course take place in the evening?"

"Of course, and at as late an hour as practicable. Your visitor will come in the evening, but not late, lest he should be refused admittance; and he must remain with you here, probably until as late an hour as nine o'clock."

"If anything should occur to require more precipitate action?"

"Of course you will be guided by circumstances, your friends outside being warned to be ready at any moment, yet patient enough to wait quietly as long as may become necessary. They must be prepared too for an instant alarm and pursuit when the rescue is achieved. A stout carriage and fleet horses, with frequent relays, must serve them until they gain a safe place to embark.'"

"Should we not instantly seek the river at the nearest point?"

"Certainly not; your boats must be at some distance from the city, for the whole town will be aroused by the tumult and the chase, and it will only be when you have fairly distanced both the pursuit and the clamor, that you can safely leave your carriage. Any attempt to do so within the city, where an enemy might spring up at any point, would be dangerous in the extreme. If your embarkation were not altogether prevented, your boats would be fired into, and your lives endangered."

"I see that you have fully digested your plan, and that it cannot be amended by me. All these details I suppose you will communicate to Gertrude, or possibly, to the man who becomes the leader of this forlorn hope."

I shall confer with the leader of the rescuing party, if possible, but it must be under such circumstances of disguise or darkness as shall preclude all possibility of his recognition of me, if we should ever meet again. I trust my secret confidently to you and your fair friend, but to no more."

"Honor and gratitude will alike bind us to eternal secrecy, unless your own consent should at some future time permit us to name our benefactor."

"A not improbable contingency; for, if our scheme succeeds, I feel assured the time will come when I shall make open boast of what I do now under a cloud."

"I regret that you deem it necessary to leave the city before the attempt is made. I fear something may occur when the influence of your presence is wanting, to prevent our obtaining the full benefit of the privileges you are to bespeak for us."

"I am not decided to go. I will think further of it ; but, if in the city, I must be at a distance from you, and where I could be of no service in an emergency. Indeed, if I were at hand, I could do little to remedy a misstep."

The young men conversed at considerable length, and it was not until the jailer had twice unlocked the door and looked in upon the colloquists, that Hadley relieved his impatience by rising to depart.

"I have learned a good deal from this man," he said to the officer, as he went out, " and it is possible that I shall wish to converse with him again."

"Certainly, sir, at any time before next Friday. We can't make any engagements for him later than that, you know," replied the keeper, with a grim smile.

"Of course—of course; I shall probably find leisure to see him before that day."

"Or, if you should not, you may find others here who are equally able to give you the information you may wish."

"Very true. Then, as to this Mr. Vrail, if that is his name, he wants a favor of you, which I presume you will be quite willing to grant. Indeed, you may find it greatly to your interest to oblige him, as he is reputed to be a man of great wealth."

"Certainly, sir; if it is anything proper, I shall be very glad."

"Oh, he only wants to make his will; and he expects a lawyer here from the States to draw it for him. Perhaps he may leave you a valuable legacy for your civility."

"Oh, indeed! I am sure I should be very glad to do anything for the unfortunate man, but it is not much that I can do. He has no appetite, though we send him daily meals that are fit for—for a lord, sir. Three-fourths of the dishes come back untouched, sir."

The jailer omitted to mention that this choice fare was trebly paid for by his involuntary guest.

"When his counsel comes," continued Hadley, "he will, of course, want to see him alone, and perhaps for several hours. This room, which I have just left, will suit their purpose, and if it will not be disturbing your family too much to give up possession of it, I suppose you will allow them to occupy it."

"Oh, certainly, sir; they shall have it, and be quite welcome. I will just station a turnkey or two in the hall here, sir, as I have to-night. You know that is proper, sir, if it is only for form's sake."

And with many obsequious bows, the warder waited upon the young gentleman to the door, and expressed his sense of the high honor which his visit had conferred upon him.

CHAPTER XLIII.

THE OUTLAW AND HIS FOLLOWERS.

Miss Van Kleeck and her cousin, to whom, on their way to Ogdensburgh, she had fully disclosed the object of her errand thither, and who had zealously promised a hearty co-operation in her plans, repaired immediately after their arrival in that village, to the hotel in which Thomas Vrail was sojourning. They found the young man in a state of great grief and consternation, for he had received tidings of his brother's fearful doom, and he had not dared to anticipate any favorable result from the application to the governor. Gertrude herself, although buoyed by this new hope, and relieved by the necessity for continual action, had her moments of torturing anxiety and fear, far surpassing any that such a mind as the younger Vrail's could ever experience. Yet she came to him in the character of a comforter, whose office it was to solace and sustain.

She at once imparted to him as much of the new and daring project as she was at liberty to reveal, and, with an eagerness betokened by the trembling of voice and frame, she as speedily inquired if he knew anything of the present abode of that celebrated man, whose co-operation in their plan Harry had considered so essential to its success.

Her hopes fell with his reply.

"Johnson left here a week since for Oswego and other frontier villages, to visit and advise with the lodges in regard to future movements, but it is impossible even to guess at his present place of sojourn, and weeks might be spent in a fruitless search for him."

"He *has been* here, then," replied Gertrude, sadly, "and might have been detained—oh, that I had known it !"

There was an implied reproach in this remark which Thomas felt, and he at once perceived his own great remissness in not having tried to secure so powerful an ally for any contingency which might arise in relation to his brother's fate.

"Let us go in search of him," continued Gertrude, promptly; "if we fail to find him in Oswego, it will at least be as easy to enlist other aid there as here, and it has the advantage of being nearer Kingston than this."

Without rest, without delay, even for a meal, the travellers, accompanied by Thomas Vrail, immediately set out by express coach, and by the aid of frequent relays, they completed their hurried journey in the evening of the same day, although at too late an hour to admit of instituting any inquiries until the next morning.

The day was Tuesday, and but two more remained beside it for all the momentous action which was yet needed to give even a chance of success to their great enterprise.

Gertrude counted the hours as the miser counts the golden pieces which are wrung by torture from his grasp, each seeming more valuable than the last, and fleeter in its progress.

"You will make immediate and earnest inquiries for Johnson," she said to her friends, "and learn, if possible, if he is still here; or, if he has left, in what direction he has gone. While there is hope of engaging him, we will look for no other."

"Yet his name must not be mentioned," replied Thomas. "Hundreds who may have seen and conversed with him yesterday, would deny that they had ever met him. Ask only for "——

"For whom ?" inquired Gertrude, impatiently.

"I had almost forgotten that I am not at liberty to tell the name by which alone he is now known, if here. But you may safely leave all inquiries to me. If he is in town, or if he has been here within the last few days, I can learn it without fail, and probably within a very few minutes. Hunters here are plentier than blackberries in August."

Vrail, in fact, telegraphed his landlord at the breakfast table, learned that he was one of the secret fraternity, and within a few minutes after the meal was ended, they were closeted together. Familiarly addressing the stranger who, by a motion of the hand, had been converted into a friend and ally, Thomas said,

"I wish to find Mr. Miller, the Commodore's friend and agent, whom, of course, you know. I parted with him a week since at Ogdensburgh, and he expected to visit this place."

"He was at the lodge night before last," replied the other, and gave us a full account of the affair at Windmill Point. He assured us, too, of Johnson's safety, of which we had great fears; but Mr. Miller has actually seen him on this side since the battle. The house rang with cheers at the announcement."

"I doubt it not. He fully deserves his great popularity. I, also, can vouch for his safety, if need be, having crossed the St. Lawrence in his company."

"Is it possible? You, then, were in the battle?" exclaimed the other, extending his hand and grasping his companion's, as if that circumstance gave him a new claim upon his regard.

"I was, and at another time I will relate to you, or to your lodge, if they desire it, all the information in my possession; but at present I have the most urgent business with this Mr. Miller, and I must speedily find him, if it is possible to do so. Important interests are involved in the success of my search. Can you assist me?"

"I will certainly do all that I can," was the zealous reply. "In two hours I can see all our people, and if he is here you shall see him; if he is gone, you shall know whither."

The two hours did not elapse without the complete fulfillment of the promises of the good-natured landlord, who not only found the disguised outlaw, but triumphantly brought him, "much amazed, and wondering much," into the presence of Vrail.

They were left alone in the room of the young man, who, greeting him warmly, expressed his great gratification at the meeting.

"Your messenger was just in time," replied the other; "in half an hour I should have started on my return home, for I have seen our friends in a dozen villages, and I am convinced that nothing can be done at present; we must at least lie still for a few weeks, or do you bring better news from other quarters?"

"I bring no good news, but I am at least glad that you are disengaged. I have travelled express from Ogdensburgh to find you."

"My disguise, then, is discovered; I am pursued? Or, still worse, my children"——

"No, nothing of this. Your children are safe; your disguise is unsuspected. It is for myself, or rather for poor Harry's sake that I have sought you. He is to die on Friday, if there is no possibility of rescue."

Johnson shook his head slowly, as he replied, "If rescue had been possible, Van Shoultz should not have died, nor Woodruff, nor Abbey. I would have risked my life for either of those gallant men, had there been the shadow of a chance to save them; but there was not. And your poor brother will share their fate. Do not for a moment indulge any other hope. We may avenge, but we cannot save him."

"I fear you are right," replied Thomas, sadly; "but before you decide fully on this, you must see Miss Van Kleeck, who is here with me, and who, indeed, has done all that has yet been done towards assisting Harry. She has much to tell you, and something that even I am not to know."

"Her conduct is most praiseworthy, yet I am sorry she is here

14*

with any hope of help from me. It will be painful to disappoint her."

"You will see her, and hear what she has to say?"

"I would willingly do so, if it were not uselessly confiding my disguise to another party. She knows me only as Mr. Miller."

"You need not fear to trust her. By design, of course, she cannot betray you, and whatever may be the result of this dreadful business, we shall both in a few days return to our distant home, where an accidental allusion to your secret, if we should be indiscreet enough to make it, would do you no harm. I beg that you will see her."

Johnson reluctantly complied, and Gertrude was admitted, trembling, to his presence. Great was her astonishment to learn that the hero, whose name was in so many mouths, and whose deeds had been blazoned so far, was the same quiet and gentlemanly man whom she had met on her first arrival at Ogdensburgh, and who then had so kindly and mildly counselled her in regard to her course of action in Canada.

His manner was not essentially different now, until she had related to him, in an earnest and impassioned manner, the particulars of Lieutenant Vrail's trial, and until she began to impart to him her reasons for hoping that a rescue might be effected.

As these were gradually disclosed, the countenance of the outlaw underwent a rapid change, and when she had told him all that she was at liberty to reveal, and had assured him of the rank and influence of her ally in Canada, his demeanor exhibited the utmost interest and excitement.

He asked her numerous questions, to which she replied, as she had uttered many of her previous remarks, in an under-tone, which even Thomas, who had seated himself apart from the eager colloquists, was not allowed to hear.

"I will see this man," he replied, at length, with strong emphasis, rising from his chair as he spoke, "if he will meet me on

Grand Island, or on any smaller island near to Kingston. I will hear all his plan from his own lips, and if there is half the chance for rescue which you fondly imagine, I am ready to make the attempt with half a dozen followers, if they can be found of the right material. It would be a triumph to snatch one victim from the jaws of this devouring lion—yes, a triumph to be remembered through life. It would repay some of the many humiliations and defeats we have been compelled to suffer."

Gertrude's relief was inexpressible at this announcement, and she vainly tried to speak her thanks to the valiant man, nor did Thomas exhibit scarcely less satisfaction.

But the deportment of the outlaw clearly showed that his thoughts were far less occupied with the idea of saving a single life, however valued, or of winning the gratitude of his companions, than with the renown of the anticipated achievement, and the mortification it would inflict on the officials of the Canadian government.

"But," he said, suddenly, "we must go as fully prepared for the undertaking as if it were already decided upon. There will be no time to find men and means after consultation with your noble friend. All must be done here, and now. Yet it will be difficult, perhaps impossible, to procure sufficient volunteers for this work on so short notice."

"We have considered all this," replied Gertrude. "We cannot expect that the fame of a noble action will of itself be a sufficient inducement to common men to enter upon a perilous enterprise. But while you can doubtless find those whom the renown of the exploit, and the honor of following so distinguished a leader, will in a great degree repay for their risk, we are prepared to add the additional incentive of a liberal pecuniary reward. Neither shall there be any stint of means for any of the expenses of the expedition. In this purse," she continued, extending a bulky *porte-monnaie* to Johnson, and pressing it into his hands, "you will find a large sum, yet not so large but that it can be doubled or quadrupled at a moment's notice, if necessary for our purposes. Use it as freely as you find occasion for, and call on me when you need more."

Both Johnson and Vrail looked in astonishment at the noble girl, and the former, after a moment's pause, replied,

"This is the ring of the true metal; could we infuse your spirit into our men, we might almost count on certain victory. I will take this money, and I will use it as you desire, freely; nor do I doubt that by its aid I can secure as many able and reliable followers as we can safely use. What remains of your treasure shall be returned to you, for I will take none of it."

"There will nothing remain," replied Gertrude, "which could be a fitting reward for services like yours; yet I shall hope to find means to induce you to change your resolution hereafter, and to accept for yourself at least as much as I have given you to dispense."

"Hope it not. I could do nothing great from such a motive, or while liable to the suspicion of sordid views. No, I will yet redeem my country, or I will remain an outlaw and an exile, but never a mercenary soldier, nor a recipient of charity. Lieutenant Vrail is entitled to all the aid I can render, and Sir George Arthur to all the annoyance I can inflict, and I will take pay for neither the one nor the other."

Gertrude did not press a point which gave such evident pain; but resolving in some way to requite so great an obligation, she consented to dismiss the subject for the present.

Little time was wasted in further consultation. Johnson immediately began his quest for assistants, and fortunately his extensive acquaintance with the warlike members of the Oswego Lodge enabled him at once to select in his own mind the very persons who would be most useful and reliable for such an enterprise as that on which he was bound.

They were all men of much physical strength and of proven courage; they had all enlisted for the war, and like hundreds of others, having proceeded to Ogdensburgh, had only been restrained from crossing by the defection of their leaders. To these men he went privately and made himself known, although with some difficulty, for they could not easily dispel the hallucination which had made two men of one, whom they intimately knew in both characters.

Their delight was equal to their astonishment at the discovery, and such was their enthusiasm for and their confidence in the heroic leader, that out of six men to whom he applied, he readily secured the services of five, without revealing to them anything but a very indistinct outline of the enterprise upon which he was bound. This number he considered quite sufficient, together with Van Vrank and the negro, whom Gertrude had assured him could be fully relied upon for an active participation in the work.

More he was convinced would only encumber his movements and jeopard secrecy, without increasing the chances of success. A small band of resolute men was what he needed, and it is saying much for his recruits to record that he was fully satisfied with them.

Having secured this important step, he next turned his thoughts to selecting a place of conference with Hadley, and to the best mode of reaching it with his men. A small island, well known to him, which was near the foot of the lake, and near the city of Kingston, was selected for this purpose, but how to reach this point, nearly sixty miles distant, in the necessary time and with the requisite supply of boats and munitions, became the most serious object of inquiry.

He hastened to the harbor, and learned that a small steamboat, which had been used for coasting voyages, was lying idle in port, and could be chartered for a few days for any part of the lake, though at an expense so large that he feared even the liberal Gertrude would shrink from encountering it. He was, of course, mistaken. He found her not less rejoiced than himself at what seemed a Providential supply of the very means best adapted for the prosecution of their daring enterprise.

With this vessel at their command, they could proceed directly to their desired rendezvous, taking with them the smaller boats which would be required to effect a landing, both there and on the Canadian shore, and all else that was necessary or might prove useful in their expedition. Provisions were hastily laid in, and weapons were carried on board in strange shaped boxes, which defied the attempts of the curious to divine their contents, and by sundown the little steamer, well "wooded and watered," and with her fires lighted, lay quietly beside the wharf, ready for instant departure. Her mysterious passengers did not come on board until after dark, and not an unnecessary minute was lost after their arrival in casting off the hawser and putting out to sea, the wondering crew being as much at a loss as the idlers upon the wharves as to the design of these unusual proceedings.

No difficulty was encountered in their voyage. The captain received instructions to sail for the upper end of Grand Island, and when near that point, which was long before dawn of day, Johnson was at his side to give minute directions for the remaining part of their course. It was not yet light when the adventurous voyagers landed, by means of their small boats, on the southern side of a very small island, less than half a mile from the Canadian shore, and but a few miles from the city of Kingston. This little territory was inhabited in the planting and harvesting seasons by a single farmer, who cultivated its few acres of productive soil, but whose home was on the main land, where he was now sojourning. The island was therefore now uninhabited, and had the additional advantage of a tenement, though of the poorest class and of very diminutive size.

These facts were known to Johnson, (whose roving life had

made him familiar with almost all the isles of the lake and river,) and they had influenced him in selecting this place of landing.

As it would have been unsafe to risk attracting attention to his quarters, by allowing the steamboat to be anchored near at hand, he instructed her captain to proceed at once down the river, and to return and pass the island at intervals of a few hours through the day, at as great a distance as would admit of observing a concerted signal, which was to call him, if needed, to his employers. If not sooner required, he was to approach the island after dark, although no immediate service was anticipated for the vessel.

Speedy measures were now taken to convey Gertrude and Van Vrank to Kingston, in order that the former might meet Hadley, and make arrangements for an interview between him and the venturous leader of the American party. Johnson had resolved to cross in the evening, and proceed to the city, where he was to take quarters at an obscure inn, under his assumed name, Miller, and await Mr. B—— or his messenger, if he chose to designate any other place of meeting. The name and locality of the inn were communicated to Gertrude, who also well knew the *alias* of the outlaw, and early in the forenoon she started for Kingston, in a small boat, accompanied by Garret and by two other men of her party. They rowed far enough down the lake, before turning shoreward, to avoid indicating by the direction of their approach to the land the point from which they had set out, and they selected a spot for landing, remote from any habitation, and several miles from the city. Only Garret and Gertrude left the boat, the oarsmen immediately returning to the island, and leaving the two former to complete their journey as best they could. This was no difficult matter to accomplish. They proceeded to the nearest farmhouse, and readily procured a conveyance to the city, where they at once sought their former hotel, and were received by the anxious Ruth with tears of mingled joy and sadness.

Gertrude had little time to weep. She heard her young friend's hasty narration of what little she had to tell about poor Harry's condition, whom she had daily seen and conversed with during the absence of Miss Van Kleeck, and when Ruth, in turn, looked anxiously to her friend for some word of encouragement, the latter dared only to repeat her former vague and unsatisfactory answers, intimating, indeed, that all hope was not abandoned, but leaving the child in a maze of wild conjecture as to the source of anticipated help.

CHAPTER XLIV.

NOBILITY IN DISGUISE.

GERTRUDE had not seen Hadley since her first and only interview with him in Toronto; she did not know whether he was in Kingston or elsewhere, and she could not but feel the greatest solicitude lest he might have entirely abandoned the cause to which he had been pledged, and for which his aid was so essential. Of his visit to Harry she as yet knew nothing, for it had taken place after her departure for Ogdensburgh, and she prepared at once to visit the prisoner, both to learn from him if he had yet seen their powerful ally, and to impart to him the encouragement which her success thus far was calculated to inspire. But before doing this, she addressed a note to Hadley, in pursuance of a preconcerted plan, in which she informed him of her return to the city, and of her place of sojourn, and obscurely hinted at the favorable result of her mission, to which she did not dare allude in express terms, lest her letter might fall into other hands than those for which it was designed.

For the same reason she was afraid to name the place at which he could meet Johnson, however vaguely she might speak of the man, or the object of the appointment.

But she wrote that "the man whom he desired to see" was in town, and that she would give his name and address to any messenger bearing a token from Mr. B——, by which she should know that he was authorized to receive them. Gertrude took this precaution because she feared that her distinguished friend, although he might be in the city, and anxious to aid her, would not be willing to increase the suspicion which he must in any event incur, by having an interview with her so recently before the *dénoûment* of the daring plot. She knew it would be almost impossible for a person of his celebrity to visit her at the hotel, however briefly, without it becoming known, and being made a subject of comment, for her own relation to the condemned prisoner, and her merciful, but supposed fruitless errand in Canada, were well known to many a sympathizing inmate of the house in which she sojourned.

Her letter, without external address, was sealed and enclosed in an envelope, on which she endorsed a name unknown to her, but which she had received from Hadley, and had carefully preserved for its present use.

This mysterious epistle, containing neither the name of the writer, nor of the person intended to be addressed, having been dispatched to the city post-office, Miss Van Kleeck hastened to a more painful and exciting duty.

It was necessary that her visit to Harry should be brief, to enable her to return home in time to receive the expected messenger from Hadley, who might come at any hour.

Garret accompanied her as before, and, as before, she saw her unfortunate friend only through the grated door of his cell. The reflection that, if the hazardous scheme of rescue failed, there remained only two days of life for the young and vigorous man who stood chained between the strong walls of that dark and narrow room, scarcely less dark and narrow than that dread abode which it seemed to typify, imparted an agonizing interest to the brief interview which ensued. They would meet there but once more, and on that momentous morrow which was either to break down the barriers between these separated friends, or was to establish others which only the Archangel's trump could remove. Let us draw a veil over these harrowing scenes.

Hurriedly and with whispered words they conversed, and although each had encouraging tidings to impart (Gertrude of the success of her mission, and Vrail of Hadley's visit), they stood too close within the shadows of that awful Future which they could not fail to contemplate, to admit of infusing anything like inspiriting hope into the breast of either.

In that Golgotha-like building, where the vacant cells seemed yet vocal with the last farewell of their slaughtered inmates, and where airy forms seemed to flit, beckoning, along the dark and silent corridors, what room was there for cheering influences, or for bright anticipations? But they talked of hope, and concealed, as far as possible, their doubts and misgivings; and Gertrude, before departing, promised her friend that she would see him again the next morning, when she hoped to have further and more encouraging tidings to impart.

Returned to the sunlight of the outer day, Gertrude felt something of its reviving influence, and upwards through the shining highway rose the unspoken orisons of her gentle soul, to that celestial city where man's great Intercessor hears the prayer of faith.

Notwithstanding her visit had been brief, and although she hastened back to her hotel as rapidly as the driver of her waiting carriage could be induced to proceed, she was too late to see the bearer of a note from Hadley, which she found awaiting her return. Yet, encouraged by the speedy answer, indicating the vicinity and the vigilance of her ally, she hastily broke the seal, and read only the following words, without date or signature:

"I will see you at seven in the evening, in your own room. Your cousin may be present."

She counted the hours until then, and punctual at the appointed time, a visitor was announced. She received with trembling eagerness the card, which bore an unknown name, and which was quickly followed by a person whom she believed, at first, to be equally strange to her.

Closely muffled in a cloak of no existing fashion, slightly stooping, as if with decrepitude, and leaning upon a heavy cane, the visitor entered the room, and casting a hasty glance around it, to see that no one was present but those whom he had appointed to meet, he closed and locked the door. He next threw off his faded cloak and his slouched hat, and resuming an erect position, the transformed and handsome young man quickly advanced to Gertrude, with extended hand, and with his usual winning smile.

"You will excuse me for coming to you in this manner," he said, "since you know the necessity for caution. Before I say more, let me ask if this gentleman "——

"He is my cousin of whom I spoke to you; you need not fear to speak freely before him."

Hadley bowed to Van Vrank, and continued,

"Tell me, then, quickly, if you have succeeded in your errand to the States. Your note speaks of but one man, and you have returned so soon, that I feared "——

"Fear nothing on my part," replied Gertrude, promptly, and with a sudden flashing of the eyes. "I have seven strong men bound almost by an oath to do this deed, and at their head a man who is himself a host in strength, and skill, and courage. He is now on Canadian soil, waiting to learn from your lips whether there is sufficient prospect of success to warrant him in bringing his brave comrades over."

"Where are his followers? How soon can they be obtained? Is he quite certain of them?" asked the young man, quickly, and with an appearance of great interest.

"Not an hour's journey from the city, they await his orders on an uninhabited island. They are provided with arms and with boats; and a steamboat, chartered for their use, is waiting to receive the retreating party when their work is done—or is abandoned."

Gertrude's voice trembled as she uttered the last three words, and she raised her handkerchief to her eyes to hide the starting tears.

"Truly, you have done your work well," replied the young man, with enthusiasm, "and you fully deserve the success I cannot doubt you will obtain. But I must not waste words nor time. I must see this disguised hero at once, and, unless he is very skeptical, I can convince him of the practicability of our scheme, if boldly and adroitly managed, and if marred by no accident."

"Those 'ifs' are separate daggers to my heart," replied Gertrude. "Pray, do not you, who have been so sanguine, talk of 'ifs.'"

"To you, indeed, I ought not, but your followers must know the difficulties of the enterprise, in order to be prepared to overcome them. Tell me now the name of your champion, or rather the name by which he is known here, and the place in which I am to seek him. I must find him at once, for at nine o'clock I am expected at Colonel A.'s, who entertains a party of friends, and at a later hour I am engaged to attend a military ball."

"And to-morrow evening?" asked Gertrude.

"For to-morrow evening I have accepted an invitation to visit the theatre, and see Macbeth murdered by some provincial actors. There I must act my part, too, and receive the intelligence of this great outrage with becoming astonishment and indignation. I should not be surprised if the play should stop and the audience disperse under the alarm of an invasion."

Gertrude trembled with agitation at every allusion to the great event of the ensuing evening, and she with difficulty composed herself sufficiently to give her companion the required address of Johnson. She gave his assumed name, of course, which, together with the name and location of the inn at which he could be found, she wrote on a slip of paper and handed to Hadley.

"And now for yourself, and your valiant little friend, Ruth," he said, "what arrangements have been made? You must be out of the city, you know, before the *dénoûment* takes place."

"Out of the city? Most certainly, we shall not leave it until the great question is decided."

"Most certainly you must. You would be unsafe here a moment after the rescue is effected."

"Unsafe?"

"Why, do not you think that you would be suspected of inciting this movement? You, who who have done so much in other ways to save your friend?"

"Doubtless I might. But is it a crime to assist a friend in distress—to rescue an innocent man from vindictive enemies, and from unmerited death? My men have the strictest injunctions to take no life, and to avoid all unnecessary violence."

Hadley smiled at the simplicity of his companion, as he replied,

"However justifiable your conduct may be in a moral point of view, it will certainly constitute a grave offence against the laws, and one punishable with much severity. There can be no doubt of this."

"What, then, shall we do?" asked Gertrude, after a moment's musing.

"Cross to Grand Island to-morrow, by the ferry, and there await your friend; or, better still (for, if the pursuit should be hot, they might not be able to stop for you), let Miller send his steamboat to the island to meet you. You can remain on board the vessel till your friends come."

"Yes, that is doubtless our best course," said Gertrude, with hesitation, for she reflected, with a shudder, that if the attempt at rescue should fail, she would then have seen Harry for the last time. She could not return to bid him a final farewell.

"Tell this to Mr. Miller," she continued, "and tell him that I must see him to-morrow, when his plans are matured, that I may communicate them to Mr. Vrail, whom I shall see once more before I leave. And you—when shall I see you again?"

"I shall travel through your country before I return home, and I shall certainly find you, or, if anything should prevent my doing so, the loss will be wholly mine. Farewell."

"I will not attempt to express the extent of my thanks for your kindness. You must comprehend the vastness of the favor you have sought to confer, and be assured my gratitude is proportionate to the obligation. Will you not see dear Ruth, that she, too, may thank you?"

"It is better not. I will do my best to see you both in your own home. Farewell."

Hadley resumed his ancient cloak, his heavy cane, his slouched hat and his stooping gait, and unlocking the door, he departed with remarkable celerity for a man of his seeming infirmities.

CHAPTER XLV.

A LAWYER WITH A SMALL LIBRARY.

In a small upper room of a dingy hotel by the river side, a middle-aged man, well dressed, and apparently much at his ease, sat smoking an unexceptionable Havana, and looking listlessly into the cheering fire which burned in a grate at his side. On a table near at hand lay a volume of New York statutes and another legal book, while a bulky portfolio beside them indicated the presence of writing materials within. These implements of his assumed profession had been furnished by the forethought of Gertrude, and Johnson had brought them with him now, in order that he might familiarize himself with their presence, and perhaps receive some hints from his more clerkly confederate as to the skillful handling of such strange tools.

His reverie, which seemed by no means a painful one, was interrupted by a knock at his door, and scarcely had he given permission to enter, when the disguised Hadley, who had been shown up by a servant, walked in unannounced.

Johnson's eyes glanced momentarily towards an overcoat which hung on the wall, in an inner pocket of which were the weapons he usually carried closer to his person, but which his legal dress did not admit of receiving. The singular apparel and deportment of his visitor had induced him to doubt whether he could be the man whom he was expecting to see, but at the next instant his misgivings were dispelled by an expressive smile on the stranger's face, and by the lady-like hand, flashing with a brilliant diamond, which was extended towards him.

"Your name is Miller, I believe?" said Hadley, taking a seat which was offered him, but without removing either cloak or hat.

Johnson bowed assent, and threw the remainder of his cigar into the fire.

"You are a barrister from New York?"

"No, sir—a lawyer; there are no barristers in our State."

"Right—it is well to remember the distinction. You have brought your library with you, I see, Mr. Miller."

The outlaw again bowed and smiled, as he observed the searching look of his companion.

"All of it, I presume?" again asked Hadley.

"All of it."

"I believe there can be no doubt that you are the man I am sent to. But you will excuse me, if I seek to make assurance doubly sure, before entering upon business of grave concern. There is a name which may serve as a watchword between us."

"Gertrude Van Kleeck."

"Right. It is a name, too, although strange to Anglo-Saxon ears, which the bravest knight of the days of chivalry might have been proud to bear to tournament or battle-field. If you were such a champion, she could not repose higher confidence in your valor and skill than she already does."

The outlaw smiled with evident satisfaction, as he replied,

"She is worthy of a brave man's fealty; yet I fear I should not be here to-night, had I not other motives than her service. It is something to inflict a humiliating blow, however slight, upon a tyrannical government."

It is unnecessary to detail the conference which ensued between these dissimilar confederates, which a subsequent narrative of its results will sufficiently explain. Let it suffice that Hadley was able to give his companion such satisfactory assurance of the promised

15

facilities for a rescue as to fully decide the latter upon making the attempt.

A little before nine o'clock in the evening they parted, the one to become the "observed of all observers" in a fashionable and brilliant assembly, the other to rejoin the concealed comrades, who waited to bear him back to their island refuge.

While these events were taking place, there were still two parties who were deeply interested in the fate of Harry Vrail, who as yet knew nothing of the intended rescue. In vain had the unhappy Ruth sought, again and again, to obtain from Gertrude some clue to the mysterious hopes at which she hinted, and which seemed sufficient to sustain her from despondency. The child had long ceased to ask, but her tear-filled eyes turned often with appealing glances to her friend, and she watched with strange interest every minute event which might throw light upon the clouded subject. She had some indistinct idea that Gertrude's visit to the States had been for the purpose of invoking the aid of her own government for its imprisoned citizen, and this hope grew and took shape in her mind, until it entered into her dreams, and she saw vast armies, with starry banners, come to demand the freedom of her unfortunate friend. From these visions she awoke to grief enhanced by the brief illusion.

"You shall know all to-morrow, dear Ruth," said Gertrude, on the evening of her last conference with Hadley, from which the wondering child had been excluded. "Be patient until then."

"I will try, Gertrude," she replied, faintly; "but oh, I am so frightened as the time draws nigh. Is there nothing that I can do?"

"Yes, Ruth, you can pray."

"Night and day—night and day!" exclaimed the frantic child, with clasped hands. "Oh, do you think He will hear?"

"Yes," replied Gertrude, with sudden enthusiasm, inspired by the beautiful picture of passionate supplication before her; "yes, Ruth, I believe that He will hear."

She drew the gentle child to her side, and together the fair young friends wept long and in silence.

With grief scarcely less deep or sincere, though more rudely expressed, did the faithful servant bewail his young master's fate, and his own impotency to aid him.

"I don't know, Massa Garret," he said, "what it all means. Dare is a great deal of comin' and goin' and talkin', but it don't amount to nothin'. These Britishers will hang Massa Harry day after to-morrow, as sure as a gun."

"I fear they will, Brom."

"'Course they will sir; he'll walk out of that back door I showed you, Massa Garret, and he knows it, too, only he don't want to scare Missa Gertrude by tellin' her so. She had better go home, she and little Roof, and then we'll come afterwards, and tell 'em he's only transported, and will come back one of these days, ten or twelve years from now."

Brom showed much emotion, and was quite in earnest in his proposition.

"It won't do, Brom," replied Van Vrank; "we could never deceive them in that way. They must know the worst, whatever it is."

"I bin thinking," continued the negro, after a little pause, and speaking in an embarrassed manner, as if he feared he might be presumptuously overrating his own importance, "I bin thinking whether dey wouldn't take me back and let Massa Harry off. I think I would do it, Massa Garret, for poor Missa Getty, that I've trotted on my knee when she was a baby, and who was always jis so good and kind. She'll die if Massa Harry dies, I know. You don't know all that I do about dis ting, and I ain't gwine to tell you—but I sartingly think I would do it. Do you think dey would swap?"

"What, and hang you instead of Harry?"

"Yes—I am a strong man."

"No, my good fellow, they would do no such thing; they would not hang you any way, not if you should ask them to."

"Dey are a set of heathens, den," replied Brom, indignantly, "and I am sorry we ever had anything to do with them."

CHAPTER XLVI.

THE WILL.

From the moment that the outlaw's interview with Hadley, terminated, all irresolution and indecision was banished from his mind, and he set himself earnestly at the task which he had undertaken, not, indeed, with a full confidence of success, nor entirely without personal apprehension, but with the conviction that the opportunity for a great achievement was one which a brave man ought to embrace.

At an appointed hour he met the boat which had been sent for him by his friends on the island, and returned to them to mature his plans by consultation, and to bring to the city that part of his daring band who were to take part in the attempted rescue.

An immediate council was held, at which some portion of the plan of operations was fully decided upon, while other points were necessarily left to the decision of the leader on the eventful morrow. Two of the small force were appointed to take charge of the boats, and bring them, at the appointed time, to a designated spot, a few miles from town, to meet their flying friends (for Hadley's warning, not to attempt to embark within or very near the city, had been regarded); yet for this least perilous service, it was so difficult to find volunteers, that Johnson was compelled to settle the question by his authority. Thomas Vrail, who, at Gertrude's earnest request, had been forbidden by the leader to touch Canadian soil, was placed in temporary command of the steamboat, with instructions to meet the returning skiffs as near shore as the captain, who was also the owner of the vessel, would allow it to venture. That personage, whose proclivities were all with the patriot cause, had entered fully into the spirit of the exciting enterprise on which his companions were bound; but he was a Yankee, whose first instincts were for the "main chance," and who well knew that his vessel would be forfeited, if taken by the Canadian authorities while employed in its present business. Not that he had any other fear of capture, excepting that which resulted from the peril of night navigation in an unknown channel, in which the boat might easily become stranded, and thus rendered a certain prey to the enemy on the ensuing day. Whatever he could safely do, however, he freely promised, and with an evident zeal, which left no doubt of his fidelity to the cause.

The remainder of the venturous party, only four in number, including their leader, crossed to Kingston a little before daylight on the ensuing morning, and each proceeded to take lodgings at a separate inn, and all at inferior ones, with the exception of a man by the name of Gordon, to whom was assigned a special service. He was to stop at the best hotel, and enact the part of a man of wealth, in order to enable him to purchase, without exciting suspicion, the necessary carriage and horses for the flight of the party after leaving the jail. Gordon was also to communicate with Miss Van Kleeck, informing her of the position of affairs, and was to arrange a meeting of all the confederates, including Garret and the yet uninitiated Brom, immediately after dark, when each might receive from the leader his assigned task.

The long day of anxiety and expectation wore heavily and slowly away for all but Gordon, whose *rôle* required vigilance, activity and sagacity, and who well performed his allotted part.

Gertrude made an early and brief visit to the prisoner, and, with pale lips and trembling voice, exhorted him to that courage which her own terrified heart almost refused to entertain. His bearing was calm and dauntless, yet it was the courage of fortitude rather than of hope. He was equal to the emergency of the hour, whatever might be its issue, yet it was agony to him to see the wretchedness of his friend. Their interview was short, their adieux were almost unspoken. Her ungloved hand, gliding like a sunbeam between the dark bars, rested a moment in his, was pressed a moment to his lips, and—she was gone.

Within an hour from that time, Gertrude and Ruth, accompanied by Van Vrank, had left the city, and were on their way to Grand Island, it having been arranged that the steamboat should approach that island early in the evening, and that a small boat should be sent to take them off. Van Vrank, after seeing them safely quartered at a small inn, returned to Kingston, still long before the close of day. The closely-watched skies, flecked with many passing clouds, gave promise of an evening of favorable obscurity; but whether the heavens should be overcast or not, the confederates had the consoling certainty of a moonless night for their daring enterprise.

Soon after twilight they met in an unfrequented spot on the shore of the river, where Gordon, the only man of the party who had gone openly about town, made report of his proceedings, and of whatever he had learned which might have a bearing upon their momentous undertaking. He had purchased a strong carriage, and a span of fleet horses, which he said he had already proved, by driving them at the rate of twelve miles an hour on the very road which they would have to travel that evening.

"With an empty coach, and you alone on the box," said Johnson.

"By no means—a gentleman of my cloth would not look well on the box," replied Gordon, who was richly dressed. "No, we had a driver, and there were four inside—the man of whom I bought the horses, two of his friends, and myself. We were five in all."

There will be seven to-night, including Vrail," said Johnson, musingly, and seeming to entertain no doubt of bringing off the prisoner.

"That is nothing; the coach is new and strong, and the horses I will be surety for. If I am a judge of anything, it is of horseflesh. As to the number, four can go easily inside, one can ride with me on the box, and we can put Cuffy on behind for ballast."

"Put yourself on for ballast, Massa Gordon, and speak more 'spectf'ly of colored gemmen."

This remark proceeded from an entirely invisible source, but it gave evidence that Brom was somewhere around in the darkness.

"I beg your pardon, Brom," replied Gordon, laughing; "I didn't know you were here; I meant no offence."

"Berry well, den I 'scuse you; and as to ridin' behind, ef we only get Massa Harry, I'll ride anywhere, I don't care ef it is on the hub of the wheel."

Johnson hastened to stop this unnecessary conversation, and to inform each man as distinctly as possible of what would be required of him. To Van Vrank, who was unarmed, he furnished a brace of loaded pistols, remarking that he did not anticipate any necessity for the use of them in the first instance, but that they might become necessary in case of a pressing pursuit. Humanity, as well as prudence, he said, dictated that no deadly weapon should be used upon the jailers, who, whatever the fault of their superiors, were but discharging their official duties. Brom he dared not intrust with fire-arms, lest he might indiscreetly use them, but he knew that his great physical strength might prove abundantly serviceable in the struggle they must have, and he cautioned him to stand ready to fight for his master when the proper time came, and not to be frightened by the sight of a few officers of the prison, even if there should be a half-dozen or more.

"I give you stout cords instead of pistols," he said, "and some of the rest of us will have the same. We may want to knock down and bind a man or two, and it is best to be prepared."

"Dat's a fact," replied the negro; "dese is jes de bery thing. Dis one to tie his hands, and dis ere stouter one to tie his legs. Brom will fix one on 'em, I bet. What's dis ting?"

"That is a gag. Did you never see a gag before? Very likely there will be no time to use these things, but it is prudent to have them. Whatever you do after the fight begins, must be done very quickly. Let all remember that."

Brom tried the gag in his own huge mouth, which nearly closed over it, and it scarcely proved an impediment to his speech.

"It's too *small*, Massa Miller," he said, without removing the wood, "dey can hollow like blazes for all dis."

"No it isn't, Brom," said Gordon; "all mouths ain't cellar-doors like yours."

"It ain't no use, I 'clare," answered Brom; "I could swaller it easy."

Again Johnson interfered to produce silence, and he proceeded hastily to instruct each member of the party as nearly as he could in the duty which would be expected of him, and to exhort them to a resolute and unflinching determination to effect their object. He cautioned them particularly against any sudden panic, whatever turn their adventure might take, or whatever unexpected opposition they might encounter.

"Be brave and cool, my boys," he said, "and we shall be certain of success.

All the confederates manifested much enthusiasm and ardor, not excepting the somewhat phlegmatic Van Vrank, who could not refrain from wondering at himself, transformed by gradual steps, and almost of necessity, from a quiet farmer on the banks of the Hudson, with no ambition but to mind his own business, to a member of something like a military band, about to storm a stronghold in a foreign country, which a few weeks before he had never even expected to see. But he was zealous now in the cause, not only for Gertrude and Harry's sake, but for his own, for he saw no better way out of the entanglement than to push matters bravely through to a successful termination.

When discussion was at an end, and the programme of proceedings was fully understood by all, the party dispersed to their several hotels, Johnson to prepare for an immediate visit to the prison, and Gordon to get up his coach and horses, and carry him there in a style befitting his assumed profession and errand. The others were to remain at their quarters until about half-past nine in the evening, when Gordon was also to call and convey them to the jail; in front of which, as if only waiting for the lawyer, the coach was to stand, like the wooden horse before ancient Troy, silent as the grave, but full of armed men.

Darkness had fully set in, though it was yet early. in the long autumnal evening, and less than half an hour sufficed for Gordon to rein up his champing steeds in front of Johnson's inn, and receive the latter (ostentatiously displaying his legal books and his bulky portfolio) into the carriage. He was entirely unarmed, for he knew there was a possibility of his being searched before being admitted to an interview with the prisoner; but his men were provided with weapons enough both for his use and their own, if exigencies should require them to be produced.

At the prison door, when he alighted and made inquiry pompously for the keeper, he was careful again to make a display of his books, and he was much relieved, on the appearance of the principal jailer, to find that few words were required to make himself known as an expected visitor, whose business was understood.

"You have come at the eleventh hour," said the keeper, when Johnson had almost unnecessarily told his assumed errand, "and I would much rather your visit had been made by daylight.

Perhaps even now there will be time in the morning, if you call early. It does not take long to draw a will, and he is not to be turned off until eleven."

"Impossible! He will be engaged with the ministers in the morning, and he will be in no suitable frame of mind to dictate so important a document. Besides, his will will doubtless be a long one, as he has a very large estate, and many relations and friends. I expect a thousand dollars myself for a fee, and I will of course see every one well paid who is put to any trouble in this melancholy business."

"Thank you, sir. I suppose you must see him—in fact, I have already promised as much to a friend of his, who thought, too, that you would require a larger room than his cell for your purpose, and I have made arrangements to give you this apartment."

He led the way, as he spoke, to the room which has been described, the entrance to which was out of the main lower hall, and but a few feet from the principal door of the building.

Johnson noted everything carefully as he followed the keeper into the room, which had apparently been prepared for his use. A decaying fire burned in the grate, giving evidence of having been lighted early in the day; a table, furnished with writing materials, stood in front of the hearth, and a chair was placed on either side.

Again complaining of the untimeliness of the visit, and saying that he feared he would be censured for permitting it, the jailer inquired what length of time would be required to complete the work.

"Two or three hours, at the most. Indeed, I have ordered my carriage to call for me at half-past nine, and you may depend on my having everything finished in that time."

"You will want witnesses. How many do your laws require? I can bring you half a dozen of my men, if you wish, when you get through."

"No, I thank you," replied Johnson, a little too eagerly for discretion; "it will not be necessary. Indeed, it would not be sufficient by our laws, as they do not know the signer. I shall bring in two of his acquaintances in the morning to witness the will; it will take but a few minutes."

"In the morning! Very well; that will do. We certainly should admit no more to-night."

So saying, the man withdrew to summon assistants, and with their aid to conduct the dangerous prisoner, weak and shackled, from his cell in an upper story to the lower room.

Johnson sat down and awaited his arrival with much real perturbation of mind, yet with a schooled air of *sang froid* which would have been unsuspected as feigned by the closest observer. His fears arose from an incertitude as to what extent Vrail was in the secret of the plot, or whether, if uninitiated, he might not penetrate his disguise, and give way to some exclamation of surprise which would excite suspicion, or possibly entirely betray him.

His own *rôle* was unmistakable. He must meet the prisoner as an old acquaintance, and as one who had a business appointment with him, and he doubted not, that if Vrail were unadvised of his assumed errand, he would at least be discreet enough to remain silent until he could give him the right cue for reply.

But Harry had fortunately already safely passed one dangerous ordeal, which had fully placed him on his guard, and rendered the present peril of self-betrayal comparatively slight. The garrulous keeper had spoken to him during the afternoon about the non-arrival of his American lawyer, and although for a moment surprised, he was too astute not to comprehend that it had reference in some way to Hadley's scheme of rescue. Again, when the jailer now went to conduct him to the lower room, he naturally explained to him the cause, and informed him that his counsel had come, and although in neither case did the prisoner make more than a monosyllabic reply, his taciturnity while in so wretched a condition was a mattter of no surprise. His eyes were, indeed, partly opened to the pretence under which his rescue was to be attempted, and whatever might have been his scruples against devising or counselling it, he did not feel at liberty now to thwart his generous friends, much less to peril their safety by a backwardness in accepting their aid.

Anxious to follow the strict line of duty, yet perplexed with doubts as to its requirements, if he erred, let us censure him lightly, for the love of life was yet strong in his young heart. We are recording the story of a good and amiable man, but by no means of a perfect one.

His guards were, of course, curious to behold this meeting between him and his friend from the States, and they lingered a moment, after bringing the prisoner in, to catch the first words of greeting under such melancholy circumstances.

The salutation was a sufficiently natural one on the part of Johnson, who knew that he was closely watched, and Vrail availed himself of the privileged taciturnity of grief to avoid saying anything until the keepers had withdrawn.

He extended his hand in silence to meet the welcoming grasp of his visitor, and received his expressions of condolence with emotion that certainly was not feigned.

Johnson, in the meantime, grew loquacious, to cover his friend's supposed alarm, and to prevent the necessity of his speaking in reply.

"I should have been here yesterday," he said, "but I was about five minutes too late for the boat, and I lost a whole day by the delay, so that I have to come to you in the evening; but I think if we set about our work in good earnest, we can accomplish it all in a couple of hours, and leave you time for a good night's rest yet, Mr. Vrail, which I have no doubt you will be able to take, notwithstanding to-morrow.

"The turnkey who goes the twelve o'clock rounds in his hall, says he always finds him asleep," said the jailer, nodding approvingly towards Vrail, and evidently intending a compliment.

"He certainly will rest none the worse for having so important a piece of business completed," replied the pretended lawyer, opening his portfolio, and taking from it half a quire of paper, on the outer sheet of which the formal commencement of a Last Will and Testament was already written.

"I have begun my work, you see, in order to save time here," he said, seating himself at the table, and drawing from the same receptacle which had contained his paper, a supply of red ribbon, sealing-wax, and other articles, supposed to be essential to the formal completeness of a solemn legal document. He hoped the attendants would take the hint thus thrown out, and leave them to their privacy. But they did not. He next opened his golden pen, and dipped it into the ink, yet still they lingered— nay, more, they whispered together by the doorway, glancing at him askance as they did so.

Vrail did not observe this ominous circumstance, but Johnson, who did, was certainly greatly alarmed. He was entirely within the power of his enemies, who, if he were suspected, would not even have the trouble of arresting him, for he was already in jail. They had only to close the door upon him, and turn its massive bolts, and he was secured beyond the possibility of escape. He preserved, however, an exterior of perfect equanimity, and seemed not to notice the alarming signs around him.

While he awaited the issue, the jailer stepped suddenly forward, and approached him rapidly, but with a nervous manner, and said :

"It's rather an unpleasant duty, sir, but really, before leaving you alone with the prisoner, I ought to search you, to see that you have no weapons about your person. I hope you will excuse me."

Harry was now, in turn, frightened, for he supposed it certain that his visitor was armed; but Johnson, greatly relieved, gave utterance to a loud and natural laugh, quite unsuited to the solemn presence of the condemned man, as he replied,

"Search me? Oh, certainly, you are quite welcome to do so; you will find nothing more dangerous about me than my pen. A lawyer's pen is his weapon, you know, and sometimes a pretty effective one, too. Where will you begin? Come, all of you at once, that it may be soon over, and no time lost."

He threw off his coat and vest as he spoke, and withdrew his boots, handing each of these garments to one of the men to examine, and then he requested the principal to come nearer, and make a more thorough examination of his person.

The search thus freely invited was of course but slightly made, suspicion being at once allayed by the stranger's manner, and in a few minutes the anxious friends were left alone in the room. The door was locked from the outer side by the retiring guards, one or more of whom, they knew, would patrol the main hall during the whole of their interview, and might re-enter at any moment to see that all was safe. Nay, for aught they knew, there might be secret apertures for looking in and watching their movements, and it became necessary to exercise the strictest caution and vigilance in all that they said and did. So impressed was Johnson with the importance of this prudence that he deemed it necessary to sit constantly, pen in hand, and to employ the greater part of his time in writing. What he wrote it would be difficult to say, but it was nothing that interfered with the conversation which, in a low tone, was kept up unremittingly between the two friends.

He informed Vrail fully of every particular of the arrangements made for his rescue, and (for there was abundant leisure) of many things besides. He told him of Gertrude's resolute and unwearying labors in his behalf, of her first interview with himself at

Ogdensburgh, of her second visit to him at Oswego, and of the arguments by which she had prevailed on him to undertake his present enterprise. Every new evidence of her labors and sacrifices for him, gave new pleasure to the young man, and increased the strength of that tender emotion with which he could not fail to regard her. But, alas! it increased also his painful anxiety lest he should never recover that liberty which alone would allow him to acknowledge or requite such transcendent kindness.

Harry, in turn, had much to tell, which his companion had not heard, of his eventful experiences, and some messages to charge upon his memory for Gertrude and Thomas, and his old grandfather, in case their schemes should be frustrated and Johnson should reach home in safety. Thus, much of the painful interval of suspense was passed, while they awaited the hour of trial. They discussed every dangerous contingency which they could imagine as liable to arise, and how to meet it; yet, with all their forethought, they felt sensible that there might be some fatal obstacle to their plans yet undiscovered.

A little before nine, a turnkey entered to replenish the fire, or, under that pretext, to see that all was safe, and Johnson's pen at once began to display unwonted activity.

"Mr. —— wished me to inquire if you had nearly finished your business?" said the man.

"I think we shall have done in about half an hour," replied Johnson; "you must have a little patience in such a case as this."

"Oh, yes, sir—but—he is pretty particular about having everything snugly locked up before this hour usually. But we can wait, I suppose, till ten o'clock, if it is necessary.

"I do not think I shall keep you quite so long; but I will knock on the door when I wish to come out."

The man retired, and the town clock struck nine as he went out.

The friends resumed their colloquy, but it was broken by many anxious pauses, as the few remaining minutes, freighted with such terrific interest, flew by.

"If it were only possible to rid me of these shackles, I should have far more courage," said Harry, in a whisper. "Is there no way to do it?"

"No, it is impossible here, but there will be tools in the carriage with which to knock them off as we go along. Never fear."

"I shall be so helpless, so unable to assist you. I cannot step farther than six inches at a time."

"Never fear, I say. All that has been calculated and provided for; only use your eyes vigilantly, and your judgment coolly, and we will see to the rest. There may be a chance for you to give us some important suggestion or direction, for you will be able to survey the whole scene, while we may be all engaged in the *mêlée*. Why, Vrail, you are certainly trembling."

"I am, but it is Hope that has taught me to fear. I should not tremble if suspense were past, and I knew that I was to die to-morrow. I should not tremble if I stood unbound at your side, attempting for another this very achievement."

"I understand you; you are right."

"Am I not calmer now?"

"There is not even a quaver in your voice. It was but a passing emotion."

"Believe me, it will not return; I am altogether self-possessed now. But these two long hours of dreadful endurance have been far more trying to the nerves than if they had been passed on the battle field."

"It is true—most true."

Johnson looked at his watch as he spoke. It wanted but ten minutes of the time appointed for the arrival of his men. He walked to the window, and looked out.

"I cannot see far, but we shall doubtless hear them when they drive up. They are certainly not here yet."

"Is it any darker than an hour since?"

"No—the clouds are scattered, and the stars shine brightly."

"It is just as well—perhaps better so. We shall be able to see our way."

Johnson returned to the table, and some minutes passed in silence. It was interrupted by the sound of a town-clock striking the half-hour, and all again was still. A few minutes more elapsed, and Vrail's quick ear caught the sound of wheels.

"They are coming!" he said.

The outlaw again walked quickly to the window, and looked out.

"They are here," he replied. "So far, all is well."

He returned coolly, gathered up his papers and placed them in the portfolio which he clasped with a steady hand. Calmly he closed his open law books, threw his overcoat across his arm, and walking to the door, he knocked loudly for egress. Ere it could be opened, he stepped quickly back to Vrail, whose hand he was grasping as the guards entered.

"Good-night," he said. "Keep up good courage to the last, my friend. It is the fortune of war, you know, and you are only treading the path which many a brave man has trod before you. Good-night. I will see you in the morning, of course—good night."

As he spoke, he advanced gradually towards the door, and Vrail took a few short steps in the same direction, clanking his chain dismally at each movement. Johnson left him standing in about the centre of the room, and turned to the jailer, who had entered, with two of his men, while two more could be seen lounging in the hall.

"My work is done, and my carriage is at the door," he said, "so that I will not detain you a moment longer. In the morning I shall see you again, when I shall have something to communicate which will be of interest to you personally. You understand?"

The man *did* understand the allusion to the promised bequest, but he made no other reply than was contained in a very pleased look.

"You are leaving your books and papers," he said.

The outlaw turned around, a little embarrassed; but at the next instant he replied,

"No, I have the will in my pocket. I will leave the other things in your charge until morning."

Johnson purposely made a little delay, fearing that his men might not be quite ready, and feeling safe in doing so while as yet no movement was made to re-conduct the prisoner to his cell. But while he tarried, events were taking place outside, which require a brief narration.

CHAPTER XLVII.

ROUGH VISITORS.

IMMEDIATELY before the carriage stopped, Gordon, who was driving, observed that they passed a man who was slowly approaching the jail, bearing some light burden, and who, in fact was a domestic in the family of the keeper. He approached the vehicle when it became stationary, and, without speaking, stood looking at it for some moments, much to the alarm of the driver, who feared that he might discover its occupants, although the windows were closed.

Gordon hesitated a moment as to the proper course to pursue, but as it was important to gain time, and he expected Johnson's appearance momentarily at the front door, he remained silent as long as the reconnoiterer did not speak. He did speak soon, however, and inquired in a careless way whom the carriage belonged to.

Gordon replied,

"It's a livery-stable hack, and I've come for a Yankee that I brought here early in the evening. He's some friend of the poor fellow that's going to swing to-morrow."

"Oh, yes," drawled the man, sauntering a little nearer, and looking attentively at the coach and horses.

"You've seen this Vrail, I suppose," Gordon continued, thinking to engage his attention, so as to keep him from looking into the carriage.

"Oh, yes, I've seen 'em all. I've seen eleven hung. Twice I saw three strung up at a time. There's only to be one to-morrow; that's nothing."

"Do you mean to see it?"

"Yes."

The fellow, whose proximity to the carriage had become in the highest degree alarming, started suddenly at this point of the conversation, as if he had seen or heard something which surprised him, and if he had uttered a word indicating suspicion, or had started to go into the house, Gordon had resolved to leap down and seize him at all hazards, and to secure his silence by threats or by force. But the man instantly resumed the conversation, quite in his previous manner, and after continuing it a little while, he turned slowly about, and walked on his way toward a gate which led to a back entrance into the building. Gordon was in a most painful state of indecision, since to stop him forcibly might cause an alarm which would prove fatal to their project, while if his suspicions had been excited, it was equally dangerous, nay, far more so, to allow him to proceed. But believing that his own fears had deceived him, he chose what he thought to be the least risk, and allowed the man to depart. As he went, however, he called to him, asking him if he would inform the gentleman inside that his carriage was ready and waiting. The man replied in the affirmative, but quickened his step as he did so, and instantly disappeared through the gateway. Had Gordon seen his changed manner then, he would have known how great was the cause for alarm. Darting quickly forward, he entered a basement door, and hurriedly inquired for the jailer, and when informed that he was in the main hall, he hastened up stairs, and to the side of his employer, to whom he said in a loud whisper,

"There's something looks wrong outside, sir; a carriage quite full of men, all very still, and the driver is a Yankee, I know by his talk, though he says he belongs to a livery-stable in town, and that he is waiting for this man. It may be all right, but it ain't a livery-stable 'turn-out,' I know, for it is too stylish for that."

The alarmed jailer cast a hurried look of suspicion on the pretended lawyer, and then suddenly called out to the men in the hall,

"Don't open the front door, but step around the back way and see. There may be another Theller plot here."

An electric-like light flashed from the outlaw's eyes, and his frame seemed to dilate and tower while the hasty alarm was spoken, but ere the words were ended, he leapt almost at a single bound, to the door, turned back the huge bolts with the key, which remained inside, and swung wide the massive portal.

"Now, my boys!" he shouted, "quick, for your lives!"

The carriage-door, though closed, had been left unfastened, to admit of instantaneous egress when the signal should be given, and instantly at the call, four men leaped out, three of whom, together with Gordon, rushed up the steps and into the hall. Yet quickly as they came, Johnson was attacked on all sides before they reached him, but he stood with his back against the opened door, only solicitous to keep it unclosed until his comrades came, and regardless of the blows he received in maintaining his post. The *mêlée* instantly became general, but the keepers had no firearms, and the outlaw's party used none, so that the contest was one only of physical strength, in which no fatal wounds were like to be received. In numbers the opponents were equal, for the terrified servant had fled at the first onset of the assailants, chiefly from fear, but also for the purpose of giving the alarm, and bringing more aid to his master.

If the belligerents were numerically equal, however, they were far from being so in strength, for Johnson, when roused, was quite a match for two ordinary men, and his own followers had been chosen for their great muscular power, as well as their courage, while young Van Vrank was certainly no trifling antagonist for any one to encounter. Brom, much to his chagrin, had been left in charge of the horses, and he found sufficient employment in restraining the restive animals, which were frightened by the tumult, from running away.

It was not enough, however, for the assailants that they could master their opponents, unless they could do it very speedily, and make good their escape with their prize, for a few minutes, at the most, would suffice to bring a powerful addition to the enemy, which no strength of theirs could oppose. Unfortunately it takes many words to tell what really occurred in a few seconds of time. No sooner did the leader see his friends at his side, than he called to them each to engage his man, and setting the example, he knocked the nearest down, and was hesitating how to keep him so, when he heard the voice of Vrail, who had shuffled himself along to the doorway of the room in which he had been left.

"Draw him in here," he said, "and drive in the rest, if possible. We can lock them in ; there is no time to bind them."

"It is well thought of," replied Johnson, dragging the prostrate man to the door, and shoving him in, with threats of instant death if he attempted to rise.

Gordon was scarcely behind him with another fallen foe, and Van Vrank, who had attacked the jailer himself, pushed him rapidly backwards to the door, and thrust him in, yet standing, but tumbling over his prostrate companions as he entered.

"Lock it now—we can quickly deal with the others !" shouted Johnson, and the door was immediately closed and fastened, and the key removed.

The two remaining men, who had thus far fought well and maintained their ground, did not longer keep up the unequal contest, but threatened by a suddenly drawn pistol in the hands of Gordon, which he did not mean to use, they both turned and fled.

Scarcely had they done so, when the herculean Johnson caught up Vrail in his arms, carried him out, and placed him in the carriage. The remainder of the party instantly followed, and as every man knew his post, no time was lost in taking places. Van Vrank and another followed Johnson into the carriage, one climbed with Gordon to the box, and Brom, after resigning the reins, got up behind. The driver's call to his horses was lost in the louder shout of alarm which was already resounding through the building, but the steeds felt the tightening reins and the crackling thong, and they started forward at an encouraging, though far from their greatest speed. It was too dark to admit of a headlong velocity, when an accident might prove so fatal to their hopes, and Gordon rather restrained than urged his mettled chargers, while as yet there was no actual pursuit. Within the vehicle all was excitement. Johnson, on his knees before Vrail, was busily engaged, with tools brought for that purpose, in breaking the lock which fastened the fetters upon his ankles. Under his skillful blows they soon fell clanking to the floor of the coach, and Harry, in ecstasy, exclaimed,

"Is it possible that I have the free use of my limbs once more, and that I am outside of a prison? I cannot realize all this—it seems like some wild, bright dream."

"Ay, you are outside of a prison, and behind a pair of fleet horses, too," replied Johnson; "yet it seems to me we are not going over fast. I say, Gordon," he continued, addressing the latter through the open window, "are these your twelve mile horses? What is the matter?"

"Nothing is the matter," replied Gordon. "Would you have a quiet party of ladies and gentlemen, on their way to Col. B——'s party, go dashing through the streets like mad? We don't want to raise an alarm, you know, as long as we are not chased. Besides, it's unsafe to go faster in this darkness."

A church-bell, which seemed to be very near them, rang out at that instant a loud and startling peal, like that which usually

"It is well thought of," replied Johnson, dragging the prostrate man to the door, and shoving him in, with threats of instant death if he attempted to rise.—
PAGE 359.

UNIV. OF
CALIFORNIA

gives warning of a conflagration, and a shout of many voices was heard, crying indistinctly in the distance.

"That means us," said Gordon, cracking his whip, and urging his horses into a quicker pace; "now we'll show you what we can do."

By this time another bell began to respond to the first, and a third and fourth almost instantly joined the clangor, while the tumult and shouts in the streets rapidly increased.

"They will send a party of horse after us if they know which way we have gone," said Johnson. "Can't your span do a little better than that?"

"Yes, they can do a great deal better when it becomes necessary," replied the imperturbable Gordon.

"It is necessary *now*," returned the outlaw, with a suddenly changed air. "Put them to their utmost speed this instant, I command you, and keep them so until we reach the boats, or until they drop!"

Gordon complied without reply. Indeed, his whole attention was required, for the road over which his flying chariot was passing, and with which, of course, he was not familiar, although he had travelled it twice that day.

"If we break down," continued Johnson, addressing his friends inside, "the horses must be cut loose, when they will easily carry two apiece, and the rest must follow as best they can; or, if the horses themselves should fail, we must all take to our feet across the fields and to the river. They are really coming," he said, as the increased and nearer sound of pursuit was distinctly heard. "How could they so soon organize a force and get upon our track?"

"You forget that one man fled and gave the alarm at the moment of your first irruption into the jail," replied Vrail. "It does not take long to call out a Canadian police."

"I fear we have something worse than a police behind us. It does not take long to call out a British troop of horse. The fire-bells have brought every body into the streets, and then the true cause of alarm has been quickly spread by shouts and cries. It is well that we are out of the city."

"Hark! that certainly was the report of a musket," said Van Vrank.

"It was fired to frighten us, then," replied Vrail; "they are certainly too far off to see us, much less to do us any harm, and they will not gain upon us while we go at this rate."

"It is best not to make too sure," answered Johnson; "we may have to sell our lives yet for what they will fetch. I think I am good for three men at least. But we forget, Vrail, that you and I are both unarmed. Where are our pistols?"

"They are here, all ready to speak for themselves," said Van Vrank, producing a couple of brace from the seat of the carriage which he was occupying. Each took his weapons, and while doing so, a voice was heard through the back window of the vehicle.

"Better hand over one or two dem pop-guns out here, Massa Harry. I shall be de fust man 'tacked, and I got nothing to fight with but a rope and a gag."

"You shall have them, if necessary, Brom," said Johnson; "keep cool, and don't get frightened. Do you see any lights down the road?"

"No, Massa; but I hear a gun, and think I hear a officer call 'Forward!' bery loud."

"I think Gordon could get a little more 'go' out of these horses," said Van Vrank, though we are certainly travelling very fast."

"I wish he could," answered Johnson; "for it is not enough that we reach the boats ahead of our pursuers; we must be far enough from shore when they come up to be out of the reach of their guns. But I fear to urge Gordon too far, for I can't deny that he knows far more about horses than I do."

"Another gun! and another! Do you hear that? What can it mean?"

"It is sheer folly if it is meant to intimidate us. It only shows us where they are, and enables us better to escape them. There is another!"

At this moment the headlong velocity of the carriage suddenly subsided into a moderate speed of six or seven miles to the hour, and those within hurriedly inquired the cause.

"We are approaching a turnpike gate," replied Gordon, "where they will be sure to suspect something wrong if we come up so fast, and they may shut down the gates."

"That, then, is what the shots are for," said Vrail quickly; "to give the alarm to the gate-keeper."

"Aha! is that the game? Go on then, Gordon!" shouted the outlaw; "faster! faster than ever! I have the tickets here which will carry us through."

As he spoke he thrust one arm out of the side window of the carriage, and held a pistol, pointing to the ground, but ready for instant use. With all their former speed, and more, they dashed forward and approached the gate, with a momentum that had well nigh precipitated the horses against it before they could be checked. It was shut, and the keeper, lantern in hand, stood beside it, while his wife and three or four children were assembled in the doorway, attracted by the extraordinary arrival.

"What's the matter? What's the matter? What's all this firing?" said the man, without offering to perform his usual office.

"Step this way, and I will tell you," replied Johnson coolly.

The man came near the door, when he was suddenly seized by the outlaw with one hand, while with the other he presented a pistol to his breast.

"Bid your wife open the gate instantly, or you are a dead man."

His terrific voice reached the trembling woman, who did not wait the bidding of her husband to pull up the gate, and give free passage to so dangerous a customer.

"I was jis goin' to get down and open it myself," said Brom, as the carriage again rattled on, "but he won't give me a chance to do nuffin."

The delay had been brief, but it was sufficient to considerably lessen the distance of the pursuers from the flying party, and the incident would also serve, unfortunately, to make them more certain they were on the right track.

It was no longer necessary to listen closely to hear the sound of pursuit. A cavalry gallop makes itself audible a long way, and the enemy was certainly not very far behind the fugitives, and was momentarily gaining on them. Gordon's boasted team had doubtless accomplished all that he had claimed, on his first trial of them, but that was done by the full light of day, and with a load materially less than that which they were now drawing. He had great difficulty now in keeping them at a speed which he estimated at ten miles an hour, and so pantingly was even this task performed, that he feared to urge them beyond it, lest they should altogether break down. But, on the other hand, far more than half their brief journey was already accomplished, and if they could maintain even their present rate of progress for the remaining distance, there was no danger of being overtaken, unless it might be by some of the random shots of the foe.

All hearts grew sanguine of reaching the boats in safety, but many fears were entertained lest they should not be able to obtain a secure "offing" before the arrival of the enemy on the beach.

"There will be nine of us to go in the boats," said Johnson, "and we all know how little speed we can make with a loaded skiff. At the best, we shall be within musket shot of the shore for many minutes, unless Captain —— has ventured the steamboat far nearer the land than we have any reason to hope."

"Do you think our pursuers are dragoons?" inquired Vrail.

"Certainly, judging from the musket reports which we have already heard, and we know that there are several companies of dragoons now in Kingston. Doubtless this is a detachment of them."

"If we are to be exposed for several minutes to the fire of all their guns, we can scarcely hope to escape."

"It looks doubtful, certainly—but we must hope for the best. It is too dark for any certain aim, and those who are not rowing must lie on the bottom of the boats. The oarsmen, of course, must be exposed."

"And at that post we may all be shot down in turn," interposed Van Vrank.

"Dat are is a fact, Massa Johnson and gemmen, what Massa Garret tells you," said the negro, who, with head partly protruded through the rear window, had listened to the conversation; "we shall all be shot down like crows off a dry tree. Now, you jis listen to me; I haven't done nuffin' yet for Massa Harry, 'cept hold the hosses at de jail, and I ain't satisfied. I can *drive* hosses too, jes as well as Massa Gordon, 'zactly. Now, what you gwine to do with these horses and carriage when you go to the boats—leave em to the inimy, ain't you?"

"Of course," answered Harry, who knew Brom too well to doubt that he had something important to say.

"Bery well—you all get out quietly when we get near the boats, and Brom will drive on a mile or so furder, and all de sogers will follow me—don't you see?"

"Capital!" exclaimed Johnson.

"And when dey come most up to me, I jump off and run across lots to de river, and back to de same place, where you can send a boat for me."

"Brom, you are certainly a noble fellow, and your stratagem is worthy of a wiser head. I have no doubt of its perfect success for all excepting yourself. But if you are willing to take the risk, we will do all we can to bring you off afterwards."

"I take de risk, Massa Johnson, not for you, but for Massa Harry. I know what I'm doin'—I take de risk."

"If my life alone were at stake, my good friend," said Harry, addressing the negro, "I should hesitate long before accepting your generous offer; but I do not feel at liberty to refuse it now. I believe we shall be able to save you. Certainly we will not desert you, while the shadow of a hope remains.

The carriage had proceeded with undiminished speed during this conversation, and they were now within a minute's drive of their stopping place, which minute was devoted to giving some directions to Brom, and to concerting a signal by which he should indicate his position on the coast when the boat should be sent for him. The call of the screech owl, which he knew well how to imitate, and which is not an unusual sound in a Canadian forest, was agreed upon for this purpose.

Near two tall maples, which partly overshadowed the road, the carriage stopped, and when the noise of its motion had ceased, the sound of the galloping troop behind was more distinctly heard, and seemed frightfully near. All instantly alighted, and Brom, hastily climbing to the vacated seat of Gordon, drove immediately off more rapidly for the lightening of the carriage, and with a flourish of the whip, and an encouraging cry to the steeds, which was intended not so much for the animals, as to attract the attention of the foe.

Vrail and his friends, elated to exhilaration by the new aspect of affairs, clambered quickly and silently over the roadside fence, and ran across a vacant field which alone interposed between them and the river, where, to their inexpressible joy, they found their boats waiting, ready for instantaneous flight.

No word of inquiry or of congratulation was spoken; all was understood, as the running fugitives leaped into the boats, and the ready rowers dipped their broad oars into the water, and bent silently to their task.

In less than a minute, with emotions it would be impossible to portray, they heard the galloping dragoons dash past on the highway, and then for the first time they knew that they were safe—safe from the utter ruin which had impended over them, and free as the chainless waters across whose calm surface they were gliding towards a land of freedom. *Harry was rescued!* The horrible gallows, with all its attendant terrors, had passed from before his mental vision, which for so many weeks it had not ceased to haunt by day and night, and never again was its fearful shadow to fall upon his young heart.

With what exultation was that heart now beating; with what boundless gratitude to the great Deliverer; with what inexpressible thankfulness to the heroic friends at his side; with what tender and melting emotions towards her whose agents they were, and who in turn was but the agent of Heaven, in accomplishing his deliverance.

Five minutes' rowing brought them within sight of the steamboat, upon the deck of which Gertrude, and Ruth, and Thomas Vrail were awaiting, with distressing solicitude, the return of the boats. Three boisterous cheers, which rang far and wide across the still water, announced to them the perfect success of their approaching friends, and Gertrude, overcome with the sudden transport of joy, was carried, swooning, below. Ruth danced, and clapped her hands in glee, while the large tears rolled unheeded down her cheeks, and Thomas sent back an answering shout which spoke his own delight, and imparted new rapture to the heart of his affectionate brother.

These spontaneous greetings were the result of irrepressible feelings, which had rendered all parties momentarily oblivious of the prudence which should still have influenced their actions. One of their number was yet on Canadian soil, and the chance of bringing him off would certainly not be increased by their shouts of triumph, if they should unfortunately reach the enemy's ears. But elated by so great success, it was no longer possible for the triumphant party to feel apprehension, and as soon as they had reached the steamboat, one of the skiffs, manned by two volunteers, of whom Gordon was one, returned in pursuit of Brom.

To depict the scenes which, meanwhile, followed the arrival of Harry upon the vessel's deck, and to portray the emotions with which he and Gertrude met, would be a task in which the most graphic pen would fail, or, if successful, would still be outstripped by the imagination of the intelligent reader.

But unutterable as was the joy of each, it could not be complete until they knew that the generous and devoted servant, who had so nobly risked his life for his friends, was safe. Nor was this addition to their pleasure long denied them. The negro was readily found, by means of the signal which had been agreed upon, and was brought off without difficulty, exulting almost to madness in his success. He had decoyed the enemy about a mile and a half beyond the place of embarkation, and had only quitted the carriage when he plainly heard the musket-balls whistling past him.

"I tought it time to go den," he said, "'kase I knew Massa Harry must be safe enough den, so I jis jump off, and hit de nigh horse a tremendous whack, which kept 'em going a good while yet as fast as ever. De dragoons warn't more'n fifty rods behind, and so I jis climbed over de fence, and laid down mighty still until dey gallop pass, and den I up and run like a wild Injun, right straight for de river."

"Were you followed?"

"No, sir—nobody seed me; dey all went on chasing de carriage. Besides, 'twas berry dark, and Massa Gordon says I'm so black I can't be seen after sundown. Ha! ha! I glad of it dis time."

"What did you do when you reached the river?"

"I run right on down stream until I tought I got about to de right place, and den I climb a tree, and screech every little while."

"What did you climb a tree for?"

"'Kase de owls allers screech in de trees; dey don't come and sit down on de ground and screech."

"Oh, very true. And you did not have to wait long?"

"Oh, no; 'twan't long afore I heard de oars, and den I come down and wade out to meet de boats."

Brom found himself a great hero when he reached the steamboat, and he was astonished to learn how highly his services were estimated. He did not seem to think he had done anything very wonderful, and his delight was not a little allayed by the reflection that the beautiful carriage and horses, which had cost so much money, had been lost. If he could only have brought them off, his satisfaction would have been complete.

CHAPTER XLVIII.

CONCLUSION.

The return voyage to Oswego, which was commenced the moment that Brom was received on board, occupied the remainder of the night, and a brief and sleepless period it proved to the relieved and delighted travellers.

Assembled in the cabin, they discussed, with no thought of rest, and with little abatement of their joyous excitement, the various incidents of the eventful enterprise which had terminated so happily. Harry had much to tell of his capture and of his prison experiences, but he had far more to learn of what had been done for him, of countless details of which he was as yet necessarily ignorant. Gertrude, indeed, said little of her own achievements, but there were enough to blazon them; and in regard to many events, including the interview with Governor Arthur, the impulsive Ruth, when questioned, became the eager narrator. The story of her own solitary travels was also drawn forth; of the treacherous guide who robbed and deserted her, and of the more treacherous kidnapper, from whose grasp the valiant Van Vrank had saved her.

Thomas, also, had his story to tell, scarcely less replete with interest, and which, like much of the other narratives, necessarily abounded with compliments to the heroic Johnson, who, wakeful enough to other tales, went fairly to sleep (may our readers not do the same) over a spirited recital of his defence of Rainbow Island.

The brothers had, indeed, reason to confess that although they had tired of a monotonous and peaceful life at home, their few months' experience of war had been crowded enough with incidents to fully satisfy their longings for a change, and to content them hereafter with more peaceful and laudable pursuits. Each had seen sufficient reason to change his convictions in relation to the merits of the cause they had espoused, to which, indeed, Harry had been rendered a convert, rather by his fraternal affection, than by the deductions of an unbiased judgment. But they considerately concealed these new sentiments from the heroic man to whom they owed so much, and whose opinions and prejudices, they well knew, were rooted too deeply to be shaken by argument or influenced by example. To him, indeed, a wronged citizen of the country he sought to revolutionize, the subject had far different relations, and might justify a far different conduct.

It was with much grief that the brothers and Miss Van Kleeck parted, at Oswego, with this valiant and generous man, whom no persuasions of Gertrude could induce to receive a reward for the great favors he had conferred. A costly memento, indeed, she gave, which as a memento only he received and cherished, nor would she suffer her benefactor to depart until she had extorted a promise from him that, when better days should come, and he should no longer be an object of governmental vigilance, he would visit her at her own home on the quiet bank of the Hudson. On his brave followers she bestowed an additional bounty beyond the large remuneration which had been advanced to them, and this she accompanied with kind words and judicious praise, which, far more than the gold, won their enduring gratitude and remembrance.

If Harry felt humiliated to see himself thus ransomed, as it were, by a lady, like a prisoner redeemed from Arabic captivity, while he stood penniless by, the feeling was only of momentary duration. All Gertrude's conduct had borne evidence of the promptings of a noble philanthropy, with which he felt that he would scarcely have the right, if he had the power, to interfere.

To some extent he would have the ability, on his return home, to discharge his pecuniary obligations to her, and there was a future in which, the promptings of ambition told him, he might yet repair the shattered fortune of his fair friend—shattered for his sake. But he knew that if he could do all this, he would still fall immeasurably short of requiting his obligations to Gertrude, to whom he would ever remain a willing and a grateful debtor. But with a revived affection stimulating a long dormant hope, it was impossible that Harry should long remain ignorant of the grand mistake of his life, originated by his blindness, and perpetuated by his indiscretion, until it had so nearly proved utterly irreparable.

Reason and reflection had long since convinced him that Thomas had been an unsuccessful suitor for the hand of Gertrude, and this belief was changed into certainty soon after the re-union of the brothers, by the distinct avowal of the younger.

He not only freely acknowledged his own deserved repulse, but, with still unextinguished vanity, he imputed it solely to the circumstance that the young lady's heart was pre-occupied by Harry, who, he said, had long before made an unknown and undesigned conquest of it. Harry doubted still, but Thomas, with many earnest assurances, half convinced him of what he so earnestly hoped for.

"But you, Tom," said Harry, "you should not yield to one repulse—and I certainly will never be your rival."

"No, you never will. You need not fear that; and as to *one* refusal, I think, if I recollect aright, I had three or four. No, no; Getty and I have a very distinct understanding now; and, to tell the truth, I cannot say that I ever was really in love with her, or with any one else. You know very well it was only a question of policy with me. I was a fortune-hunter, which you never were, and never could be. I deserved all that I received ; and you, Harry, richly deserve all that I am very sure you are going to receive, and that is the heart and hand of Gertrude."

Harry was now more convinced than ever that Tom was the noble fellow he had always believed him, and although in that opinion he was still in error (yet not so widely as once), let him be pardoned the blindness produced by an excess of light radiating from his own generous heart.

A stage-coach journey homeward, which confined the travelling party to narrow limits, and compelled a common sociability, relieved in some degree, the embarrassment which the unavowed lovers could not fail to experience in each other's presence.

A few days of travel brought them home, where the intelligence of their safety had preceded them, and where they received the glad greetings of friends and neighbors, who had long given up Harry for lost, and who, as yet, had no knowledge of the mode in which his release had been accomplished.

The good old Guert Rosevelt, who had long been suffering from serious illness, found sudden strength again at the sight of his favorite boy, whom he clasped, weeping, in his arms, and addressed volubly in Low Dutch, the only language in which he could express his violent emotion with a rapidity necessary to his relief.

"I should have died with you, my boy," he said, "if they had killed you. But now I shall live another year—another year to see you."

"Twenty of them, grandpa—twenty of them, I am certain. Why, you will soon be well ; we are going to take the best of care of you, and next spring you will be as strong as ever again "

The old man smiled, and whatever may have been his presentiments, he would say nothing farther to mar the happiness of that joyous hour. If it was with a more moderate welcome that he greeted Thomas, it was less from favoritism to the elder, than because he had long known of the other's safety, and had entertained no solicitude in his behalf.

Aunt Becky, although very glad to receive her niece again in safety, was greatly disappointed to learn that she was not married to Van Vrank, and that there was no probability of such an event.

She soon had other cause of perplexity in the renewed visits of Harry Vrail, who rightfully resolved that Gertrude should at once know the whole history of his love—his presumptuous love, if such it were—and that his painful doubts should be dispelled, even although by a more painful certainty.

By that same bright fireside where he had spoken his hasty farewell, where her tears had been with difficulty concealed from his view, as she responded to his adieux, there did they meet again, alone, with the shadow of that sad hour yet resting on their young hearts.

Need it be said how quickly that cloud was dispelled—how effulgent was the light which succeeded it! Gertrude knew all; not only that she was now loved, which might have been the result of gratitude alone, but that for years she had been the one object of Harry's most fervent and faithful affection. And richly did this consciousness alone repay her for all that she had suffered and sacrificed. Not less complete was Harry's bliss, the memory of whose past sorrows rendered doubly bright the serene skies which now smiled upon him.

In the first hour of their unselfish joy, their happy hearts turned to that sweet child of a foreign land, to whom they jointly owed so immeasurable a debt, and whom each was henceforth to regard and cherish as a sister. As such, the delighted Ruth was formally and fully recognized, discarding forever the abhorred name of her pretended relative, and assuming henceforth the patronymic, not euphonic indeed, but dear to her, of Van Kleeck.

"There will be need for some one to take it, if it is to be long preserved," she said, archly, to Gertrude, calling a rich blush to the cheek of the *fiancée*, and a gay smile to the lips of Harry.

Within a few months indeed, when spring began to put forth its rich promise, making all nature glad, and bringing to the patriarchal Guert that restored strength which the voice of affection had predicted; when May, bright May, brought again its verdure and its flowers, Ruth and Dame Becky bore the Flemish name alone.

Gertrude became a bride, and amid the festivities which marked that occasion, none was more gay than the rejected Thomas, who had learned from the perpetual examples of generosity before him to rejoice in the happiness of others. What a roystering time he and Van Vrank, aided by some village *confrères*, made of that wedding evening; and how the happy grandsire enjoyed their mirth, and grew young again in heart amidst this festival of youth and love. Even Aunt Becky became gracious beneath so many genial influences, and, to the dangerous merriment of Garret, was coaxed into dancing a minuet in the style of the preceding century. Brom, stationed beside the sable musicians, richly enjoyed the scene, and became himself the object of no small share of attention. All had a pleasant word for him, for all knew his fidelity, and the invaluable services he had rendered Harry.

Ruth, now a blooming school-girl, exuberant in innocent glee, was the bridesmaid, and if she had not ever been forgetful of self, there might have been something in the scenes around her to carry her thoughts a few years forward to a similar event in her own destiny. If she thought not of these things, however, there was one who did, and whose honest heart warmed with emotion whenever his eye fell upon the beautiful child.

Stimulated by ambition to make himself worthy of her, Garret, during the years which were yet necessary to ripen Ruth into all the graces of womanhood, found time and means for great personal improvement, and in no small degree for mental cultivation. He found time, also, to win the heart he so much prized, and without any promptings from Aunt Becky, who had long given him over as a dolt, he conducted his courtship to a triumphant issue.

The patroon-like estate which had descended to Gertrude, although shorn of some of its fair proportions, was far from being entirely sacrificed by her generosity. A few valuable farms were sold to discharge the incumbrances she had imposed upon them when starting on her heroic expedition, but the great bulk of the property still remained to her, and by the aid of those very unromantic improvements so deploringly depicted at the outset of this narrative, it soon acquired an increased value, nearly equivalent to all that had been lost. From these great possessions the young and generous owners did not cease freely to dispense. On Garret they early bestowed a farm adjoining his own, for the hoped purchase of which they knew he had been long carefully hoarding his gains, and Ruth's dowry, when at length her wedding day came, was, of course, a noble one. Much, too, had been lavished on her education, and although she became a prize sought by many aspirants, and capable of making what the world calls a splendid alliance, Gertrude and Harry did not desire to see her affections diverted from the honest heart she had chosen. Nor had she, fortunately, any such weak ambition to interfere with her happiness, which has remained unmarred by regrets, and unclouded even by the remembrance of her early griefs.

Thomas found a brother's ready aid, and was afforded opportunities of professional advancement, which he embraced with commendable zeal, forgetful of his military aspirations, and achieving a success which enabled him to laugh at his grandsire's moderate predictions in his behalf.

To that venerable man there remained a long, serene evening of life, with its tranquil memories and its blissful hopes, for his was the Christian's confidence, which grows stronger at death's approach. The hour of his exultant departure brought the first real grief to Harry and Gertrude, of whose family he had ever been a cherished member, happy and dispensing joy.

Hadley did not visit his American friends, as he had given them reason to hope, having been recalled to England sooner than he had anticipated, by an urgent summons from his father; but Gertrude had the satisfaction of receiving a letter from him, congratulating her on the success of her great enterprise, and highly complimenting her heroism and generosity. He related many amusing incidents connected with the alarm in Kingston on the night of the rescue, but said he believed he had been fortunate enough to entirely escape suspicion of any collusion with the brigands.

Brave old Commodore Johnson made good his promise of visiting his young friends, and beholding the happiness he had done so much to promote, and great was the gratification of the veteran soldier, as together they recounted the vicissitudes they had mutually experienced, and the triumph they had achieved. But although entertained with a noble hospitality, and urged with almost filial affection to prolong his stay, the old hero could not long be detained from his island world, where, since the border war had ceased, and his high hopes had been relinquished, he had found a quiet and peaceful home. There Harry, in turn, accompanied by Thomas and Van Vrank, made him an autumnal visit, and spent a week in the exciting pleasures of the chase; and many were the rich presents they bore, in the name of Gertrude and Ruth, to their benefactor and his family.

It remains only to say a word of sable Brom, who, notwithstanding that the munificence of Gertrude has rendered him independent of labor, has ever remained in her family, nominally a servant, but virtually his own master, and to some extent the controller of all around him. His military career and its consequences have made him an oracle in all the neighborhood, and he takes delight in recounting his experiences, whenever he can find a listener to whom the tale is new. But his most attentive and delighted auditors now, who never tire of his repetitions, are some juvenile representatives of the houses of Vrail and Van Vrank, who address each other as Hadley, and Getty, and Ruth, and who become compliant to all requests, on being promised a story of the war. They grow wild with excitement over its details, and fully sympathize with the regrets which are invariably expressed by Brom at its close, that he was obliged to abandon the beautiful horses and coach to the British dragoons.

THE END.

www.ingramcontent.com/pod-product-compliance
Lightning Source LLC
Chambersburg PA
CBHW030359230426
43664CB00007BB/667